THE ARKANSAS
PROJECT

FROM THE UNITED STATES JAYCEES TO THE UNITED STATES DEPARTMENT OF JUSTICE AND WHITEWATER

DAVID W. HENDERSON

The geographical range of most Arkansas Project activities depicted in this book is on the cover. From Tulsa, Oklahoma to Olive Branch Mississippi and from Memphis, Tennessee to Fort Smith, Arkansas and everywhere in between. Some other localities not covered by this map were: Arlington, VA, Washington, D.C., Manhattan, NY, Lulu, MS, Shreveport, LA, Orlando, FL, Pittsburgh, PA, Church Hill, MD, Springfield, VA, Dallas and Fort Worth, TX, and of course, large amounts of the wonderful Chesapeake Bay.

THE ARKANSAS PROJECT

But, yes, she is out there and she has the money to buy silence, obedience, and fealty...since 1992. Never has anyone come so close to Richard III in life who left a similar wake of wakes.

~ Jim Peck

Contents

PREFACE

In January of 1998, the President of the United States was adroitly dodging yet another bullet fired from his own gun. Scandals had plagued his administration from the beginning. Indeed, his first and second campaigns for President had both been scandal plagued. So had the twelve years that he had served as Governor of the State of Arkansas. President William Jefferson Clinton was, in many ways, predictable. He had built a political career on his ability to dodge bullets fired from his own gun. He had mastered the political skills necessary to cause aides and hangers-on to fall on their swords for him. They were the great enablers, and the enabler-in-chief was his own wife, Hillary Rodham Clinton. Theirs had been a symbiotic relationship. It seemed to work for them.

The most recent bullet that left his gun was an unfortunate dalliance with a White House intern. Unfortunate, because it had been found out. Discounting the long-running Paula Jones case, this revelation had more impact than any other since the Gennifer Flowers' tapes during the 1992 presidential campaign. That one had been dealt with by a joint appearance of the Clinton's on CBS's Sixty Minutes. The Clinton formula was to be repeated. True to form, an interview with Matt Lauer on NBC's Today Show was quickly arranged and as always, NBC was a willing player for the Clinton interests.

Appearing with Matt Lauer on the morning of January 27, 1998, Hillary Clinton mustered a defiant defense of her husband's behavior. She maintained that she believed his denials that there had been no relationship with the intern and then threw in this tidbit: "I mean, look at the very people who are involved in this. They have popped up in other settings. That is...the great story here... for anybody willing to find it and write about it... and explain it is... this vast right-wing conspiracy that has been conspiring against my husband since the day he announced for president. A few journalists have kind of caught on to it and explained it. But it has not yet been fully revealed to the American public. And actually, you know, in a bizarre sort of way, this may do it."

That was not the first time that she had spoken of a "vast right-wing conspiracy," and it was no accident that she had done so this time. One of the Clinton's aides, Sidney Blumenthal, had urged her to do this. They already had a plan in place, and her job was to raise the profile for things to come.

Soon to follow would be news stories accusing several people, myself included, of the crime of bribing a federal witness, followed by demands for a federal investigation. Eight days after Hillary's appearance on the Today Show, Joe Conason, writing a screed in The New York Observer on February 4, 1998, set the tone for what was to follow. United States Senator, Bob Torricelli, a Democrat from New Jersey, appeared on "This Week with Sam and Cokie," the popular ABC Sunday News talk show, where he blew on the smoldering embers created by Joe Conason. That was on Sunday, February 8, 1998, twelve days after Hillary's proclamation.

The next day I met a friend from London in the Watergate Hotel restaurant. Shortly after we were seated a familiar Washington insider who had also been on the "This Week" program walked in and he was seated at the table next to ours. It was George Will. He was obviously there to meet someone because he waited alone for the next few minutes, and soon US Senator Bob Torricelli arrived and joined him. They had talked the previous day on the set of the TV show about following up, so here they were, following up. It was very difficult for me to concentrate on my friend's conversation because it was also possible to hear what was being said at their table. To this day my friend, Dan M. Burt, does not know about that conflict I had listening to both tables.

Next to come were several stories by Karen Gullo, an Associated Press writer, soon followed by a scurrilous series of stories in Salon Magazine, an internet or e-zine publication, which at that time, was virtually unknown. There was a common thread between the articles by Karen Gullo, carried by The Associated Press and those by the writers of the Salon articles. They were both based on stories told to them by a fortune teller which would lead to a series of events that I detail in this book. Joe Conason and Gene Lyons, an Arkansas newsman and Clinton crony who already had picked the title for a book they were planning to write: "The Hunting of The President," for reasons explained in this book, Clinton Hollywood friends Harry Thomason and wife Linda Bloodworth-Thomason were preparing to produce a movie by the same name, which they eventually did, however, it took much longer than they expected.

Naturally, The United States Department of Justice was eager to participate. The United States Attorney General, Janet Reno, not usually known as one to make quick decisions regarding investigations, (do we see an emerging pattern here?), moved as if in an Olympic sprint event. On April 9, 1998, she announced that there would be a federal investigation.

These were not random events. They were carefully planned by a small group of Hillary Clinton's underlings, under her supervision. Once started, it had a life of its own. It had taken this entire process just seventy-two days to go from an "aside" in an interview to a formal Department of Justice political investigation. *The American Spectator* had investigated and published stories about Whitewater. Now we were in Reno's raging water. We were falsely accused of conspiracy, witness tampering, and bribing a federal witness. These are federal crimes. So is obstruction of justice. So is politicizing the Department of Justice and the FBI. It all happened to some of us associated with *The American Spectator.*

What I will relate to the reader herein, I have previously sworn to, under oath, twice, before a federal grand jury. The same information was conveyed to a team of Federal Prosecutors, FBI, and IRS agents, also under oath.

After an exhaustive investigation, lasting, in my case 365 days exactly, we were all cleared. What we had been accused of never happened. That was not a problem for Hillary. The damage had been done to reputations simply by being subjected to highly public charges. As a former Secretary of Labor, Raymond Donovan said, after being cleared in another investigation, "Where do I go to get my reputation back?" I choose to do it in these pages. I invite you to join me.

I wrote the draft of this book in 2000/2001 while those events were fresh in my mind. Now it is 2016 and a Presidential Election Year. I hope this story will shed some light on the already heavy evidence of Hillary Clinton's relentless destruction of those who get in her way. I did make one effort to publish this book shortly after I had finished writing it. Knowing Al Regnery of Regnery Press, I asked him to have a look at my manuscript. He took it and some time later told me that I had a book, but no one would buy it because the Clinton's were leaving office and they would not be of interest to the readers since they were finished in Washington. Sure they were!

This book is part history and part autobiography. The reader will gradually begin to see that the story told here is the beginning of a decades-long corruption of the justice system in the United States. The protective apparatus of the Department of justice is available to the elected leaders to use and abuse in order to gain power and wealth and The current election cycle 2016 brings it into focus.

I had an unblemished reputation in Washington having been in the Public Affairs Consulting business for 20 years and was well known to the Press, frequently featured in stories in the Washington Post about my outdoor activities i.e., hunting, fishing, and boating. Most notable was my defense of General William C. Westmoreland by preparing and managing his press reaction to the CBS Broadcast, The Uncounted Enemy, A Vietnam Deception. I became his unpaid press spokesman and PR agent throughout the three-year period that culminated in Federal Court in Manhattan. I donated my time and covered my own expenses throughout that period. That reputation was destroyed, leaving me unable to earn a living due to the untrue press accounts of and about the so-called "Arkansas Project." Also, I didn't want to expose any of my congressional friends to retaliation from the Administration. The Clinton's were still co-presidents.

Sidney Blumenthal and David Brock were among Hillary's scandal team, then and now, and as history has shown, they remain in the dirty act of protecting Hillary from exposure of her criminal activities while reaping huge monetary benefits from it.

Soon after Bill Clinton was elected to the Presidency of the United States, stories began to circulate that he had no interest in money. He and Hillary lived in a modest home and they were just an average young couple. That was what they wanted everyone to believe.

I had contacts with dozens of members of Congress in both parties. A Democrat member of Congress who represented a district in Arkansas made that claim when I was visiting in his office. I had a friendly relationship with the member so his explanation to me was unguarded, and I found it to be very amusing. It was also believable considering the stories of his relationship with Jennifer Flowers. He said that Bill didn't really care about money and there were only two things that he was interested in. They both started with the letter "p" and one of them was pizza. A few years later during a government shutdown I was reminded of that story when It was revealed that an Intern named Monica was working in the White House and among other things, the President ordered Pizza for the young staffers.

Of the people subjected to this investigation dubbed The Arkansas Project by some of the staff at *The American Spectator*, I am the sole survivor.

Deceased
Steven S. Boynton August 24, 2007
Parker Dozhier August 29, 2012
Richard M. Larry July 6, 2013
Richard Mellon Scaife July 4, 2014
Rex Armistead December 24, 2015

Also deceased; my grandson, Jonathan Kelly, June 13, 2013

"Hillary is the best darn Change Maker I ever knew," said Bill Clinton, speaking at the DNC July 26, 2016. Oh yes, she is. She can change the life of anyone who threatens her gravy train: man, woman or family.

CHAPTER ONE ~
FORTUNE

It is a short cab ride from the corner of Connecticut and L streets, N.W., in Washington, D.C., to an office building on Pennsylvania Avenue that housed the newly assembled Office of Special Review, a team of federal investigators under the supervision of Michael E. Shaheen. With me was Richard Leon, a partner in the law firm of Baker Hostettler. Dick Leon and I had been brought together because of a Fortune Teller in Arkansas, Caryn Mann, had been relating a story to several reporters who desperately wanted to believe her. In fairness to Caryn, I must add that she did tell fortunes, but she also sold cemetery plots, read Tarot cards, and professed to be from a Chicago Mafia family. It was in connection with that later claim that she once told me and a few others that she knew where Jimmy Hoffa's body was buried. You will be pleased to know that Jimmy's final resting place is beneath a swimming pool in Fort Lauderdale, Florida. According to Caryn, the concrete was poured immediately after the body was placed there. An instant Headstone was thus created. That revelation was made at a restaurant in Hot Springs, Arkansas. True story, cross my heart; I have witnesses.

Oddly enough, I felt calm when we arrived at that nondescript office building and went inside. The main reason for that calmness was the sure knowledge that there had been no violation of the letter or spirit of the law by either myself or the others being investigated. The second reason was the reassuring presence of Dick Leon. Dick is a big man with a bigger personality. He was also my attorney. I was about to go on a long voyage, in uncharted waters, and he was my navigator.

To understand how and why I found myself in this situation it is necessary for me to retrace a sizable amount of my personal history. You will soon see the need for this. I will introduce some of my friends from my past personal and professional life, and explain how, many years later, some of us came together in a fateful venture, and how, and why, we were politically targeted for destruction... by the Wife of the President of The United States...the woman who would become co-president.

Richard J. Leon is now a federal judge for the United States District Court for the District of Columbia. He has served on the court since February 2002, when he was confirmed by the U.S. Senate after a 2001 nomination by President George W. Bush.

Thirty years earlier, after twelve years of honorable service in the United States Air Force, I made a career change. Upon discharge from the Air Force, I became Executive Director of the Virginia Jaycees, a state-wide civic and service organization. In the sixties and seventies, the Jaycee organization was at its zenith and enjoyed a place of prestige in communities throughout the nation and around the world. After three years in that post, I had the unbelievable good fortune to be selected to be one of the few senior staff at the Jaycees national headquarters in Tulsa, Oklahoma.

Federal investigators would ask me countless questions in 1998 that could only be put in context by explaining events that occurred during those Jaycee years in Tulsa. It is, therefore, necessary as well as heartwarming to continue.

Arriving in Tulsa in July 1970, my wife Peggy and I were about to embark on the most memorable and pleasurable part of our lives. We were in our early thirties and childless. I was involved in exciting work with talented and highly motivated young people at the helm of a 350,000-member national organization. Life was good and about to become better. In the first year that we were there, I was traveling on all but five weekends. In the three years there I would travel to forty-three states, some of them many times.

There were hundreds, even thousands of people to meet and work with. Not all of them were Jaycees. The organization had a broad base of support from corporations and foundations. A survey taken in the early seventies revealed that seventy-six percent of the members of congress were or had been Jaycees. It certainly was a useful affiliation to have if you were a young politician on the rise. It was totally nonpartisan, and both democrats and republicans existed in friendship and harmony. Among other things, I directed the Governmental Affairs program.   Other programs that were in my portfolio were equally representative of the political and philosophical breadth of the organization. I found myself at varying times dealing with the Ford Foundation, The Mott Foundation, Fortune 500 companies, and the White House, all in the same day.

A meeting that would change my life dramatically, both then and in the future, took place at our Tulsa Headquarters not long after I had arrived there. A young man, near my age, visited our office in the late summer or early fall of 1970. He was Richard M. Larry and he represented the Scaife Family Charitable Trusts. He had come to Tulsa to meet with the people who would administer and conduct programs that his Foundation had funded. As luck would have it there were two programs that the foundation had funded. They were Environmental Improvement and National Security Education. Both of those programs had been assigned to me. We were excited to have our visitor there and pleased that he was so down to earth. Not all of our contributors were.

I mentioned the "Big Tent" philosophy of the Jaycees, and it is time for full disclosure. I am a lifelong Republican and a political conservative. Richard Larry and I had something in common. The Scaife Family Charitable Trusts were and are longtime supporters of conservative causes. There are a lot of other things that Dick Larry and I have in common, including the fact that thirty years later he, too, would be swept up in this politically motivated federal investigation. He was to become President of the Scaife Family Charitable Trusts a few years after we met.

I didn't meet Dick Larry's boss right away, but I did work with his staff and had their full support. Eventually, though, I did meet Dick Scaife and instantly liked him. I have met several super rich people who are household names and believe me, they are different than you and me. So is Dick Scaife, but that would not be your first impression when you met him. He makes people comfortable and puts them at ease with his ready smile and genuine interest in what they have to say. Dick Scaife would become the biggest target of all in the forthcoming politically motivated Federal Investigation.

CHAPTER TWO ~
FUTURE

Writing about Tulsa and our Jaycee experiences there brings back memories of the most pleasant kind. Our daughter Marcail was born there on November 3, 1971. She is our only child and now is the mother of our only grandchild, Jonathan Kelly.

Two more people whom I met while a staff officer with the United States Jaycees would become pivotal characters in a drama unlike any seen in my lifetime. This drama would involve a President of the United States. And it would lead to his impeachment.

In 1970 a young man met me at the airport in Indianapolis, Indiana, and drove me to Bloomington, Indiana, to the home of R. Emmett Tyrrell, Jr. The Vietnam war was raging, and on campuses across the country, students were rebelling. The emerging counterculture was in full bloom, and it was common for students to bring college administrations to their knees, often with the guidance and assistance of their professors. An underground press was thriving on and off many of the nation's colleges and universities. Their avowed enemy was "the establishment," and to them, the Military personified the Establishment. Dick Larry had told me about a group of graduate students at the Indiana University led by a recent graduate, R. Emmett (Bob) Tyrrell, Jr.

Bob had founded an off-campus magazine called The *Alternative*. He and his friends had become counter-counterculture publishers, writers, and editors. They extolled traditional values and actually defended "the establishment." That was incidentally the name Tyrrell chose for his headquarters and his home, "The Establishment." the name of their headquarters, and Tyrrell's home. At that period of time, The United States Jaycees were pro-establishment as the definition implied, yet we were not all Republicans. Many politicians of both parties owed their success, in part, to the Jaycees. United States Senator Wendell Ford, D-KY, had been National President of The United

States Jaycees, then returned to his home in Kentucky and was elected Governor before becoming a United States Senator. United States Senator Sam Nunn, D-GA, often stated publicly that he owed his success to the Georgia Jaycees, and without their organizational skills, he would not have become a senator. United States Senator Dale Bumpers, D-AR, had been propelled to both the Governor's office and the Senate by the Arkansas Jaycees. It is a very long list, including both political parties.

During World War Two, the Jaycees almost folded because so many of their young leaders volunteered for service. Some of them became Generals. You could say of the Jaycees that "we had a dog in this fight." We had our own Vietnam veterans on staff. Among them was Marine veteran Lloyd Bandy. He provided considerable support to a new initiative of the Jaycees. Our National President, Gordon B. Thomas had initiated a campus tour and he, along with his assistant Herb Conyers, and our Director of Public Relations Tom Cantrell was speaking before groups on college and university campuses around the country. Their purpose was to identify and try to understand the motivations of those who were ripping the country apart and to simultaneously offer the Jaycees as an example of what was right with the young people in America.

While Gordon was touring campuses, I was conducting meetings around the country with civic leaders. My purpose was to bring groups of community leaders together to meet with and hear from speakers who could both educate and motivate them. For that job, I had some world class help in the person of Frank Barnett. Frank was a Rhodes Scholar who had been General Lucas Clay's interpreter when the allies met the Russians at the Elbe River near the end of World War II. After the war, he founded The National Strategy Information Center, in New York, and carried on the vital task of national security education for the remainder of his life. Frank had the skill and stature to surround himself with some of the finest leaders ever to serve this country. Among them were countless retired Generals, Admirals, Ambassadors and university professors. There were gifted speakers and writers who had an amazing grasp of world affairs. Frank Barnett made those people available to me.

Bob Tyrrell and I visited at his home in Bloomington where I explained the things being done by the Jaycees and Bob told me about *The Alternative.* Thus began what would become a friendship that would last for decades. *The Alternative* would become *The American Spectator* some years later and begin its march into history.

A few months earlier, in June of 1970, Peggy and I went to St. Louis, Missouri, to attend the fiftieth annual convention of The United States Jaycees. The organization had been founded there in 1920. I was still Executive Director of The Virginia Jaycees but had already accepted the offer to join the national staff. Thomas R. Donnelly, Jr., then Executive Vice President of The United States Jaycees, had written to me and invited me to accept a staff position at the headquarters in Tulsa. That offer was immediately accepted. Tom, his wife Chris and their three sons, Tommy, Derek and Terry would become like family to us over the next few decades. Among other accomplishments, Tom would later become Assistant Secretary of Health and Human Services in the first Reagan administration. During President Reagan's second term Tom moved to the White House as an Assistant to The President of the United States.

The 50th annual convention became momentous, taking on an importance beyond the other 49 before. Andre LeTendre was finishing his year as President of The United States Jaycees, and he would preside over the convention that would elect his successor and ten National Vice Presidents. Each of these Vice Presidents would represent five states and serve on the Executive Committee. The highlight of the convention was an address by The President of The United States, Richard M. Nixon. President Nixon had been a member of the Whittier, California Jaycees in his earlier years and was very fond of the organization.

The President and Mrs. Nixon were introduced to the assembled delegates in Kiel Auditorium by National Jaycee President Andre LeTendre. The President's popularity at that time was weakened, in part because of the continuing Vietnam War, but before he could utter his first word he received an eleven-minute standing ovation. It was estimated that there were over seventeen thousand people in Kiel Auditorium at that time, far more than the auditorium could seat. Delegates were standing on every available square inch of floor space.

I was standing near the press box and could see surprise turn into astonishment on the faces of those in the press who cover Presidential events. They travel with the President everywhere he goes and report each word that he utters. What they were witnessing took them by total surprise. This President, in the view of many in the media, did not deserve this show of respect and recently he had not been getting it. What they were seeing and not understanding was a celebration by Jaycees of one of their own. As the applause died down the President raised his hands in a gesture suggesting that the welcome had been appreciated and said: "Thank you." At the sound of those first two words, he received another standing ovation that lasted over five minutes. Nothing specific that the President said that day is etched in my memory, but the emotion of what happened will always be there.

Gordon B. Thomas was elected the fiftieth President of The United States Jaycees and would be taking office on the first of July. That is a very heady honor for a young man who must achieve it before he becomes thirty-five years old. The president-elect and his family must move to Tulsa, Oklahoma for one year and he becomes a full-time leader of the organization. Life is made easier for the president and his family by a staff of about one hundred and thirty and a residence called "The Little White House." The home is completely furnished and all they have to do is empty their suitcases. As one president arrives another one leaves. The one leaving, in this particular instance, was Andre LeTendre. He, his wife Mary Jean and their children were about to get the shock of their lives. President Nixon had returned to the White House a restored man. His staff reported to us that he couldn't begin a meeting for weeks without asking if everyone had seen the reception that he had received by the Jaycees. There were numerous press reports about the event in St. Louis. The President was about to return the favor. Andre received the call before he left Tulsa. Would he come to Washington as Deputy Assistant to The President of The United States?

Peggy and I arrived in Tulsa the same day that Gordon Thomas did. There was another arrival that day that would enrich our lives. Robert S. Dunbar, his wife Vivian and their children, David, Robin and Daniel had come down from Minneapolis, Minnesota. Bob Dunbar would be replacing Tom Donnelly as Executive Vice President. The Executive Vice President was responsible for the day to day operation of the organization including the supervision of the staff. As such, he was my boss, and a very good one.

We adjusted easily to the frenetic pace of our new environment. Our future was being shaped in ways that we couldn't then understand. There were friendships to be made with our fellow staff officers, most of whom had come from other states. Each of us brought different skills and backgrounds but we all had a common bond. We were Jaycees. Since we were all from somewhere else, we became like family to each other, temporarily replacing families left behind.

There was not time to be trained. We were there because of our initiative and each of us was expected to be able to do whatever was asked of us. We were also expected to bring new ideas and new ways of doing things. After all, this was an evolving organization whose leadership was completely replaced each year. The exception to that was the staff. It was the continuity of the organization.

Elections take place each spring at all levels of the organization. State and local chapters hold their meetings and conventions prior to the national convention. They not only elect state and local officers, but certain state officers serve as national directors. National Directors and State Presidents from each of the states make up the Board of Directors and at the beginning of each new administration, a board meeting is held in Tulsa. It is from within this group that future national leadership develops. *Future Magazine* was the official publication of The United States Jaycees, and never had a publication been more aptly named.

It was at one of those meetings that I met a young man from Arkansas. He was a lawyer and in a few years, he would rise through the ranks to become President of The United States Jaycees. He would become famous, though for another reason. His name was David Hale.

His future would include a fateful linkage to a future President of The United States, a Judgeship, and imprisonment.

CHAPTER THREE ~
MY "PRISON" RECORD

The summer of 1970 went at a furious pace leaving no time for acclimation to my new duties. We completed our July Board of Directors meeting. It had been an interesting period as we met and worked with fifty new State Presidents, ten new National Vice Presidents, and a few hundred National Directors. During that week Gordon Thomas hosted several social events at "The Little White House." We rapidly became acquainted with both our fellow staff officers and their families. We developed working relationships with the Executive committee and the State Presidents. Our travel commitments grew during that period. Several State Presidents and National Vice Presidents worked us into their state meetings. I had a seminar to conduct with the Charles Stewart Mott foundation in Flint, Michigan, in a couple of months, so a trip to Flint was scheduled for preliminary meetings and planning.

The Ford Foundation was a major Jaycee contributor, and since we had entirely new leadership, none of whom had met or was known to the Foundation's personnel who administered our grant, Gordon Thomas, Bob Dunbar and I went to New York for a meeting with Roger Wilkins, then an executive with The Ford Foundation and son of the civil rights pioneer, Roy Wilkins.

That summer I received a most welcome phone call from an old friend and mentor from Virginia, John O. Marsh, Jr. He was a US Congressman whose district encompassed most of the Shenandoah Valley in Virginia. Jack, as he was known to his friends, had been a Virginia Jaycee and had once served as its Legal Counsel. That was an appointed position that each State President filled during his administration, and naturally, it was a non-paying, volunteer job. Jack was a Democrat in his fifth term. The congressman was calling to tell me that a conference was to be held at The White House a few days later and he suggested that I be there. The conference would be attended by several very important people and he wanted me to meet some of them. He offered to have me invited and I accepted.

I was to witness a brilliant career unfold over the next several years as Jack Marsh made one important move after the next. First, he declared himself an Independent. Next, he announced that he would not seek reelection. He was named to the newly created post of Assistant Secretary of Defense for Legislative Affairs by President Nixon. A short time later Vice President Spiro Agnew was forced to resign and President Nixon named Congressman Gerald Ford of Michigan as his new Vice President. Though Jack had been a Democrat and Gerald Ford had been a Republican, they served together in congress and they were very close friends. Vice President Ford called on Jack Marsh to leave his Pentagon post to become his National Security Advisor.

When President Nixon resigned and Vice President Ford became President, one of his first announcements was naming John O. Marsh, Jr. as Counselor to the President with Cabinet Rank. When President Ford lost his re-election bid to Jimmy Carter, the former Governor of Georgia, once again President Ford tapped Jack Marsh for a job of national importance. He named him to head the transition between his administration and the Carter Administration. During Jack's time as President Ford's Counselor, he had been a strong advocate for Richard Cheney to become the president's Chief of Staff. Dick Cheney was named to that position and served with distinction. But John O. Marsh, Jr. of Virginia was not through, nor for that matter, was Dick Cheney.

Less than four years later, Ronald W. Reagan was elected President of the United States and would serve two complete terms. He appointed John O. Marsh, Jr. as Secretary of the Army. Jack would serve in that post for the full two terms of President Reagan and a few months into the Presidency of George H. W. Bush. No one in history had ever served in that position for that long. During the latter part of his tenure as Secretary of The Army, he would be reunited with his old friend Dick Cheney because President Bush had appointed him Secretary of Defense. Dick was then Jack's boss.

If you are wondering how and why Jack Marsh would take the time to see that I got off to a good start in my new position with The

United States Jaycees, I'm not surprised. I even wondered about it myself for a few years. Then one day, as Jack and I were meeting in his office, he recalled the circumstances under which we had met. I remembered it well, but Jack knew something I didn't.

This is what I knew. While I was on active duty in the Air Force, I spent several years on an Army Post. Fort Lee, near Petersburg, Virginia, was headquarters for the Army Material and Logistics command. There was a small Air Force squadron tucked away in one corner of the post. It was the nerve center for the Air Defense of much of the East Coast. It was there that I had become involved with the Petersburg, Virginia Jaycees. Very few military personnel were involved in the local community, so for that reason alone I stood out. The Petersburg chapter had a history of strong leadership and close ties to the community. Philip H. Kirkpatrick had been State President a couple of years before I joined the organization, and he had remained very dedicated to his home chapter in Petersburg. He was, by temperament and training, a teacher. Doctor Philip H. Kirkpatrick would complete his government career years later as the civilian head of the U.S. Army Logistics School at Fort Lee, Virginia. Phil took an interest in me for a variety of reasons. Among them, I am sure, was the novelty of having an active duty non-commissioned officer holding office in a host community civic organization.

Phil Kirkpatrick was in constant demand as a speaker to Jaycee chapters around the state. He accepted as many of the invitations as he could. He had found me to be a willing student so he began to invite me to accompany him to his speaking engagements. The hours on the road consisted of many conversations about many subjects, but mostly, it was a history of the Jaycees. All of the fifty state Jaycee organizations recognized their "Outstanding first year Jaycee" and that honor was determined by both written and oral examinations. The level of participation one had during the first year and one's understanding of the organization's history was the determining criteria. Phil was determined that I would be selected for that award, and with his help, I was. This brings us back to Phil Kirkpatrick's friend, Congressman John

O. Marsh, Jr.

There is a Federal Prison just outside Fort Lee, Virginia. It is the Prince George Federal Reformatory. Sometime in the nineteen sixties a young man, Gary Hill, from Lincoln, Nebraska, conceived the idea that a novel and effective prison rehabilitation program would be the creation of Jaycee Chapters in prisons. There the same organizational and communication skills could be taught to the inmates and possibly, upon their release from prison, the former inmates would become involved with their communities. If it worked it would be what was known in those days as a win-win situation. Recidivism would be reduced, crime would decline, at least among those who chose not to return to their old ways, and the Government would have reduced the cost of prison administration.

The Petersburg Jaycees chose me to chair a committee to create a chapter in the Prince George Federal Prison. I accepted the task and proceeded to get it done. As always, Phil Kirkpatrick was there to help make the impossible take less time. After a few months of evening and weekend visits in the prison, we had an organization ready to go. We chose the date for a charter banquet in the prison. The prison administrators had been more than helpful and had arranged for us to bring our chapter's members and spouses to the dinner. That had caused a mild stir among Jaycee wives because civilian women in a prison tend to evoke visions of scenes from the movie, "Silence of the Lambs."

Phil Kirkpatrick insisted that everything be done first class. He volunteered to secure a speaker of distinction for the evening. We arranged with a local radio station to broadcast the program live from the prison. Phil wrote to Congressman John O. Marsh, Jr., and invited him to be the guest speaker at the most unique dinner ever hosted by the Petersburg Jaycees. Jack Marsh accepted, and we were ready to proceed. As chairman, I was the master of ceremonies and also had the honor of introducing the guest speaker. Upon his arrival at the prison, Jack and his wife, Glenn Ann, were ushered into the dining room by Phil Kirkpatrick. Phil guided them directly to me and introduced us. I believe he said something to this effect, "Dave is the one who made all of this possible. He will be the master of ceremonies and will introduce you this evening." As we sat in his office that day many years later Jack told me the-rest-of-the-story. As I was preparing to leave the Air Force to accept the position of Executive Director of The Virginia Jaycees, Phil Kirkpatrick had called Jack at his office in the Capitol. Phil asked if he remembered the young man who had introduced him at the Banquet in the Prison some months earlier, and the Congressman said that he did. Phil then said, "Dave is getting out soon and he is going to become Executive Director of The Virginia Jaycees." Phil had assumed that he had told Jack that I was on active duty in the Air Force or maybe he had told him and it had been forgotten.

Anyway, "getting out" had two meanings. The first words out Jack's mouth were, "Can he be bonded? Will he be handling any money? Boy, you guys are taking that program seriously, aren't you?" Until that phone call from Phil Kirkpatrick, Congressman Marsh had thought I was an inmate who had been allowed to wear a suit for that one evening while all of the other inmates wore their prison uniforms. Phil quickly realized his earlier failure to communicate and corrected or expunged my record, so to speak. When Jack told that story to me, he said that he had been too embarrassed to tell me sooner. By that time, he felt that we knew each other well enough to appreciate it. Not only did I appreciate it, there were a few times afterward when I had occasion to introduce Jack as a speaker and I would always tell that story, to the amusement of Jack, the audience and myself. Little did I know that my "prison record" while a Jaycee would, years later, be repeated... as I visited a friend in need...in another Federal Prison.

CHAPTER FOUR ~
BIT PLAYER

It was my first visit to the White House, the seat of power for The United States of America, and I didn't have to wait in line. True to his word, Jack Marsh had seen to it that I was invited to the conference. We were there to hear about the war in Vietnam. That war had caused the former President of the United States, Lyndon B. Johnson, to refuse to seek a second term. It was also eating away at the current occupant of The White House, Richard M. Nixon.

This was the first of my many visits to the White House. I was to become a bit player on one of the biggest stages in the world. In the coming months, I would meet some of the most influential people in our nation. This was exciting and highly improbable for someone who had been an Air Force non-commissioned officer just three years earlier.

Ray Roper, one of my fellow Jaycee staff officers and I were invited to serve on the White House Council on The Aging. Then I was placed on The Advisory Board of National Organizations to The Corporation for Public Broadcasting. My travel from Tulsa to Washington became almost a weekly event.

The seminar in Flint, Michigan went well and was a personal thrill. I had the opportunity to meet one of the industrial giants of the twentieth century. Charles Stewart Mott was one of the founders and probably the biggest shareholder in the General Motors Corporation. He was a billionaire and he was ninety years old when I met him. I was to have a very pleasant relationship with his foundation, The Charles Stewart Mott Foundation.

Mr. Mott was legendary. My favorite story about him merits telling here. He was attending a Board Meeting of General Motors. During a break in the meeting, he and some of the other board members were standing in a hotel lobby. The other board members were paying rapt attention as Mr. Mott was speaking. Suddenly he stopped in mid-sentence and his eyes began to follow a beautiful young woman. He continued to follow her with his eyes until she went out the door and out of sight. After a brief lingering look in the direction she was going, he turned back to his colleagues and said, "Ah, if only I were seventy- five again." I hope that is a true story. It was too good not to be.

Our time in Tulsa went by with lightning speed. The first year was wonderful, and we had two more administrations to work with before our odyssey with the Jaycees ended. By that time, we had formed the closest relationships that we would likely have in our lifetimes. Gordon Thomas, from Toledo, Ohio, was succeeded by Ronald G. S. Au, an attorney from Honolulu. Ron was succeeded by Samuel Winer, a businessman from New Martinsburg, West Virginia. There were more conventions to attend, more seminars and national board meetings to plan and conduct and more than enough travel. I had taken on the Governmental Affairs duties and each year one of my responsibilities was to plan and conduct the Annual Governmental Affairs Leadership Seminar in Washington, D.C. That was probably the most popular event of the year. Only the National Executive Committee and State Presidents attended.

Dick Larry called in the Spring of 1971 and told me that there was to be a graduate course in Public Affairs at Freedoms Foundation at Valley Forge. It would be conducted by Texas A&M University and it was a three credit-hour course. He suggested that I consider attending. It was to be during the summer, and my time was not committed, so I made arrangements to attend. Dick's reason for suggesting that I attend was based on the people who were to be giving the lectures. He correctly felt that I could possibly identify new speakers for some of the programs being conducted by the Jaycees.

Freedoms Foundation at Valley Forge is in a beautiful setting and my stay there was memorable. Its President was a man whose face I had seen in every building on Fort Lee, Virginia. While I had been Sergeant Henderson he had been General Harold K. Johnson, Chief of Staff of the U.S. Army. A farm boy from North Dakota, General Johnson had graduated from West Point. He had a brilliant military career. He was one of the survivors of the Bataan Death March and had suffered enormously as a prisoner of the Japanese for forty-three months. While I was attending the course I called his office and asked for an appointment with him. My request was quickly granted. Entering his office, I was warmly greeted by the man with that ever so familiar face. Everything about him was impressive, but especially his voice. I would hear from and see him many times during the remainder of his life. I cannot describe all the kindness he extended to me or the friendship that we would develop. I had read many accounts of Generals who held non-commissioned officers in high esteem, and though I was no longer in the military, he was aware of my background. I would have the sad honor of attending his burial at Arlington National Cemetery in 1983.

A strange and puzzling invitation arrived one day in Tulsa. It was addressed to me and was an invitation to a luncheon in New York at the St. Regis Hotel. The invitation had been extended by David and Nelson Rockefeller. Naturally, I accepted. Arriving at the hotel with some trepidation, I squared my shoulders and walked in. Then I fully understood what culture shock was, I knew it immediately, and I was the one in shock. A receiving line was in place and it was astounding. It included not only the famous Rockefeller brothers, Nelson and David, but Henry Ford and Ross Perot were there, as well as John Y. Brown. Apart from those in the receiving line, there were fifty-one other people in that room. Fifty of them were Chairmen of the largest Corporations in America. I was number fifty-one. Moving along the receiving line there were perfunctory introductions and handshakes until I came to Hubert S. Humphrey, United States Senator from Minnesota and former Vice President of The United States. Each person was wearing a name tag and I was wearing something else that caught Senator Humphrey's eye.

As I approached him, Humphrey stepped toward me with that trademark smile on his face, took my hand warmly and said, "David, I see that you are a Jaycee." For an instant I was taken aback by that remark, then realized that he had seen my lapel pin. He continued talking in that mile a minute style of his. "Muriel and I certainly enjoyed our years in the St. Paul Jaycees." I knew that he had been President of the St. Paul Jaycees when he was younger. "If I can ever be of service to you just call me." He meant it. "Come by my office when you are in Washington and let's visit." I never did and I regret that. The Happy Warrior was just that. Everything that I had ever read or heard about him was validated in those few seconds. Most people liked Hubert Humphrey whether they agreed with him politically or not. I never did agree with him politically but joined a long list of his admirers that day.

After lunch was served the Rockefellers both made comments, as did Henry Ford and Senator Humphrey. Ross Perot was not at the head table, nor did he speak. That seemed to rankle him. The reason for the luncheon soon became clear. America had hundreds of prisoners of war in Vietnam, peace talks were going on in Paris, and there was the expectation that the prisoners would soon be coming home. The people in that room were there to arrange a "welcome home" for our prisoners of war. Then I knew why I was there. They had the money and the clout. We had the manpower.

Unfortunately, history was not on our side. Things didn't work out the way they were expected to, and the prisoners didn't get their nationwide hero's welcome home. They had to settle for a tent on the White House grounds.

In a gesture that I perceived to be genuine, H. Ross Perot approached me and asked me to meet with him in the hotel lobby. Everyone in America knew that Ross Perot had moved heaven and earth for our military forces in Vietnam. That is why something that he said to me in the lobby that afternoon has stuck with me all of these years. We probably talked for fifteen minutes or more. I could tell that he felt slighted for not being given more exposure. He seemed to feel that he was not considered an equal in that company, and he projected some insecurity for that reason. The conversation with Mr. Perot mainly consisted of him speaking, and me listening. He pointed out to me that we would wind up being the ones who did all of the work, and the others would take all of the credit. That was OK by me but I didn't get the chance to tell that to Ross Perot. The words that followed told me just how insecure he was. He said," Those beady-eyed bastards in there won't even know who we are after we leave this luncheon." I never heard from Ross Perot again. I wonder if he forgot who I was?

CHAPTER FIVE ~
A CHILD IN AFRICA

Our tour with the Jaycees had been a rewarding and exciting time made even more so by the splendid young men and their families who lived and worked in Tulsa. Those people were the heart and soul of the organization that inevitably became a force in the lives of all its members. We would only be with them for a short time in Tulsa, but as fate would have it, we would become intertwined in friendship for the remainder of our lives.

Both the Democrat and Republican conventions were held in Miami Beach, Florida in the summer of 1972. I was excited that I would be attending both of them. The Republican convention came first and I was to be there for the platform hearings as well as the nominating convention. The prospect of two weeks in Miami Beach in the sweltering heat of July wasn't at all a daunting prospect in view of the fact that I had already spent eighteen months, while barely more than a child, wedged between the Libyan desert and the Mediterranean Sea at Wheelus Air Base in Tripoli, Libya. Granted, that had been a long time ago, long enough ago that I had seen the British and French bombing armada cross the Mediterranean Sea en route to its target, the Suez Canal.

From our vantage point on the southern coast of the Mediterranean, our radars were able to track the invading force all the way into Egyptian airspace. That was in 1956 and occurred shortly after I had arrived for my tour of duty as a radar operator. That such a momentous and historical occurrence should happen while I was on duty to witness it left an indelible impression on me, as would something that would occur the following year in the endlessly volatile Middle East. That was a border dispute between Syria and Turkey, an event that quickly escalated into an international crisis which brought the forces of The Soviet Union and NATO into a face off. My unit at Wheelus Air Base had an added responsibility as a quick response team to go to the aid of NATO countries who came under hostilities. The escalating hostilities between Syria and Turkey triggered the need for the establishment of emergency radar facilities at Incerlik Air Base in Adana, Turkey, as well as the manpower to operate it.

In the fall of 1957, I found myself boarding an Air Force C-54 in early morning darkness, with one week of clothing and other necessary supplies, with no idea of where I was going. Others on board that flight and the Air Force C-47 following us were as unenlightened. Many hours later in the slow moving C-54, an unidentified Air Force Lt. Colonel, carrying a briefcase handcuffed to his wrist, emerged from the front of the aircraft to announce to us where we were going, and what we would be doing there. We were told that The Soviet Union had announced its support of Syria and that The United States would be as resolute in its support of Turkey. Our radars had two purposes. The primary purpose was to provide surveillance of the air space over the borders in dispute and to direct interceptor aircraft to targets should that become necessary. Second, the geographical location from which we would operate would allow us to cover a sizable area in the Soviet Union.

As history will attest, the Syrian and Turkish dispute ended without erupting into a major conflict, and to me, that was a happy ending. For fifty-seven days our radar crews maintained vigilance over the skies without incident. At least without reported incident at that time. There was something going on in the sky that none of us had seen before and something that we could not reveal. Each day at the same time a radar target would appear, outbound from Incerlik Air Base, with flight characteristics, unlike anything we had been trained to recognize. From the first appearance of the target as it emerged from the ground clutter of our radar the target climbed at a steeper rate than we thought possible.

No known aircraft at that time had the capability to do what this one did. It would climb completely above the upper limits of our height/range radar (HRI) by the time it had reached ten miles from takeoff. Primitive as they were by today's standards, those were pretty impressive capabilities in 1957. Our height/range radars (HRI) at the time could detect flying objects up to 60,000 feet. We did not lose radar contact with the target after it climbed above our height range indicators, HRI because our surveillance radars, by their design, were able to view targets at a much greater range and elevation. Given the ability of the surveillance radar, we were allowed to continue to observe the strange behavior and destination of this "unknown" aircraft. Turkey borders on the southern edge of the Black Sea, and each day our departing target would head directly to and across the Black sea where it would assume a pattern that could be described as "loitering" over the southern Soviet Union. The ground speed would be reduced to a point that would seem to defy gravity, and there it would remain for several hours until it would return to Incirlik Air Base.

Needless to say, those of us who were fascinated with this aircraft each day had plenty of questions. Those questions went unanswered. They also went unasked. We had orders about not talking to anyone about what we were observing. Since we had three shifts working around the clock, all of us had plenty of free time. My free time and my curiosity led me to long walks around the periphery of the runways and hangers and I soon noticed an aircraft hangar unlike the others around it. The extra security around that particular hanger was in some ways subtle, but as someone who knew that unusual flight activity was occurring from this airfield, I knew that I had located the source of these secret comings and goings the moment that I spotted the hanger. It was located just a few hundred feet from the main runway and a taxiway led directly from the hanger, slightly diagonal from the hanger, to the end of the runway, in such a way as to facilitate the rollout and takeoff of an aircraft, and aircraft that could not afford to be seen on the ground, or from the sky, for more than a few seconds. There were also the "doors." It had been my observation that aircraft hangers had massive doors, high and wide enough to allow the passage of aircraft for maintenance or storage. Those doors are usually permanently hung, and can be rolled open or shut, depending upon the use to which the hanger is being put at the moment. Those doors, because of their mass and weight, tended to move slowly when opened or shut.

Not so the "doors" on this special hanger. They consisted of huge louvers sitting in front of the hanger opening and not attached to the hanger itself. Rather, they had several axles, similar to automobile axles with rubber tires mounted on them upon which the louvered "door" rested. The tires ran parallel to the opening of the hanger in such a fashion as to allow the louvered "door" to be pulled away from the opening, presumably in a more efficient manner than the usual hanger doors. Another advantage of this arrangement, it would seem, would be to allow an aircraft to operate its engine or engines in an atmosphere of ventilation without being exposed to prying eyes from the outside or above.

I was drawn back to the vicinity of that hanger more than once for further observation and to satisfy my natural curiosity. Soon enough I found myself nearby on one of my days off and a few minutes earlier than our daily detection of those outbound departures. My reward began soon when I heard a powerful jet engine start up in the hanger. The sound continued for a few minutes as the engine warmed up and suddenly a jeep arrived at the end of the louvered "doors" and attached what appeared to be a short metal bar appended to one end of the "door" to a trailer hitch. It was show time. The roar of the jet engine inside the hanger reached a crescendo that coincided with the sudden forward movement of the jeep as it moved the louvered door quickly and smoothly away from the front of the hanger. At once there emerged from the hanger a strange looking aircraft already building speed for a takeoff. The fuselage was small, about the size of the T-33, a common jet trainer plane of that era, but the wings were something to behold. They had an enormous width and almost dug into the taxi-way at their tips until the increasing speed of the racing plane caused them to lift. There was the telltale exhaust of a single jet engine as the aircraft merged smoothly from the diagonal taxiway onto the main runway and suddenly it was aloft. It had reached liftoff speed almost as soon as it had reached the main runway, and I then had the rare pleasure of watching from the ground what I had seen before on radar.

The aircraft that I had just witnessed in takeoff was the U-2, the spy aircraft, and may have been piloted that day by Francis Gary Powers. That personal observation was three years before the rest of the world learned of its existence when a Soviet missile brought it down over Soviet territory. Having honored my security oath, I had never breathed a word of the U-2's existence until that day when President Dwight Eisenhower admitted it to the world.

It is important to remember, in those years, our country had only been free of massive armed conflict for a very short period of time. While most Americans were occupied with building lives which had been interrupted by a depression and wars throughout the first half of the twentieth century, there was still a very real threat of war between East and West. In the 1950s, as it had always been, the sons and daughters of the poor were manning outposts around the world, providing a bulkhead against forces who were intent on destroying, or disrupting, the engine of capitalism, the great threat to the ideology of socialism. Families in the United States were finally free to begin making better lives for themselves and their communities. They were building homes, and with heroic sacrifice, educating their children in ways that only the affluent had previously been able to do. Common people were able to do uncommon things, and their children were as dedicated to those efforts as were their parents. The schools lent their support and efforts to what may have been the most important social development in this nation's history.

Sons of farmers, mechanics, bakers, machinists, railroad workers and other working classes gave all of the sweat from their bodies to help achieve the great promise of democracy. That, after they had already given so many of their sons. Those who survived, however, joined a new class. No matter what one's background had been, a degree from an American college or university provided entry into a new world of privilege. It was manifestly true in the armed forces. Second Lieutenants, sons, and daughters of the marginally less deprived families of that period would become Colonels and Generals within the next two decades. And many of the returning veterans of World War Two and the Korean war, would, with the aid of the GI bill, become national leaders. There had been no country in history to match ours.

Those old memories returned to me as I contemplated the forthcoming conventions in 1972. Strange? Not at all. If anything was at the center of national thought at the nominating conventions of the two national parties approached, it was war. It had been less than a generation since the end of World War II and in those short intervening years, we had seen the Korean war come and go only to be followed by the current and all-consuming Vietnam war. I was not yet 35 years old and had personally been brushed by all three conflicts. As a preschooler, my family had moved to St. Louis, Missouri. My father had been unable to pass an induction physical, so he moved his entire family two hundred miles, to another state, in order to work at a small arms munitions plant. It was his contribution to the World War II effort. The Korean war ended before I was draft age, but we had friends and family in that conflict. My last few years in the Air Force were during the Viet Nam war, though I did not serve there. Some of my friends did. Anti-war demonstrators were already publicly promising to tie up Miami Beach during the conventions. How could one not be awash with anticipation as events such as the upcoming political conventions were about to unfold?

I would be attending these conventions as an officer of the United States Jaycees. Our organization had as big a stake as any other in the democratic process. We impetuously reminded others that our national conventions were as big and as exciting as the Democrat and Republican ones. They were as big, and certainly as exciting to us, but ours paled in importance to the nation in comparison to these "Super Bowls" of national politics.

CHAPTER SIX ~
WINDS OF "ANTI" WAR

The Fontainebleau Hotel dominated Miami Beach, Florida during July and August of 1972. Situated across Collins Avenue from the Intercostal Waterway, the grand old hotel had been selected as the headquarters hotel for both the Democrat National Convention and the Republican National Convention that same year. Fortunately, they were held on separate dates during consecutive months. Otherwise, the streets of Miami Beach would have been much hotter than normal that year. As it was, it was plenty hot. And not only the weather. From a yacht, El Presidente docked directly across Collins Avenue from the Fontainebleau Hotel, a visitor had an unrestricted view of the pomp and splendor of a national political convention. El Presidente was a grand old lady, over 100 feet, and her Captain looked every bit the equal of whatever might come his way. A burly man in impeccably starched and pressed whites with gold braid, he was as much a part of the atmosphere as were the politicians and their followers who came to Miami Beach that summer.

From the spacious and elegant salon of El Presidente to the afterdeck and the staterooms, John H. Perry, Jr., would entertain visitors throughout both conventions. He was the former owner of the largest chain of newspapers in Florida and a unique man in all respects. Inventor, visionary, philanthropist. All those words described John Perry, but in and of themselves they didn't do him justice. He had pioneered the development of mini-submarines and manufactured them at Perry Submarine in Riviera Beach, Florida. He conducted research for Perry Oceanographics on his private island in the Bahamas. He had pioneered the computerization of newsprint. He was a graduate of Yale and the Harvard Business School and he attended the London School of Economics before he left to become a pilot in The Army Air Corp during World War II. In the summer of 1972, John Perry was fifty-three years old and a very rich man. He lived in Palm Beach, Florida, in a thirty-two thousand square foot home.

John Perry had chartered El Presidente for the conventions. He had secured the best possible place to have it docked. Not being a flashy or flamboyant person, he would rather charter a jet than own one. The same with yachts. His boats were as big, but they were working vessels. His aircraft were also used for work, and they were propeller driven. He could fly airplanes, as he had during the war, but he hired pilots to do that. John Perry needed time to think, and he chose to use his time for that purpose. It was, after all, his mind that had allowed him to accomplish so much in his lifetime and there were many years ahead.

I had met John Perry the previous summer and had instantly liked him. He had been working for several years on an economic plan that he had named The National Dividend Plan and it was deserving of attention. The United States Jaycees had adopted his proposal as part of an economic education program. He had invited me to join him in Miami Beach for the conventions and I had accepted. I would be helping him in making presentations to the platform committees of the respective political parties, as well as meeting with delegates to the conventions, elected representatives, and the media.

From the deck of El Presidente, I was able to see events unfold during those historic days that would lead to political upheaval for the nation. We would smell tear gas when the Miami Beach Police fought to establish order during the frequent demonstrations. Many of those demonstrations occurred just in front of the Fontainebleau Hotel, and by consequence, in front of El Presidente. We made the Miami Beach Policemen who patrolled the area welcome aboard the yacht where we would provide soft drinks and an occasional sandwich. It was a comfort to have them around during those times. On one occasion the Captain of El Presidente stood at the gangplank of his vessel with a twelve-gauge shotgun to repel demonstrators while they chanted their version of "Down with the Capitalist Pigs."

To no one's surprise, Richard M. Nixon was re-nominated for a second term as President of the United States during the Republication convention. At the Democrat convention the following month it took all night to name the candidate to challenge President Nixon. A Jaycee friend from Louisiana was a delegate to that convention and he and I were staying in the same hotel (I didn't have an overnight berth on El Presidente). He returned to the hotel after a long night of balloting and stopped by my room. I asked him what had happened, as I had gone to bed before the nomination, and he replied, "We nominated George McGovern and reelected Richard Nixon."

When I returned to Tulsa after the Democratic convention, I was considering the fact that my self-imposed three years on the staff of the Jaycees would end in less than a year. I wasn't sure just what I would do the following July but was not particularly concerned about it. I was also remembering a conversation with John Perry on the day before leaving Miami. He had asked what I planned to do when I left the Jaycees and I had told him the truth. I didn't know. He flattered me by asking that I talk with him before making a decision.

Shortly after returning to Tulsa a phone call from Andre LeTendre arrived. He said that he was calling from the White House, where he was serving as a Deputy Special Assistant to the President. He asked if I would be willing to take a leave of absence from the United States Jaycees and come to Washington for thirty days as a consultant to the President's Cost of Living Council. He said that the President had asked him to call. I didn't believe that then, and I don't believe it now, but Andre, God rest his soul, was a world-class salesman. In my naiveté, I did buy the thirty-day part. Further, it would be a presidential appointment, and I would be compensated at the rate of a GS-15. What did I know? I hustled downstairs to see Robert S. Dunbar, my boss and Executive Vice President of the United States Jaycees.

Bob Dunbar approved my leave of absence. He was soon to be leaving his position with the Jaycees to return to Minneapolis, Minnesota. Whether he thought it possible to accomplish anything in the federal government in thirty days is a question that I have never asked him. I must make it a point to do so. Whatever Bob Dunbar or I thought or believed about federal speed is irrelevant. It cannot be done.

And it wasn't done. I did take the appointment in good faith and went to Washington. It took thirty days just to do the entry paperwork. My job was to arrange speaking engagements for presidential surrogates so that they could explain the president's economic policy. In other words, it was an election year.

As the thirty days drew to a close, and the paperwork was nearing completion, my supervisor called me in for a chat. He asked that I extend my leave of absence for another thirty days. Not an unreasonable request in my mind since little had been accomplished during the first thirty days. We now had a new Executive Vice President in Tulsa, Ray Roper. Ray had been one of my fellow staff officers since I had arrived in Tulsa. He had been selected to succeed Bob Dunbar. I posed the question of an additional thirty days to Ray, and without hesitation he granted it. That time soon expired. My heart was still in Tulsa. At the risk of being redundant, so was my family.

Again, my supervisor called for a meeting. This time, I heard a question that was becoming more frequent. "How much more time do you have with the Jaycees and what do you plan to do when you leave?" When I answered that I had until July 1, 1973, he offered a helpful suggestion. To wit, I could receive a schedule C appointment in the Nixon administration and continue in my current position. After all, I was nearing the end of my role with The United States Jaycees, and why not just cut the cord early? My response was imperfect and perhaps not well thought out, but I immediately declined. I muttered something about having unfinished business in Tulsa. The questions led to a possible replacement for me with the President's Cost of Living Council, and I had the perfect answer. Thomas R. Donnelly, Jr., former Executive Vice President of the United States Jaycees, and the person who had hired me to come to Tulsa was then living in the Washington area. I impressed upon my supervisor my belief that Tom not only had all of my contacts and abilities but that he had superior capabilities. I asked if a meeting between the two of them could be arranged. It was. Tom replaced me and I returned to Tulsa.

Tom Donnelly did not surprise me. The door to Republican

politics had been opened to him and he made the most of it. At the beginning of the Reagan administration, Tom was confirmed by the Senate to be Assistant Secretary of Health and Human Services (HHS) for legislation. During that period, he served as acting Secretary of HHS between the resignation of Secretary Richard Schweiker and the selection and Senate confirmation of Margaret M. Heckler. Tom led the confirmation process in the Senate for Margaret Heckler and regularly attended cabinet meetings in his role as acting secretary. It was no surprise then when he was moved to the White House during the second Reagan term as Assistant to the President for Legislative Affairs.

In 1973 my three years with the Jaycees came to an end. Peggy, Marki and I returned to Virginia. This time, we located in northern Virginia, near Washington, D.C. The last few months in Tulsa had included some soul searching about what direction our lives should take, and naturally, I had talked with people whose judgment I respected. Two of those people were Richard M. Larry and R. Dan McMichael. Dick and Dan worked for the Scaife Family Charitable Trusts, and I had become comfortable with both of them. I also held them both in the highest regard. During a visit in Pittsburgh with Dick and Dan a few months before my tenure with the Jaycees ended, Dan McMichael made the convincing case that Public Affairs was where I belonged. He spoke of my past experiences and suggested that I could, and should build upon them. He correctly noted that I seemed to enjoy that work and that I should give serious thought to continuing on that path. It was wise counsel, and it was heeded.

CHAPTER SEVEN ~
CHESAPEAKE

In the fall of 1993, twenty years after moving to the Washington D. C. area, I chartered a fishing boat, "The Compensation" for a day of fishing on the Chesapeake Bay. Captain Mike Harris, skipper of "The Compensation" and I were not strangers, nor was my act of chartering his boat in the least bit unusual. What followed that day on the bay, though, would prove to be monumental in my own life and I suspect, in the lives of my guests on that fateful day.

Captain Mike Harris met us at the dock at 7:00 a.m. His forty-two foot, bay built boat, was swinging on her lines in a slip at the Rod and Reel Club in Chesapeake Beach, Maryland. It was a beautiful fall morning as we stepped aboard, full of anticipation. The prized Chesapeake Bay "Rock Fish" known elsewhere as striped bass, had made a remarkable recovery in the Chesapeake in recent years and now was abundant throughout the bay. We were ready to partake in that abundance. Captain Mike had a reputation as one who would get you "on" the fish. At the time he held the state record for the largest "Rock Fish."

One of my guests was Stephen S. Boynton. In light of our relationship the use of the word "guest" seems terribly inadequate. Steve and I had met on the last day of August 1974, in a popular K Street "watering hole" in Washington, D.C. Each of us had stopped there after work for an "adult beverage" and the Club Down Under was overflowing with people on similar missions. I had been one of the lucky few to have a seat at the bar and was preparing to leave when the press of the crowd moved Steve next to my bar stool. I told him that I was leaving, and he could have my seat. We exchanged pleasantries as I paid my check and Steve asked why I was leaving so soon. I told him that I had to go home and prepare for the opening day of Dove season, which was the next day. His face became an exclamation point. "You are a hunter?", he asked. I allowed as to how I was indeed a hunter and he pressed his business card into my hand as I was leaving and asked that I please give him a call.

I had been eight years old when my two cousins, Carl and Floyd Keith came home from World War II. Carl and Floyd were my mother's cousins, making them my second cousins, but it was a distinction that mattered not at all. They embraced me as a companion and I would exult in that role for the next ten years, until I too, would leave home for military service. Their companionship shaped me as much as any experience that I would encounter in life's journey.

We lived in a small town in the extreme western part of Kentucky, on the banks of the Mississippi River, and closer to Tennessee than to the next town. About a mile across the great river was Missouri, and Huck Finn and Tom Sawyer would have felt at home in our town. Our homes were no more than a two-minute walk apart. Not many minutes farther and we would be in the fields and woods surrounding the little town. Carl and Floyd had grown up there and like other rural depression era kids had learned to hunt and fish as small boys. They were eager to return to those pastimes and determined to share them with me. Their father, Earl Keith had supplemented his income by guiding duck hunters on nearby Reelfoot Lake, Tennessee, when they were boys. Uncle Earl made his own hand carved duck calls and they were quite effective.

Carl and Floyd had to start from the bottom with me. Though I had been fishing, thanks to my daddy, since I was three or four, guns and hunting had not yet been introduced into my life. It was not for lack of desire on my part. Hunting was a rite of passage for boys in that age, as it had been for countless centuries. My cousins could not have found a more willing student, and they proved to be more than adequate teachers. They started me with backyard schooling in firearms, beginning with a .22 rifle, and soon moving up to the heavier shotguns. First, it was a .410 and my little body didn't have a problem with the recoil, so they soon had me firing a 20 gauge. They may have waited for a day or two before introducing me to the twelve gauges, but not much more. They seemed to be as full of anticipation about my graduation to the heavier Winchester model 97 and the Winchester Model 12 as I was. I can still plainly see their grins as I shouldered the big twelve gauge for the first time. The recoil administered first to my shoulder, then to the rest of my body, caused me to take a couple of unsteady steps backward. That day marked my passage into a lifelong love of the sport of hunting. The more practical instruction in the field would last for the next ten years.

I looked at the business card given to me by Stephen S, Boynton, Attorney at Law, and saw that his office was about a three-minute walk from mine. My office was in a Town House near the corner of 17th and N Streets and his was at 17th and L Streets. I called Steve and we arranged to meet for lunch.

Steve Boynton had a passion for hunting. He explained that since he had come to Washington he had found few hunting companions and that he generally spent his time in the field with his young son and daughter, Scott and Stuart. I learned that he was from Watertown, New York, had attended Ohio State University and the University of South Carolina Law School. He then served on the staff of the Columbia Chamber of Commerce. From there, he had joined the venerable law firm of Hogan and Hartson, had been a legislative aide to United States Senator Ernest F. "Fritz" Hollings, a Democrat from South Carolina, but most of all, I learned that he wanted to go hunting. Steve had grown up on a dairy farm and his father had taken Steve and his brother on countless hunts throughout his youth. Steve was in the process of passing that tradition along to his children. We made plans to go dove hunting the following Saturday. Scott, his son, would join us.

Steve and I had grown so close during those twenty years that our friends rarely spoke of us in the singular. Their comments were more likely to be, "Steve and Dave said" or "Steve and Dave did." In 1979 Steve and I founded a hunt club of the eastern shore of Maryland, Fort Point Hunt Club. The Canada Goose was royalty on "the shore" in those days, though more recently, they have become widely dispersed. His family and my family were close and we shared in many family celebrations as well as tragedies.

Captain Mike Harris, Steve Boynton and I had spent many days together in the fields and on the water. Mike ran a goose and deer hunting guide service during the hunting season, and that was how we all met several years earlier. Mike welcomed us aboard as old friends.

Another guest was R. Emmett "Bob" Tyrrell, Jr., Editor-in-Chief of *The American Spectator*, my feisty old friend and founder of the equally feisty magazine. Bob and I had fished together for at least twenty years. His family and mine had vacationed for years on the Outer Banks of North Carolina. Whenever we could, we would arrange to be there during the same time. I had been on the Board of Directors of *The American Spectator* for several years and still was at that time. Bob and Steve knew each other casually because most of my friends had met Steve. We were "joined at the hip," after all.

Arrangements had been made for me to pick up Steve at his home at 5:00 a.m. that morning and we were to go by the Madison Hotel in Washington to get Richard M. Larry. Dick had taken the short flight from Pittsburgh the evening before in order to make the early departure to the Bay. Dick was one of the few friends that I had who had not met Steve Boynton and I wanted to take advantage of the opportunity for the ride out to the bay in order for them to become acquainted. Bob Tyrrell would get himself there.

Dick Larry was President of the Sarah Scaife Foundation. Dick and I had kept our friendship alive after my departure from Tulsa, Oklahoma twenty years earlier. Mostly, we went fishing. We made an effort to go on a fishing trip each year. Some years we were successful and some we were not. We had surf fished together on the beach in Florida and North Carolina. We Tarpon fished in the Florida Keys and trout fished on the Big Hole River in southwestern Montana in an inflatable raft. One year we went deep sea fishing off the Florida coast. Dick had joined me on the Chesapeake Bay before, when I had an old 32' Luhr's sea skiff, and we caught bluefish. Once we had tried, unsuccessfully, to catch sea trout on the Delaware Bay, when Peggy's uncle, and my friend, John Diskau lost an engine on his boat, and we spent the rest of the day limping back to port.

One deviation from our fishing trips and an unmitigated disaster was a sailing trip from Fort Lauderdale, Florida, to Bimini, in the Bahamas. With some partners, I had purchased a 41' Morgan Out Island Ketch. It was sometime in the early 1980's and Peggy and I had invited a couple who were close friends who lived near us, as well as Dick and Lois Larry to sail with us to Bimini for a few days. Arrangements for travel were made and the six of us arrived in Fort Lauderdale, Florida, the day before our departure. We went out to dinner that evening and returned to the boat fairly late. I was unable to sleep in my eagerness to be underway, and in one of my not too uncommon errors in judgment, I decided to get underway at 3:00 a.m. It was blowing hard when we left the calmness of the harbor and entered the open sea. That was not a problem for the broad shouldered Morgan, but it was for my tired and unhappy "crew." We followed a squall moving east and away from us for quite a long time and the bolts of lightning seen clearly from sky to water were unnerving.

We were under full sail for the entire crossing that lasted twelve hours. Dave and Judy Semler, our friends from Virginia were not strangers to sailing, but neither of them was able to go below decks. It was, in a word, miserable. Dick Larry fought off nausea by staying at the helm for most of the trip while I ranged above and below decks, navigating and taking care of "Captain" chores. Peggy, to the envy of all, was able to go below and sleep for a couple of hours. And then there was Lois Larry. She was the sickest person that I have ever seen, from start to finish. I felt so sorry for her, but could do nothing about it. That is until we reached Bimini. I suggested that it would be unwise for her to return on the boat and that I would not be offended if she and Dick chose to fly back to Florida. Without protest, she immediately made reservations to fly back on the Chalk Air Taxi. On the morning of our departure, we watched the Chalk amphibian aircraft taxi to a takeoff in the Bimini harbor before we cast off. The return to the Florida coast was so calm that we had to motor the entire trip, naturally!

With all aboard, and after we had stowed our lunch Captain Harris moved his vessel gracefully out of the slip and into the short and narrow channel leading out to the Chesapeake Bay. Cool, clear mornings like this one are always splendid on the Chesapeake. Passing the man-made breakwater, and approaching the first buoy, eases the stress of a city dweller and reminds him of the God who could paint with such a grand brush.

There would be thirty or forty minutes spent, at a fairly high speed, in reaching the day's first trolling location. This location would be determined by a combination of the Captain's experience and the impressive array of electronics at his disposal. He would be able to see fish and generally determine if they were baitfish or what we were seeking, the Chesapeake Bay "Rock Fish." Mike was good at finding fish and this day would be no exception.

While the Captain and his mate were cruising to our first location and preparing the tackle Dick, Bob, Steve, and I were otherwise occupied in observing the life on the bay; the birds, breaking fish, other boats, waves, and the receding shoreline. It takes a period of adjustment on each trip to fall into the pace of the day and its offering. As the eastern sun lifts through the heavens the chill fall night gives way to warmth, and the first layers of windbreakers and sweaters begin to disappear below decks. Questions are asked of the Captain as each person on board moves about the boat. Has the fishing been good this week? What does that gadget do? How fast are we going? When will we get there (as if there are small children on board)?

Soon enough the roar of the engines stops as the Captain spots fish on his electronics and he throttles back to get rods in place and bait in the water. All hands on deck quickly achieve a new mindset as expectations mount. For the next several hours the six occupants on board the Compensation will achieve harmony with the flow and pace of boat and water.

The first Rock Fish came aboard quickly followed by others, followed by slack periods of moving and searching. That is the usual pattern of fishing on the bay and inevitably the fishermen become languid and relaxed. The next strike will come "when it comes." In the meanwhile, there are other things to do. "A sandwich?" "Sure." "Did you hear about...?"

It did not take long for our talk to turn to politics and current events. Each of us, in our own way, had been molded and shaped by those subjects: Steve Boynton, as an attorney representing wildlife interests, Bob Tyrrell, a writer and head of a political commentary magazine, and Dick Larry, president of a foundation that makes grants to, among others, a broad array of think tanks, colleges and universities and one of the oldest and largest donors to *The American Spectator Educational Foundation*. Between the four of us was more than a century of combined experience in public affairs. There is no point in not stating the obvious.

There was much talk of our new President of the United States, Bill Clinton. He had been in office for eight months. Thus far his administration had been disastrous. At least in our opinion. The campaign that he had waged against President Bush had revealed much about Bill's past, and each day seemed to bring forth another revelation of unsavory conduct. There was no question that this presidency was diametrically opposed to what we believed in. At least I could say that for Dick, Bob and myself. The three of us had been long time conservatives and as far as I know, Republicans. As close as Steve Boynton and I were, I was unable to classify him. He had worked for a Democratic U.S. Senator and I had no idea what his voting preferences were. I had told Steve countless times that he had the temperament to be a judge because he had the ability to listen to all arguments in an unimpassioned way before deciding for himself.

Since much of the conversation that day centered on Bill Clinton and his state of Arkansas, it was only natural that Steve had a lot to say. Steve was the only one on board with any firsthand knowledge of Arkansas. He spoke knowledgeably about the closed society in Arkansas and the handful of powerful interests that clearly dominated the state. He revealed to us a chilling account of the Arkansas bar. The cozy relationships of the powerful with the judiciary. The difficulty facing average citizens who seek redress against the powerful. A one-newspaper state and that paper could usually be counted on to look the other way. At one point there were two daily newspapers in Little Rock, The Democrat and The Gazette, but The Gazette and The Democrat were merged into the Democrat-Gazette, thus eliminating competition and any expectation of opposition to the state Democrat party.

Steve's observations carried great force because he was speaking from experience. He had been retained to represent more than 100 plaintiffs in a lawsuit in Arkansas. The defendant was such a powerful force in the state that no in-state attorney could be found who would be willing to oppose them. The defendant was Arkansas Power and Light, AP&L, and the plaintiffs were the residents and business owners on Lake Catherine near Hot Springs, Arkansas. Another upstream lake, Lake Hamilton rests behind Carpenter dam. Lake Hamilton is the site of expensive vacation homes for Arkansas' elite. Carpenter dam holds back water that flows downstream into Lake Catherine and under normal circumstances provides a delicate balancing of water levels and simultaneously generates electricity for AP&L. On May 19 and May 20, 1990, a flood raised the water levels on Lake Hamilton dramatically, threatening the expensive homes of the rich and powerful. It is subjective judgment to suggest a causal relationship between the value of the homes and the social status of the wealthy homeowners on the larger Lake Hamilton, and the act that followed. The smaller and much less affluent residents of Lake Catherine paid the price. Lake Catherine looks more like a modest sized river than a lake. It sits between steep shorelines for the first mile or so below Carpenter Dam. Imagine a funnel...and the top... where the liquid is poured, represents Lake Hamilton and the spout where the liquid emerges represents Lake Catherine. In the early morning hours of May 20, 1990, and without adequate warning, AP&L opened all the gates wide open on Carpenter Dam to relieve the flooding on Lake Hamilton.

The first structure below Carpenter Dam was Carpenter Dam Bridge, 500 yards from the dam. The bridge had been built by AP&L in 1939 after a previous bridge had been destroyed by flooding. The concrete and steel reinforced bridge on Arkansas State Route 128 was maintained by the Arkansas State Highway Department. Accustomed to carrying millions of pounds of automotive traffic, the bridge, rising 40 feet above the normal surface of the water, was unable to withstand the force of the water flowing down through Carpenter dam, and it collapsed. The next structures below the dam belonged to a friend of both Steve's and mine. His name is Parker Dozhier. Dozhier's Rainbow Landing contained a bait and tackle shop, some boat docks and other structures. It had been a landmark since Parker's father had opened it many years earlier. It all washed away in the fury of the torrent. Below Dozhier's were homes and other small businesses. They too were destroyed. Fortunately, there was no loss of human life. Many homes and businesses were lost or destroyed. For more than thirteen months the residents, unable to cross the highway where the bridge was washed out, had to travel between twenty-five and thirty miles farther to get their children to school, purchase their food, get medical attention and the myriad of other human needs.

The Lake Catherine residents and business owners came together to seek redress from AP&L, and after a futile effort, they searched for an Arkansas Attorney to represent them in a suit against AP&L. Again, they were unsuccessful. Parker Dozhier sought out Steve Boynton in desperation. Knowing that Steve would not be beholden to any higher interests than that of his clients, he convinced Steve to take the case. The case would take a personal toll on Steve, both personally and financially. In the course of the next three years Steve commuted to Arkansas, and in some cases rented a house, in the conduct of taking the countless depositions and court filings. He became very familiar with the courts in Arkansas and no small number of lawyers there. In the end, the "little" guys lost, as they had at the beginning; not an unusual outcome in the State of Arkansas.

Parker Dozhier was a genuine "every man." His broad interests and his unusual personality made him an appealing person to be around. Like another and better known Arkansas personality, the late Jim McDougal, Parker has a theatrical presence. His voice was made for the stage and he knows it. Whenever two or more people are around, the show goes on. And it can be entertaining. Parker is also a doer, not just a talker. Steve Boynton had introduced me to Parker in 1979, at a conference at Frostburg State Teachers College, in Frostburg, Maryland. The conference was sponsored by the American Fur Industry and Parker Dozhier was a speaker. Steve had represented the American Fur Industry in Washington for several years and had come to know Parker through his dealings with fur trappers. Parker was legendary among the trappers and wrote a column for American Trapper and Predator Caller Magazine. He and Steve had traveled to Africa together, and if their stories are to be believed, it could make an interesting movie.

Parker Dozhier had written a "White Paper" detailing the unusual, unethical, and probably, illegal practices of the Arkansas Game and Fish Commission and The Arkansas Highway Commission. We discussed the "White Paper" and its implications with Dick Larry and Bob Tyrrell that day on the bay.

Over the years that we had been friends, Steve and I had made substantial contributions to the "hooks and bullets" constituency in and around Washington, D.C. It was not at all uncommon to see either or both of us quoted or featured in stories in The Washington Post sports pages. We hosted a Who's Who of politicians at our Fort Point Hunt Club. With Ted Kratovil, an aide to US Senator Lowell Weikert and now Senior Vice President of United States Tobacco Company, we planned the creation of a Chapter of Ducks Unlimited (DU) in Washington that would be made up of Congressmen, Senators, their aides and representatives of Corporations with a Washington presence. We organized early meetings with representatives of each of these groups and sold them on our idea. It has been wildly successful. Now over twenty years old, the Federal City Chapter of Ducks Unlimited raises more money for DU than any other.

Not finished, Steve then created another chapter of DU outside the beltway, The Potomac Valley Chapter. And, as if that was not enough, he and G. Ray Arnett, Assistant Secretary of the Interior for Fish Wildlife and Parks in the Reagan administration were persuasive in their efforts to establish, in the congress, a caucus representing the hunting, fishing and trapping sportsmen of the nation. I played a role in that effort, though not as great as that of Steve and Ray Arnett. The Congressional Sportsmen's Caucus was born in 1989 and now is the largest single caucus in the congress, with 240 Congressmen and 50 Senators of both political parties. I planned and conducted the first annual banquet for the caucus on October 9, 1990. Ray Arnett, Steve and I incorporated the Congressmen's Sportsmen's Caucus Foundation on December 7, 1989. Ray was the incorporating Chairman, I, the vice-chairman, and Steve, the secretary-treasurer.

With our strong conservation backgrounds, we were not at all happy about what Dozhier's "White Paper" alleged. The story, according to Dozhier, was that there was a pattern of insider deals involving the Game and Fish Commission and The Highway Commission in Arkansas involving federal funds and sportsmen's funds. It worked like this. A private landowner with land on a river or other waterway would donate a small parcel of land on the water to the Game and Fish commission for the purpose of creating a boat launching ramp. At some later date, the Arkansas Highway Commission would build a road through the private property of the generous landowner in order to allow public access to the donated boat launching ramp. The remote, private property, in most cases, would then appreciate sharply in value because of the public road building done at taxpayer expense. That is a simple explanation, but adequate.

For many years, hunters, fishermen, birders, and other outdoors enthusiasts have paid excise taxes on items such as boats, motors, guns, binoculars, fishing tackle and other products used by sportsmen. Those federal taxes were set aside for use by fish and wildlife agencies for the purpose of improving wildlife habitat and fisheries. They are referred to as Pitman-Robinson funds in the internal revenue code, named for the congressional sponsors of the legislation creating them. Those funds were allegedly being used in Arkansas to enrich politically favored individuals in this scheme. As we write, a congressional investigation is being conducted by the United States Congress into the misuse of sportsmen's funds by the Clinton Department of the Interior. Another case of Arkansas policy gone national.

As Steve and I talked about this issue there was a visceral reaction from both Bob Tyrrell and Dick Larry. Bob speculated aloud about the possibility of doing an investigative piece in *The American Spectator*. Dick Larry said that it would be difficult for the young writers at the *Spectator* to do such a project because of the cultural differences involved, after all, this was a fish and game story, not strictly a political or intellectual story. He believed that the trust necessary for a project of this type could not be attained by "twenty-somethings" who had no background or ability to meld with the outdoors types. Addressing me he said, "I could do it, you could do it, and Steve could do it, but these young intellectuals would never understand the culture sufficiently, and they would fail to gain the cooperation necessary to break a story like this. Once again, Dick Larry had hit the nail directly on the head. That quality had earned him the admiration and respect of many people who had had the privilege to know and work with him over the years. It was also the reason that he was so valuable to his employer, Richard M. Scaife. Dick had grown up in the Allegheny River Valley north of Pittsburgh, and in his youth had enjoyed the river and its tributaries. That enjoyment has continued throughout his life. Dick enlisted in the United States Marine Corp and served for four years. The quiet confidence that Dick displays is, no doubt, partly a result of those years. After his service with the USMC, he earned both a bachelor's and a master's degree. He accomplished that while raising a family. His wife, Lois, shares those accomplishments. Dick is not a hunter, but he has been around firearms for a very long time. For years he shot small bore rifle competitively and once was on the National small bore rifle championship team at Camp Perry, Ohio. He knew his subject. Dick remembers his roots!

It had been a good day. Enough "Rock Fish" had been caught to provide each of us with a couple of delicious meals. They were cleaned and packaged at the dock. Dick, Steve, and I said goodbye to Captain Harris and Bob Tyrrell at the dock and departed for National Airport where Dick Larry would return to Pittsburgh. Each of us went our separate ways, thinking similar thoughts.

CHAPTER EIGHT ~
HALE TO THE CHIEF

It started sooner than I thought. After dropping Dick Larry at the airport and driving Steve Boynton home, I went home. As I came through the door Peggy told me that Bob Tyrrell had called and wanted me to return the call. I didn't need to look for the number because Bob and I talked daily, often several times a day. Since Bob had asked me to join the board of *The American Spectator* years earlier, he frequently talked with me about matters concerning the magazine, as he did with the other directors. The board was full of luminaries, some of them were famous. I was an exception. When Bob had broached the subject of my joining the board, I was involved in what was at the time one of the biggest media events in recent memory.

I was press spokesman for General William C. Westmoreland in his long-running battle with CBS over a documentary, The Uncounted Enemy: A Vietnam Deception, produced by George Crile and narrated by Mike Wallace. The dispute that arose over the broadcast of that documentary lasted some three years and ended in a highly publicized trial in federal court in New York. During those three years, I did what I could for General Westmoreland because he was a friend, and because I believed that he had been wronged by CBS. During my daily conversations with print and broadcast reporters, I learned that many of them believed as I did. I must add, that, in my opinion, the media in general treated the General with fairness and respect throughout that long ordeal. I had donated my services to General Westmoreland and was privileged to have done so. He had deserved a fighting chance, and I had helped him fight. If not for that high profile exposure I doubt that I would have been considered for the board of *The American Spectator*.

Hearing the familiar voice of Doreen Gibbs confirmed that I had dialed the correct number. Doreen was Bob's housekeeper, a charming woman from Granada, and master of the Tyrrell household. "Mr. Tier-re-al's residence." Bob picked up the phone and immediately asked if we had further discussions about the "White Paper" en route to the airport. There are few journalists in America, since Woodward and Bernstein became famous, who are not interested in investigative journalism. R. Emmett Tyrrell, Jr. was no exception. *The American Spectator*, like most similar commentary magazines, was not profitable and depended on contributions to keep it operating. It had a very small staff and few resident writers. There was little chance under those circumstances for it to undertake investigative projects without the financial support of a donor or donors. Bob had been impressed by Steve Boynton's knowledge of Arkansas, as well as his grasp of the issues outlined in Parker Dozhier's "White Paper." He asked if I thought Steve would be interested in looking into those matters for *The American Spectator* if money could be found to pay for it. I told him that I would talk to Steve about it. My thoughts on the subject were that there may or may not be a story there and that a commitment of resources to a project like that should initially be limited to confirming whether there was proof of the allegations. If the proof was there it could be pursued. If not, it could be quickly abandoned. I had confidence that Steve Boynton could ascertain the necessary evidence. He would know where to look, who to talk to, and being a familiar figure around the courts in Arkansas, he could avail himself of court records without raising suspicion.

When I talked with Steve about his interest in the project the following day, he had some questions. He didn't doubt that he had the ability to do it, but pointed out that he had no background in journalism, didn't know how *The American Spectator* operated and had no idea about how such a project could be funded. Steve had been Editor of The University of South Carolina's *Law Review* and had many articles published, but I pointed out to him that his role would not include writing. If evidence led to the publication of a story or stories they would be written by staff writers at *The American Spectator*. With respect to not knowing how *The American Spectator* operated, I assured him that I would be in a position to assist in his understanding. Steve agreed that he would be willing to undertake the project if asked.

Later that day I called Bob Tyrrell to let him know of my talk with Steve and that he would be willing to undertake the project. The magazine had raised money for special projects many times in its twenty-five years and it could be done again. Bob had to have discussions with his colleagues at the magazine to make sure that everyone was in agreement before taking the next step. Bob moved quickly with his discussions at the office.

The decision was made to proceed if the necessary funding could be secured. There were only three or four possibilities for funding since very few foundations and businesses were known to support conservative organizations. At the top of everyone's list is the Scaife Foundations. They had been contributing to the magazine since its earliest days as an off-campus publication in Bloomington, Indiana when it was called *The Alternative*. I happen to believe that there would have been no *American Spectator* if not for the long and continuous support from Scaife foundations. Not only had they contributed longer, but they had contributed more than any other supporter.

A funding request was sent to the Scaife Foundations for "An Editorial Improvement Project" to fund Steve's work. It was a modest request and it was approved. A few years later this small beginning would be blown up into a "Vast Right Wing Conspiracy" known as "The Arkansas Project."

October of 1993 was proving to be a busy month. After the fishing trip and the subsequent decision by Steve Boynton to undertake the investigative role for *The American Spectator* I found myself spending more than the usual amount of time on magazine business. Meetings were necessary to launch Steve's project as smoothly as possible. There were logistical matters to be taken care of and there were operational considerations as well. Steve needed to be introduced to the magazine's staff in order to ensure a familiarity and comfort level for both parties. Naturally, I was the facilitator for those necessities. I had not considered my function to be other than that of a concerned board member. I was willing to lend whatever support necessary to Steve and to *The American Spectator*. And since I was the natural link to the magazine, to Steve and to the donor, it was prudent that I be involved in the beginning. During the remaining days of October and the first few days of November, my activities were limited to the ones described. I had no role in grant requests or any of the decisions necessary for the administration of the project. At that time, it was supposed that there would be a short investigation, that would either result in a story or in the termination of the project.

The Washington Post arrives at my house around 5:00 a.m. most mornings, and the first weekend of November that year was no exception. As a rule, I am awake when the paper arrives, and even though it was a weekend, I was up, the coffee was brewed and I was about to start my day in a manner that was routine. One of life's great joys, for me, is reading. It is how I had learned the fundamentals of golf, a passion of mine. Sailing also had been learned through reading about the experiences of sailors. Indeed, most of my life's accomplishments had been the result of my love of reading. Since following the news was a necessity as well as a pleasure this part of my day was my favorite time. It is always quiet in my household before sunrise and the only interruptions are from our pets. *The Washington Post* frequently launches major stories in their weekend editions then continues them in serial form during the week until they are finished. Such an article was begun on this day. The by-line was not familiar to me. The story was a reprise of an earlier story which had made an appearance in The *New York Times* during the previous presidential campaign. The story had not caught on during the campaign and I didn't get very interested that day. It was not until the second part of the story, which appeared a few days later, that my attention raced into overdrive. By now, everyone knows the story about Whitewater, a land deal in Arkansas involving the former Governor and his wife, Bill and Hillary Clinton. On that day, and in the days before many readers of *The Washington Post* were learning of it for the first time. I was about to be drawn directly into the story because of something that I read in the second or third paragraph. David L. Hale, a municipal judge in Little Rock, was claiming that the President of the United States, Bill Clinton, while Governor of the State of Arkansas, had pressured Hale to make an illegal $300,000 loan to Susan McDougal, wife of Jim McDougal, the previous owner of a failed savings and loan, Madison Guaranty.

Unless it is an emergency it is considered bad form to call your friends at 5:00 a.m. So I waited, and thought, until a more civil hour. My thoughts that morning went back many years to the days when I regularly met and talked with David Hale. When he was President of The United States Jaycees and before that. I had not talked with David in more than fifteen years and the article that I had just read reminded me that I had read in some Jaycee alumni newsletter a few years earlier that he had become a Judge. There was a unique opportunity here and it didn't require brilliance on my part to recognize it. I was on the board of a maturing national opinion magazine. There were limits to what a monthly magazine could do regarding breaking news. There were also things that a magazine could do that reporters facing daily deadlines could not do. They could explore stories in greater depth and they could be reported fully. *The New York Times*, *The Washington Post*, *The Wall Street Journal* and a few other large daily newspapers could do both. They have the money and the staff to do so. News magazines such as *Time, Newsweek* and *U.S. News and World Report*, had the time, being weekly publications, to more fully develop stories and they had been doing it for decades. Maybe, just maybe I could level the playing field for *The American Spectator* and allow it to compete with the big media on this story.

At 7:00 a.m. I called Doreen Gibbs and asked her to have Bob Tyrrell call me as soon as possible. Minutes later I received Bob's call and I suggested that he read the Post story and then call me back. Later that morning Bob called and told me that he had read the story and had, in fact, read the previous part of the story a few days earlier. I then told him that I had known David Hale for years and had a good relationship with him. I shared my earlier thoughts with Bob and he asked if I thought I could talk with David. I told him that I was confident that I could and would attempt to contact him. We left it that I would make the effort to reach David and get back to him.

Realizing that I did not have a phone number for David Hale, I immediately called a mutual friend in Little Rock, Arthur "Frenchie" Boutiette. While I had not seen or talked with David in many years, I had remained in touch with Frenchie, usually seeing him at least once each year at a golf outing or at the annual reunion of our old staff from The United States Jaycees. Frenchie had joined the staff a few months before I departed and later became Executive Vice President. He had lived in Little Rock before moving to Tulsa and returned years later, after his service with the Jaycees. Those relationships had been invaluable to me over the years. There were friends or acquaintances in every major city and town in the country, and I frequently called on them as they did me. Reaching Frenchie required only a couple of calls. I asked him if he had the Hale's home phone number and he did. He volunteered that David was embroiled in some problems and I told him that I had just become aware of it. Without elaboration, I thanked Frenchie and said goodbye.

A muffled message on the phone asked that I leave a message. Nothing more. My message followed. "David, this is an old friend, Dave Henderson, and I would like to talk with you. Please call me." And I gave him my number.

CHAPTER NINE ~
REUNION

Two days after my message was left on David and Sue Hale's answering machine, I found a message on mine. It was very brief and left in a whisper. It was David returning my call. My answering machine said that it had been received around 3:00 a.m. That alarmed me. Why wait two days to return a call and then do it at 3:00 am? Was he in some unspeakable danger? Nothing as dramatic as that proved to be the case. The timing device on my answering machine was malfunctioning. I found out those details when I finally reached David and he told me what time he had actually called.

Our conversation was very brief. I had assumed, correctly, that he was under surveillance and in all probability, his phone was tapped. My message was succinct. "David I want to come to Little Rock to see you and your lawyer. I will bring my lawyer with me." (Steve Boynton had been my lawyer as well as my friend for years.) David was as thrifty with his words. "My lawyer is Randy Coleman. This is his phone number. Call him and arrange it." We said goodbye.

I asked Steve Boynton to call Randy Coleman, assuming that David would tell him to expect a call. Randy would not know Steve, so I told him to use my name. I had been around lawyers long enough to know that they were more comfortable talking to each other. More so when one or both of them had clients in trouble. And David was in deep trouble.

Steve's talk with Randy Coleman had been fruitful. A meeting was arranged for Saturday, November 20, 1993, in Randy's office. His office was in the tallest building in downtown Little Rock, the TCBY building, so it would not be hard to find. Getting there on time, though, would prove more difficult. Steve and I had arranged for a flight out of Dulles Airport in Northern Virginia late on Friday, November 19, 1993, and it would require us to change planes in Cincinnati, Ohio. From Cincinnati to Little Rock is a flight of some hour and one-half. That is if you make the connection. And we didn't. Our flight to Cincinnati had taken place in heavy rain and there were delays which made it impossible to get to Little Rock that night. Since our meeting was to be at 10:00 a.m. the following morning, we had a problem. We were unable to reach Randy Coleman. We were unable to reach David Hale. The first flight available the following morning would have us in the skies over Kentucky when we were due in Randy Coleman's office.

The airline sent us to a motel in nearby Covington, Kentucky, as their guests. Drenched to the bone, Steve and I made it to our rooms for a quick shower and what we hoped would be a good night's sleep. It was not to be. Not long after I had gone to bed, they arrived. Who they were, I would not know until the following morning during checkout, but their presence would be heard throughout the night. There was exuberant running and shouting in the halls. Doors opened and banged shut with deafening frequency. Two calls to the front desk brought no relief. At one point I ventured to the door for a look outside in the hallway. I saw teens flowing from room to room. Their greeting calls were the equal to a thousand Canada geese at close range. Sleep came for a short time and then it was time to depart. The hallway was empty as we left our floor en route to the lobby. I mentioned the activities of the night before to the checkout clerk. He said, "Oh, we are hosting a convention of Kentucky Youth for Christ." As we boarded the bus for the airport, I remember saying to Steve that we were lucky that it hadn't been the youth auxiliary of Kentucky's Hell's Angels.

The weather had improved significantly and our flight to Little Rock that morning was smooth and on time. While I went to the car rental desk Steve went to the phone. We were more than an hour late for our meeting. We were both in doubt that we would find David and Randy still waiting. Fortunately, they were. Steve informed Randy of our situation and estimated that we would arrive at Randy's office in about thirty minutes. There were plenty of parking spaces on the street as we arrived in front of the TCBY building. I spotted a familiar face standing just outside the doors. The warm smile that I remembered greeted us as we approached. After a handshake and hug, I introduced Steve

Boynton to David Hale. David led us inside to the empty elevator for the quick ride to Randy's office.

The four of us sat at a sizable conference table and began with small talk about our trip. We expressed our apologies for making them wait. David talked briefly about our past relationship for Randy's benefit. Then I did the same, about Steve Boynton's and my relationship. We had all performed this ritual many times before. Each of us knew the value of these niceties. We were going to be laying bare our souls and intentions. It was important that each person feel comfortable.

The story we were told was not a pretty one, and it took a long time to tell. I explained my position as a member of the board of directors of *The American Spectator* and that I was there in that role. I explained that Steve Boynton had been retained by the magazine and that he and I were working together. David had not been aware of my involvement with the magazine, nor did I expect that he would since it had been many years since I had seen him. After a couple of hours of briefing by Randy, David and I left the conference room together to find a coke and to have a private conversation. We left the lawyers to their own devices.

Sitting in the small cantina surrounded by the empty offices of the law firm with its grand panoramic view was a metaphor for what was to come. Here we quickly caught up on what had happened to each of us in the intervening years since we had last met. The previous two hours had made it plain that David was in serious jeopardy. He was facing criminal charges that were certain to land him in prison. In the past several years he had operated a small business investment company, Capital Management Services. He had made loans to people in the "political family" that had not been repaid. It had been a lot of money. David said to me quietly and with a palpable humility, "Dave, I had to rob Peter to pay Paul." That was a confession to a friend, someone with a shared background and mutual trust. My heart ached for him, knowing how difficult the moment had to be for him. It was also easy to see that he had many more difficulties facing him that would be far harder, for David and his family, than confessing to someone who wished him well.

I asked David if he would be willing to cooperate with me and my colleagues at *The American Spectator* in developing this story. I assured him that we would be guided by the facts and that he would be treated fairly by us. I had wanted to ask him to cooperate exclusively with us, but it was too late. He had already been talking with the press. He explained to me that he had done it for his own protection. In his words, "there was an effort to indict me, try me, and convict me in the shortest time possible." The evidence, thus far, bore out his fears. At first, his attorney, Randy Coleman, had objected to David's exposure to the press. From my own experience that caution permeates the minds of lawyers. It is also justified in many cases. Perhaps in most cases. But David Hale was himself, a lawyer and a judge. He had been successful in many facets of life and communication was one of his greatest strengths. Randy would come to appreciate the value of David's decision. Indeed, he already had by the time Steve Boynton and I met with them on November 20, 1993.

David was genuinely happy that I had come to see him. He had had a highly successful career and was a respected member of his community. He had many friends in Arkansas and around the country. At least he did until he implicated The President of The United States in an unlawful act. And, as I was soon to learn, that was a giant no-no.

The President of the United States inherits awesome powers when elected by a majority of those voting in the general elections every four years. Historically, most of those citizens who are eligible to vote do not exercise their right to vote, and consequently, Presidents are elected by a majority of those citizens who choose to vote. Yet, all of the citizens are subject to the choice made by their more motivated peers. Perhaps we all need to be reminded of the powers conferred upon our elected Presidents. They appoint all United States Attorneys, and President William Jefferson Clinton made that one of his first acts after his election in 1992. They command all military forces, several million men and women. They nominate members of the Supreme

Court, who, along with the Congress, are the two bodies that provide "checks and balances" over the executive branch of government, personified by the President. The President has the power to spend more than one and one-half trillion dollars each year that he is in office. He presides over and appoints the people to lead The Department of Justice, which has the power to bring any citizen before a court. The entire federal police force, including the FBI, DEA and Secret Service are at his disposal. He controls the Internal Revenue Service which has the right to know what each citizen earns and what they spend. They too have police powers. The President of The United States has a personal staff of hundreds of people who do his bidding. He has the power to retain people outside of government to carry his message. There is one other check on this vast power. The media. It helps a President if the majority of both the House of Representatives and the Senate are elected from within his own political party. When they are not, there are two other places to turn. The public and the media. Without the media, the public cannot be reached. Therein lies one of the most vexing problems faced in our democracy.

These were the problems facing David Hale on November 20, 1993. He, no doubt, was more aware of them than I was. But he did commit to an old friend that he would make himself available and would, to the best of his ability, seek to make the truth known. David Hale never violated that pledge. Never did he promise anything that he couldn't deliver. Never did he make a claim that couldn't be verified. Never did he exaggerate. And in spite of the hardships involved, he would make and keep the same pledge to Special Counsel Robert Fiske and then-Independent Counsel Kenneth Starr.

CHAPTER TEN ~
ROAD MAP

It was mid-afternoon when we left David Hale and Randy Coleman. It had been an eye-opening and mentally exhausting meeting. The outside air was refreshing. We still had work to do. It would require an hour's drive southwest of Little Rock. I had never been to Parker Dozhier's home and business on Lake Catherine but had known Parker for several years. He had been a guest at Fort Point Hunt Club on more than one occasion. He was always a charming and entertaining presence. I liked Parker and was looking forward to visiting with him. Arkansas is a beautiful state and the drive was pleasant. Steve knew every turn in the road and had guided me away from the interstate highway near Malvern, Arkansas, and onto the serpentine back roads leading to Parker's.

At a sign reading "Dozhier's Bait Shop", we made a right turn onto the road that would lead us to our destination. A few hundred yards from where we turned, we arrived in front of a modest, but neat, bait shop. A few steps to the right of the bait shop was a mobile home. Across the road from the bait shop was the modest home of Parker's ailing father. Behind the bait shop and on the lake was a floating boat dock. A few small boats were tied to the dock. In front of the shop was Maggie, Parker's red Chinese Chow. Maggie walked slowly to greet the arriving guests. Inside the bait shop was Parker Dozhier, surrounded by an impressive array of memorabilia that represented his life and interests. We were here to talk with Parker about the issues raised in his "White Paper."

After a quick tour of the shop and dock, we retreated to Parker's mobile home for coffee and conversation. Parker's life revolved around these few buildings and boats. He was open seven days a week, from early until late. Inside the mobile home were his computer and fax machine, tools of a small business. There was also a sizable number of books and publications. Parker was a "backwoodsman," but a smart one. He had lived the fast-paced city life but his heart and soul were always more satisfied with the outdoors. Where I live the market value of a home site with Parker's river view would be upwards of a half million dollars, but after the flood, a disaster recovery loan by the Small Business Administration meant that the Federal Government now owned it all. It had been unencumbered before the flood. Parker Dozhier will be 82 years old when it is paid off. This was the location that Steve Boynton and I retreated to on numerous occasions.

We told Parker that we had met with David Hale and Randy Coleman in Little Rock. We were both surprised to learn that Parker knew David. He told us that he had rented an apartment in Little Rock, in 1968, from David and his brother Milas. He said that he would occasionally bump into David on the street in Little Rock. Although David had a home on the adjacent Lake Hamilton, Parker had never seen David at the bait shop. We were not able to stay very long with Parker since we had a plane to catch in Little Rock. We assured him that we would be back soon and would have more time to spend. Back in Washington, Steve and I had several hours of meetings ahead of us and they would begin on Monday. We were cautious about phone conversations based on things that we had learned while in Arkansas. For now, we would limit our discussions to face to face meetings.

On Monday, Steve Boynton and I went to the offices of *The American Spectator*, located in Arlington, Virginia. There we apprised the publisher, Ron Burr, of the results of our meeting with David Hale. Ron conducted the business affairs of the magazine. He had to know the extent of our activities because he was the one who wrote the checks to pay for them. We also briefed Bob Tyrrell, Editor-In-Chief, as well as other members of the staff. We informed them that we had a pledge of cooperation from David Hale and that we would soon return to Little Rock to begin gathering information. We asked that a writer be assigned at the earliest possible time to begin working with us and with David. Our report was enthusiastically received. It had, after all, been something of an accomplishment to have gotten that far over the weekend. It was agreed that Steve and I would continue to gather information and that a writer would be provided to work with us. This was a fast-breaking story, and we were well behind the curve. It would require a concerted effort to draw even with the competition, and we hoped, to move ahead of it.

When we arrived back in Little Rock a few days later, we found David Hale, true to his word, ready to help guide us to an understanding of the complexities surrounding the subject soon to be known as "Whitewater." Grasping the twists, turns, diversions, and misinformation already available on this subject was the equivalent of catching eels with bare hands. We began our education with a trip to north-central Arkansas. It was a gray and rainy trip from Little Rock to Marion County. It required several hours to get there. During those hours we learned a lot about the state and its politics. David Hale guided us along with both a travelogue and a dialogue. He was a living road map. He had told us that getting up to speed would require that we see documents pertaining to the land transactions of "Whitewater." He correctly explained that our efforts in that regard would be fruitless unless we knew exactly what we were looking for. We didn't and he did. He seemed to know a lot about the interlocking corporations involved in this scheme and explained it to us as we went along. One of our destinations on that day was the office of the Recorder of Deeds in Yellville, Arkansas. Yellville is the County seat of Marion County. Marion county was the site of the Whitewater Development Corporation's real estate venture. David made a list of documents which would help us to understand what all the fuss was about. This issue was fast becoming a full blown scandal and understanding the hows and whys was vitally important to us. His list contained corporate names that would never have been obvious to us. This subject was so complex that, after years of scrutiny, the general public still would not understand it. You had to be an "insider" and David Hale was, indeed, an "insider."

His list contained, in addition to the obvious Whitewater Development Corporation, 101 River Development, Inc., Arkla Land Company, a bankrupt Oklahoma corporation, and TIERCO, a business trust operating out of Massachusetts. Steve Boynton left David and me waiting in the car while he went in to request the documents. He returned after a few minutes and said that it would be a couple of hours before the documents would be ready. That gave us time to visit our next destination. A few miles northeast of Yellville is Flippen, Arkansas. As we passed through the small town, David told us that some of the city fathers and the Citizens Bank and Trust Company played a direct role in the Whitewater land scheme. Indeed, 101 River Development. Inc. had taken its name from an object that lay just before us. Just south of Flippen, we turned toward the southeast onto Arkansas State Highway 101. It was a modern, well-maintained road but that is not what made it different. A ten-minute trip on this State Highway is all you get. It crosses creeks with multi-million dollar bridges. There is nothing to be seen but the small hills and valleys of the Ozarks and then, it just quits. One wonders why.

You have no choice but to turn around and proceed back toward Flippen. A few hundred yards after the turn-around a smaller paved road on the right beckons the traveler to enter. We knew where we were going, so we took the right turn. It was David Hale's, as well as Steve's, and my first visit to this location. The paved road that we traveled would end abruptly just a couple of miles farther, at a boat ramp, courtesy of the Arkansas Game and Fish Commission, The Arkansas Highway Commission, and the ever-patient taxpayers of Arkansas, who would bear the cost of upkeep for the road and boat ramp in perpetuity.

It was lovely. Situated on a slight rise of land a few hundred feet from the boat launching ramp, with a commanding view of The White River, was an impressive home, built by Chris Wade. Nearby was the 200 plus acres of the Whitewater Development Corporation. 101 River Development's Ranchette estates shared the road as did one other substantial land owner. On August 2, 1978, the day that 230 acres were sold to Jim and Susan McDougal and Bill and Hillary Clinton, another 195 acres were sold to Robert "Red" Bone. You have heard of him. He was the commodities broker... who with Jim Blair of Tyson's ... turned $1,000 into $100,000 for Hillary Clinton.

Both of those land transactions were handled by Chris Wade,

local real estate broker, a shareholder in Citizens Bank and Trust, and shareholder in 101 River Development, Inc. Chris Wade had also donated the acre of land on the White River to the Arkansas Game and Fish Commission, and with the application of other peoples' money, both State and Federal, he saw his land value rise.

We saw what we had come to see. It was time to return to the office of the Recorder of Deeds. Steve, once again, went into the office, leaving David Hale and me in the car. He returned with a sizable number of documents, though he had been told that all of the records that he requested were not found. The clerk promised to continue the search. Steve had given her his mailing address in Virginia and a check to cover the cost of the documents and shipping expenses. We returned to Little Rock, completing the seven-hour round-trip drive.

Eager to report our findings of the boat ramp to Parker Dozhier, we made plans to visit him the following day. We asked David if he would like to accompany us in order to renew his old friendship with Parker. He was eager for the company and the extended time to continue educating Steve and me, so he agreed. David had not been to Parker's and it was a nice respite from the schedule that he had been keeping. He was under enormous strain and he was frightened. David would not use telephones without elaborate caution. He had been threatened and openly intimidated. Getting away from prying eyes and into a safer environment, away from Little Rock, was an appealing option for him.

Parker was Parker, so the four of us had a lighthearted visit. He and David enjoyed their reunion and Parker extended the invitation to him to return at any time. It was an invitation that would be accepted.

CHAPTER ELEVEN ~
RAKING UP DIRT

Throughout the more than three years that Steve Boynton and I worked together on what others would call "The Arkansas Project", we reported our findings to the appropriate persons at *The American Spectator*. We always did so promptly and in person, as soon as we returned from a road trip. Clinton apologists repeatedly referred to our work as "digging up dirt" on the President and First Lady, but they overstate their case. There was so much information to be had that digging wasn't a necessity; a light raking was usually enough. It was our practice, from the beginning, to limit our telephone calls to matters unrelated to our "discoveries." Not all reports were open to all people at the magazine. Some information was, of necessity, limited to select individuals. We trusted that the individuals to whom we reported would make the judgment calls necessary. We did not write one word about what we learned, and we learned plenty. It was also a two-way street. Writers and editors at the magazine learned things independent of the work of Steve Boynton and myself and in many, if not most cases, shared their information with us. Often, we would attempt to verify, with our sources, information passed along to us by *The American Spectator* staff. That's the way it was during November and December 1993.

The trip from which we had just returned had produced tangible results. We had documentation, with much more to come in the next few weeks. Again, we asked that a writer be assigned to begin to sift through the material that we were assembling. One writer who was associated with the magazine at that time was David Brock, and based on his track record, I had assumed that he would be a natural to be assigned to this project. Each time I broached the subject I was told that he was tied up in another project. I was impatient and justifiably so. The doors were being opened wide by a source then being courted by the "big feet" of the media. I had unlimited access to him and could provide the same to any writer that was selected. I would learn, on the same day that the rest of the nation learned, what had been occupying David Brock.

Meanwhile, Steve and I had much work to do and we were diligent about it. We were essentially self-directed. I was comfortable with that arrangement. After all, I had a long, and I assumed, trusted relationship with *The American Spectator*. I had been on the board for eight or more years at the time and had been called into service by either Bob Tyrrell or Ron Burr on many occasions. I was always pleased to assist them. Some of the employees of the magazine were infants when my association with Bob Tyrrell began. So, we pressed on. I was soon back in Arkansas, this time without Steve Boynton. For the most part, Steve and I were together. Occasionally, though, we would work alone. It depended on the circumstances.

David Hale and I had agreed upon a time and place to meet. I flew into Little Rock, rented a car and went to the Holiday Inn, across the street from Randy Coleman's office. David knew what time I was to arrive and we had prearranged a time that he would phone me at my hotel. Our plan was to take Sue Hale out to dinner. I had not seen Sue on my previous two visits and was looking forward to the occasion. The last time that I had seen Sue was in Washington, many years before. There was an hour or more before David was to call. I had checked into the hotel late in the afternoon. The book that I had purchased at the airport in Washington was not finished, so I occupied myself with reading. The time came when I was to have had the call from David and the phone did not ring. I knew him to be reliable but also understood that many things were going on in his life at the time that could take precedence over a phone call to me. My reading continued in spurts, followed by nervous thoughts. It was now more than thirty minutes beyond the agreed time. I would give it another thirty minutes before taking action. When I picked up the phone in my room there was no dial tone. The phone was dead. There was a moment of panic. Were the people monitoring David able to follow and thwart his every move? A trip to the front desk provided an answer. All of the phone service on my floor was out, I was told.

The pay phones in the lobby were working and I called the Hales. Upon hearing my voice David said, "Thank God you are okay. We were worried sick that something had happened to you. We have been trying to call you for more than an hour." That settled, we set a time for David and Sue to pick me up in front of the hotel. They arrived and I got in their car for the short drive to a restaurant they had chosen. It was a small Italian restaurant with good food and it was quiet enough for pleasant conversation. We didn't linger there after we had eaten. Neither of the Hales were comfortable in public and I understood it perfectly. When we arrived back at my hotel and before I left the car, David and I made plans for breakfast. He suggested the Kettle restaurant, near the zoo, and easy to find. After giving me directions we said good night.

Both David and I were early risers and we had agreed to meet for breakfast at 7:00 a.m. I departed from the hotel parking garage around 6:45 a.m., followed by a nondescript sedan with two men in it. A few minutes later I arrived at the Kettle restaurant just ahead of the sedan. As I parked, so did they. Inside David was already having his morning coffee and I joined him in a booth near the front window. The two men who had followed me from the Holiday Inn took a table at the rear of the restaurant. I chose not to tell David about being followed because I did not want to alarm him. After all, it could have been purely a coincidence. During breakfast, David told me that he wanted me to meet someone and he had taken the liberty to set a time for the meeting. The meeting was for a few hours later and it would take us to a rural setting near Bradford, Arkansas. Bradford is north of Little Rock and more than an hour's drive. We had a lot of time on our hands before leaving. We decided to remain at the restaurant, talking and drinking too much coffee. The two men who had followed me to the restaurant apparently had a lot of time to kill as well. They, too, remained at their table. An hour after we had finished breakfast we were still there and so were they. The second hour found each of us in the same position. Someone had to blink and eventually the two men got up and walked by our table. David seemed to recognize them and he said hello as they passed by. As they left the restaurant I casually asked him who they were. He said that he didn't know their names, but recognized them as Little Rock policemen who were frequently seen around the courthouse. Call it paranoia, but I was more than a little bit concerned. We were sitting in David's automobile the night before when we decided where and when to meet for breakfast. If what we had just witnessed was not a coincidence it could only mean one thing. David's car was bugged. And if his car was bugged, mine could be as well. It had been in the parking garage since the afternoon before. I did not immediately tell David of my concerns, choosing to wait until we were well outside.

When we left the restaurant, and before we got in the car, I told David about being followed to the restaurant by the two men that he had recognized in the restaurant. David was visibly shaken and believed that I had been justified in my concerns. I already had a plan and I explained to David that we were going to the airport to exchange cars. I further said that we should not speak to each other while we drove the ten minutes to the airport. After that, we drove to Bradford for my first meeting with Freddie and Dorothy Whitener. The Whiteners were decent and humble people who had had the misfortune to have been in business with Jim and Susan McDougal. They had been financially ruined. Their story was published in the February 1994 edition of *The American Spectator*. I had many conversations with Freddie, Dorothy, and their family over the years and I liked them immensely. What may be surprising is that Freddie could never find it in himself, in spite of the fact that he and his family had been ruined by their association with the McDougals, to speak ill of Jim McDougal. Their feelings about Susan, however, was the polar opposite.

During December 1993 the volume of materials that we had been able to amass was crying for analysis. It was obvious that a writer would be needed for this project who had a clear understanding of banks, Savings and Loan institutions, and the regulatory agencies. James Ring Adams, a former writer for The Wall Street Journal and author of two recent books on bank scandals was hired by *The American*

Spectator. He had his first meeting with David Hale and Randy Coleman at a hotel in Washington during December 1993. Jim Adams was a good choice to analyze and report on Whitewater. His two books had covered bank fraud and scandal, and they had both been recently written and published. Adams' book, "The Big Fix. Inside the S&L Scandal," was published by John Wiley & Sons in 1990. He co-wrote "A Full Service Bank. How BCCI Stole Billions Around the World" with Douglas Frantz. Their book was published in 1992 by Pocket Books of Simon and Schuster. He knew banking, he knew fraud, and he knew how politicians were involved. It was a perfect fit.

The day that Jim Adams and David Hale met was the same day we found out what David Brock had been doing. The January edition of *The American Spectator* was out, and it contained his "Troopergate" cover story. The impact of that story would continue to reverberate up to and beyond the impeachment of William Jefferson Clinton, President of the United States, because it mentioned a woman only by her first name, "Paula." Paula Jones would identify herself as the same "Paula" cited in the story, ensuring her place in history.

By early January 1994, there were several people from the magazine on the ground in Arkansas. They were researchers, writers, an editor and, of course, Steve Boynton and me. The number of people going in and out of Arkansas presented problems. Foremost among them were the mounting hotel costs. Someone suggested that a solution to the problem would be to rent an apartment. That would provide a central location for storing and reading documents as well as providing sleeping space at far less cost. Some of us began to check into the availability of month-to-month rentals. Parker Dozhier, upon learning of our needs, informed us that he had a small rental property in Little Rock that was, at the time, unoccupied. We arranged to see it and ultimately rented it from Parker for most of 1994. It was a tiny four room, one bath, single family brick dwelling. It was about one block away from Markham Avenue, one of Little Rock's main thoroughfares. Less than a block away was a McDonald's fast food restaurant. Parker furnished the house in "early attic" and we took possession. The two rooms used as bedrooms each had twin beds. We added a telephone, a fax machine, and a few file cabinets. Some, but not all, *Spectator* visitors stayed there while in town. It was not the most comfortable place in town. Little Rock had a few good hotels. The Capitol Hotel was one of them, though old and a bit pricey. A couple of our "team" chose to stay there while in town. Steve Boynton and I stayed in the rental house, usually with a researcher.

David Hale was engaged in legal maneuvering that would result, eventually, in a guilty plea and cooperation with special counsel, Robert Fiske. Until these things were finalized, David would continue to be a valuable source. Robert Fiske had been selected to take over the investigation. He replaced the Justice Department's Donald MacKay who had been sent by the Department of Justice to replace United States Attorney, Paula Casey, who, in the glaring light of press scrutiny, had to recuse herself. Paula Casey had driven a hard bargain with Randy Coleman. She had declared that November 8, 1993, was the "drop dead" day for David Hale to plead guilty. She refused to discuss a plea bargain. On that date she continued pressing Randy Coleman on whether David would agree to a guilty plea, not informing Randy until late afternoon that she was recusing herself and was being replaced by MacKay. The Justice Department piously asserted that MacKay had complete independence, but he didn't, and under growing public pressure, Attorney General Janet Reno was forced to appoint Mr. Fiske Special Counsel, effective January 16, 1994. Fiske, himself, would serve in that office for slightly over six months.

For almost two months the new Special Counsel busied himself with setting up his operation under a daily barrage of press stories. Each time that I saw David Hale I would ask him if he had talked with Mr. Fiske and his answer was always negative. A trial date for David Hale had been set by the federal judge, Stephen Reasoner, for March 28, 1994. With the trial date fast approaching neither the special counsel, Robert Fiske nor Randy Coleman, Hale's attorney had made an effort to reach out to each other. In early March, James Ring Adams had occasion to talk with Mr. Fiske about another matter, and in the course of his brief conversation he said to the special counsel that he guessed, with David Hale's trial coming up later that month, that there wouldn't be a plea agreement between the two of them. Mr. Fiske replied to Jim Adams that that was not necessarily so. When Jim told me that I immediately asked him how he had been able to talk with Mr. Fiske and he said that he just called him and that he took the call. He also told Jim Adams that one of his articles in *The American Spectator* had been helpful to him. Since Robert Fiske was aware that David Hale had been a primary source for Jim Adams' articles, it didn't seem unreasonable to me that he was reaching out to David in that manner. At any rate, I arranged to see David that night and passed those comments along to him. When we departed that night David said that he would be meeting with Randy Coleman the following morning and that he would call me in the afternoon. The call didn't come. I was not to hear from David for several weeks. My assumption was that he and Randy had talked with the special counsel and had been instructed to cease contact with the media. I was partly right.

CHAPTER TWELVE ~
DISAPPEARANCE

We were successful in securing documents from several sources. David Hale had told us all that he could before he "disappeared." Other leads had to be pursued and files mined for bits of corroboration. New stories continued to develop and new sources came with them. It was a hectic time as articles were being written and published. Now *The American Spectator* could even be found in grocery stores in Little Rock. Prior to these times, it had been difficult to place the magazine in most newsstands. Now, it was everywhere. At a popular newsstand on "K" street in Washington it began to appear in the window, so passersby could see it. The magazine had become a hot commodity and its circulation would soar above 300,000, making it the largest magazine of its kind in the nation.

Sometime in April Steve Boynton and I had a message from Parker Dozhier. He wanted to talk with us and there was a sense of urgency implied. We had retained Parker to assist us in our efforts and had found him to be very useful. He knew the state and many of its leaders and he had a keen eye. Parker, himself a writer and former Little Rock television news/camera man, knew where to look. He monitored local news reports and sifted through bits of information and shared this information with us. Through his personal contacts, he could also get answers quickly. When we were not in Arkansas and needed court filings or other documents, he provided them to us. Other news organizations were using local stringers as well. For those services, we paid Parker $1,000 each month and $800.00 monthly to rent his house in Little Rock for most of 1994. He was underpaid. Steve and I went out to see Parker at the earliest opportunity to learn what he wanted to tell us. It was worth the trip. Parker related to us that he had received a phone call from David Hale. He was asked to meet David in the Pizza Hut parking lot in Benton, Arkansas. Benton is a small town roughly midway between Little Rock and Hot Springs, about a thirty-minute drive for Parker.

Parker had agreed and a time was set. There was no further conversation between them. Parker had driven to the specified location and there he had a revelation. With David were two FBI agents from the elite hostage rescue team. David was under their protective custody. He and his wife, Sue, were being kept at an undisclosed location. The members of this team were with them twenty-four hours each day. Steve Boynton and I would soon see David under similar circumstances, though in a more familiar setting. A few days later we had another call from Parker. He told us that a "friend" wanted to see us. He would be at Parker's on a date and time certain. We intuitively knew who the "friend" would be, and under the circumstances, we were also surprised. Faced with an opportunity to learn more, we had no choice. We kept the date.

Travel to Little Rock had become routine by that time. We repeated the exercise. We picked up a rental car and drove to Dozhier's Bait Shop. When we arrived there we saw a large Suburban vehicle with black windows sitting in the small parking space in front of the bait shop. Nearby were Parker Dozhier, David Hale and two men that we hadn't met. It was a warm spring day and they seemed to be enjoying the sunshine. We greeted David and Parker with handshakes, then David introduced us to the two strangers. We all made small talk for a few minutes and the initial tension eased. David explained to us that his new "friends" would occasionally allow him to get out for a short time, but always, they would be with him. He also told us that he had reached a plea arrangement with Special Counsel Robert Fiske and had agreed to become a cooperating witness for him. It was then that he had been placed under the protection of the Federal Bureau of Investigation. That is distinct from the "witness protection" program, under the supervision of Federal Marshals from the United States Department of the Treasury. We were allowed to visit for only a short time that day. David and his escort left in the Suburban, for a destination that we could not know.

That short meeting had raised as many questions as it had provided answers. Obviously, the Special Counsel was convinced that David needed protection, but from whom? What information did he have that caused him to make that decision? Why had David been allowed to see us? Coupled with what we already knew, there had to have been something that David had revealed to the Special Counsel that we did not know.

Randy Coleman had, months earlier, made a comment that was widely reported by the media. It was one of those folksy and catchy remarks so beloved by the press. He had said, "We have to save something for the marriage." Apparently, they had. Some of the answers were provided more than two years later by Special Counsel Robert Fiske when he appeared before Judge Stephen M. Reasoner, Chief U.S. District Judge, at David Hale's sentencing. Steve Boynton and I sat in the back of the Federal District Court on March 25, 1996, and heard the following remarks.

MR. FISKE: "In early March [1994], several weeks before the trial was to begin, Mr. Coleman entered into plea discussions with our office and expressed Mr. Hale's willingness to cooperate in the ongoing investigations. He agreed to meet with attorneys from our office and agents from the FBI to answer any and all questions we had on any matters, including both the case that was about to go to trial under the then-pending indictment and any other criminal conduct that Mr. Hale had engaged in or was aware of."

"Virtually every day for the next two weeks, Mr. Hale met with attorneys from my office, as well as agents from the FBI. During those meetings, he fully admitted to participating in the criminal conduct from which he was already under indictment. He also told us about the possible criminal conduct of others in the crimes in which he was not personally involved, but that he had either known about or had heard of."

"During those meetings, he produced voluminous records that corroborated many of his statements, and he suggested various additional ways in which we would be able to obtain further evidence to corroborate his information. For example, he identified other potential witnesses as well as locations where relevant records could be found. Although we had already been in the process of investigating many of the matters that he told us about, there were several entirely new matters that he brought to our attention that we had no prior knowledge of."

"One example of such a new and unknown matter was information that he provided to us relating to an alleged tax fraud that he told us Governor Tucker and others had participated in. The investigation that followed Mr. Hale's providing us with that information ultimately led to an indictment of Governor Tucker as well as William Marks and John Haley for tax and loan fraud, and of course, that case is pending in this district."

"Following this detailed proffer to us over those two weeks, Mr. Hale agreed to plead guilty both to the conduct that was the subject of the then-pending indictment as well as the conduct that he was not under indictment for, including conduct that he had brought to our attention and of which we had been unaware. He also agreed to enter into a cooperation agreement with our office, pursuant to which he agreed to cooperate fully with the Independent Counsel's office in connection with its investigation and prosecutions of others..."

"On March 22, [1994], Mr. Hale plead guilty to the already charged conspiracy to defraud the SBA, as a result of his activities at CMS from late 1988 through early 1989. And he also pleads guilty to the additional criminal conduct that he told us that he had engaged in over the years..."

"After his guilty plea in March [1994], through early August of 1994 when I left, I could tell Your Honor that Mr. Hale fully lived up to the terms of his cooperation agreement. Over the course of the next several months, he was consistently responsive to our requests for interviews and documents. He was interviewed extensively on dozens of occasions by lawyers working in my office at the time, specifically Rusty Hardin and Dennis McInerney, both of whom are here today, and also by the FBI. In those meetings, Mr. Hale continued to provide our office with detailed information regarding many of the matters already under investigation, as well as other matters that the office as a result of his information subsequently investigated. He greatly assisted us, both in our overall understanding of many of the core aspects of our investigation and also in our specific understanding of particular transactions and events that are often very complex and quite old. "His assistance was extremely beneficial in bringing about cases that resulted in pleas of guilty, as well as in providing information with respect to cases that have since been indicted and are currently pending..."

"Mr. Hale's assistance was also extremely valuable in connection with our investigation of numerous matters. Our office was still in the process of attempting to corroborate Mr. Hale's extensive information in investigating the many leads that Mr. Hale has provided us relating to these matters when Mr. Starr took over the investigation."

"As Your Honor notes from the Government's motion pursuant to Section 5K1, several of the individuals who were subjects of the investigation of those other matters have since pled guilty to criminal charges, with most of them agreeing to cooperate with the Office of the Independent Counsel connection with its various cases and investigations. Specifically, between March and August 1994, Mr. Hale provided substantial information to our office in connection with at subsequently led to guilty pleas by the following individuals: Robert Palmer, who plead guilty to conspiracy to making false entries in the records of Madison Guaranty Savings and Loan Association; Chris Wade, who plead guilty to bankruptcy fraud and making a false statement to a financial institution; Stephen Smith, who plead guilty to conspiracy to misapply funds of CMS; and Larry Kuca, who also pleaded guilty to conspiracy to misapply the funds of CMS; and Larry Kuca who also pleaded guilty to conspiracy to misapply the funds to CMS."

Others addressed the court that day, each of them, in their own way, detailing the cooperation that David Hale had provided to the investigation during the previous two years. They were: Independent Counsel Kenneth W. Starr, Deputy Independent Counsel W. Hickman Ewing, Jr., Prosecutor Dennis J. McInerney, and former Prosecutor Rusty Hardin. They were fulfilling their part of the agreement that they had reached with David Hale. Generally, when a witness is cooperative and helpful, the investigators with whom they cooperate detail that cooperation before the sentencing judge and ask that the judge takes that into consideration when he decides what the sentence is to be. In turn, the others had their say and then Randy Coleman, David Hale's attorney, addressed the court on behalf of his client.

Then Judge Reasoner lowered the boom. David Hale was sentenced to twenty-eight months and was ordered to make restitution in the amount of approximately $2 million. He obviously was a very dangerous man, but to whom? He would remain out of prison until after his testimony at the trial of Governor Jim Guy Tucker, and Susan and Jim McDougal. He had just two short months of freedom, of sorts, and then he would take up residence in a Federal Prison in Fort Worth, Texas.

That series of events, particularly the period of time from early March 1994 until late August 1994, form the basis for the public allegations made against me and others associated with *The American Spectator* in early 1998. Those allegations led to the Federal Investigation that will be covered fully later in this narrative.

There was a brief interval between the time we met David Hale with his two FBI agents and another call from Parker saying "A friend wants to see you." He told us the date and time. Same place. Again, we made the journey. This time, David was accompanied by two different FBI agents and we were introduced to them. It was an even nicer day than the one on the previous visit, and being spring, I wanted to go fishing. A friend of Parker's, John Peterson and his son were there and they had been fishing for the past couple of days and had caught a considerable number of crappies. There is nothing that I would rather do in early spring than catch and eat crappies. I made it known that I would like to take one of Parker's boats out for a little while that afternoon. David said that one of the FBI agents had been talking about the same thing before we had arrived and that maybe he would like to go out with me. I was surprised that he agreed when I asked if he would like to join me. The other agent told him that he would be okay alone and that he should go. I volunteered that we would not have to leave sight of Dozhier's should it become necessary for us to return quickly.

The agent touched the "fanny pack" that each of them wore and said that if he was needed, he would know it. We secured some minnows and a couple of fishing rods and shoved off.

We talked and fished as any other fishermen would and in the course of our time together the agent said that he was glad that David had a place like Parker's to come to. He related to me their concerns about David's health and morale. They were aware of his former heart problems and carried emergency medical supplies. Further, he said that David was fortunate to have friends like us who he could see from time to time in light of the pressure that he was under. I did not pry but the agent said, "We are protecting David for obvious reasons." David's detractors in the "spin machine" consisting of apologists in some of the media and paid and unpaid partisans in the political environment have and will pooh-pooh any suggestion that David Hale was in any danger. Perhaps they missed what Federal Judge Stephen Reasoner, had to say on March 25, 1996, in that regard when he sentenced David to prison.

"...I don't know if I've ever seen a case where the amount of help and the results stemming from a single person's efforts has even approached anything like this. Directly related to Mr. Hale's assistance, we've had five guilty pleas and two multi-count felony indictments. I also realize, Mr. Hale, that you have become a pariah among certain of your old acquaintances and supposed who shun you now. Worse, and more troubling to the Court, I understand that you and your family have been subjected to threats...that has caused you to have to live in seclusion under FBI protection. I realize you have paid a much higher price for your cooperation than most people do..."

We were not successful at catching our own fish and soon returned to shore where John Peterson had set up an outdoor deep fryer and was cooking crappies Cajun style, with hush-puppies and Cole slaw. All of us ate the outdoor feast and judged it to be delicious. David and the two agents soon departed, but it would not be the last time that we would see them that summer. It was, however, the last time that we would see them at Parker Dozhier's. The next time we saw them was at a motel in Hot Springs, Arkansas. It was not far from Dozhier's and he joined us. Steve and I had rooms at the motel and it was there that David and his escort met us. We suggested that we go to dinner at a nearby restaurant and the agents told us that it would be all right for David to go with us, but they would stay behind. They gave us a time to be back after we told them where we would be. Again, these were different agents. Parker, Steve, David and I went to the restaurant and secured an out of the way booth. It must have been a wonderful treat for David to have that short period of freedom. We returned to the motel at the appointed time and again, the agents and David departed into the night to a location that only they knew.

There would be two more times that I would see David while he was in protective custody. Steve Boynton would be with me on one of those occasions and on the other I would be alone. The first of these and the one where Steve and I were together would be in Memphis, Tennessee. David had asked that we meet him there and we went. This was something different and we didn't know what to expect. It is possible, in light of what Robert Fiske had said at the sentencing, that David and the agents were in the area following leads in the ongoing investigation. Geographically, it made sense. When you leave Memphis traveling west you immediately cross the Mississippi River and you are in Arkansas.

David met us at our hotel and he had a friend with him that we had not met. He had been delivered to the hotel by FBI agents who were staying in a nearby location. We went to one of our rooms. David introduced us to his friend, Cal Wasson and briefly told us of their relationship and Cal's background. David told us that Robert Fiske had advised him to have something lined up to do once he served whatever sentence he would receive because it would be important to him when parole was considered. That sounded like wise counsel to me. David then told us that he had an idea that he had given a lot of thought to and that he and Sue had decided to pursue it. Their plan was to establish an organization to assist families, who, in the future, found themselves in situations such as theirs. They proposed to counsel with the families as well as to lecture and to provide support for whistle-blowers. It reminded me a great deal of another person, Chuck Colson, who had developed a prison ministry following his release from prison. Colson had been a prominent figure in the original "gate", Watergate. He had been an assistant to former President Richard Nixon and had been tried and found guilty of having one FBI file. Knowing the background of David and Sue it seemed to me that they would be naturals in such an undertaking. I wholeheartedly endorsed what they had in mind. I even named it, CLEAN, for Citizens Legal and Ethical Assistance Network. Steve Boynton agreed to and did establish a corporation in Virginia under that name for the later use of David and Sue. He paid for it out of his pocket and did it as he had done in the past for many others. The total cost was less than $500. Steve filed an annual report the first year and let it expire later when it became clear that there was no further interest by the Hale's in following that course. They had developed and examined a business plan, and found that it would have been impossible for them to cover the startup costs.

The next, and last, time that I saw David while in the company of his protective detail was in his home in Little Rock. Sue was there also. David had called and I told him that I was going to be in Little Rock the next day. He surprised me by asking that I call him at his home when I arrived at the airport. Immediately I wondered if they had been released from protective custody and allowed to return home. Arriving at the airport the next day around noon, I called and David answered the phone. I asked if he and Sue could join me for lunch. He said no, they could not, but that I should come to their house, adding that there were people with them. He told me to come to the back door and the people who were with him would allow me to come in. Disabused of the notion that they were back home to stay, I drove to their house and parked on the street, as I had been instructed.

Entering the driveway that led to a garage at the rear of the house I saw an attractive young woman on a chaise lounge who appeared to be sunbathing. She watched me approach in a manner that told me she wasn't there for the sun. The rear door was opened by David, and Sue was just behind him. I had never been in their home before and it was obvious that they no longer lived there. All of the furniture was gone, the only things left were on bookshelves, in packing boxes and lying around on the floors. There were three men in the house with them. I did not recognize any of them. Sadly, Sue and David told me that they were packing their personal belongings, accumulated over a lifetime together. They had sold their home to pay their legal bills. Their cars had already been sold and the Lake House was gone. They had nothing left. It was then August 1994. I suggested that since they were unable to go out for lunch that I would like to buy pizza for everyone. Sue placed an order by phone after getting permission. She ordered enough for the three of us and the four of them. It was telling that when they were in Little Rock the number of FBI agents had doubled.

For years, now twenty-five, Peggy and I had annually traveled to Olive Branch, Mississippi, on the week ending on Labor Day. There we met with our dear friends from our Jaycee days in Tulsa. They were the ones that we had lived and worked with and had become so close with during the years between 1970 and 1973. One of the most special couples in our lives is Jim and Marge McCauley. Jim had taken a job with Holiday Inns at their national headquarters in Memphis, Tennessee upon leaving Tulsa and The United States Jaycees in the mid-seventies. He was Executive Director of the Association of Holiday Inns. Shortly after moving to Memphis Jim made an effort to get everyone to come and visit with him and Marge. The McCauley's sent a letter to all of us and invited anyone who could come to be their guest during the last weekend of August. Several couples accepted and a good time was had by all. Jim and Marge, surprised by the number of people who came, decided to do the same thing the next year, only they would do it at one of the Holiday Inns in the Memphis area. Considering the options, one stood out above the others. Holiday Inn had a facility just outside the tiny village of Olive Branch, Mississippi, and about twenty miles south of Memphis. It was The Holiday Inn University. It was the facility used during the early years of Holiday Inn to train franchise owners. In all respects, it was a hotel. it had an eighteen-hole golf course, tennis and swimming and acres of lakes and wooded areas for the use of its guests. It was remote enough that visitors could comfortably bring children and leave them to their own devices without worry. In the beginning, we all had young children and that feature was very attractive to us. The next year more couples made the pilgrimage to Memphis and on to Olive Branch. It became a tradition and a must for most of us.

In recent years Peggy and I have arranged our schedule to arrive a few days early for this annual event. Because she has Multiple Sclerosis, travel tires her. She needs to get her energy up for the fun to follow. David and Sue Hale were not a part of our group, but they were, after all, Jaycees. I suggested to Peggy that we invite them to spend one day and night with us in Olive Branch before the rest of our friends arrived, provided they could get permission to do so.

I had extended that invitation while at their empty home and they both were enthusiastic about the possibility. They would see if they could do it. Soon David advised that it seemed to be a possibility and they would confirm as soon as possible. What none of us saw coming was the replacement of Special Counsel Robert Fiske that August.

CHAPTER THIRTEEN ~
UNPROTECTED

Bowing to public pressure, on July 1, 1994, United States Attorney General, Janet Reno applied to The United States Court of Appeals For The District of Columbia Circuit, Independent Counsel Division for the appointment of an Independent Counsel.

"In accordance with the Independent Counsel Reauthorization Act of 1994 [the "ACT"], I hereby apply to the Special Division of The Court for the appointment of an Independent Counsel to investigate whether any violation of federal criminal law was committed by James E. McDougal or any other individual or entity relating to Madison Guaranty Savings and Loan Association, Whitewater Development Corporation, or Capital Management Services, Inc..."

She recommended that Special Counsel Robert Fiske, be appointed as Independent Counsel... "so that the Investigation may continue without interruption." In a stunning order by the court, issued on August 5, 1994, Kenneth W. Starr would become the Independent Counsel, replacing Special Counsel, Robert Fiske. That same day The Department of Justice issued this brief press release.

ATTORNEY GENERAL JANET RENO'S STATEMENT

"Earlier, I urged speedy re-enactment of the Independent Counsel law so that no possible question could be raised about who appointed him. When that became impossible, I appointed Mr. Fiske under Justice Department regulations. Once the law was reinstated, I suggested that Mr. Fiske be retained in order to ensure that there would be no delays or loss of continuity in the investigation. Now the Special Division has appointed Kenneth Starr. We will provide full cooperation to him, just as we did to Mr. Fiske, who gave selfless and distinguished service to that task."

STATEMENT OF ROBERT B. FISKE, JR.

"It has been a privilege to have had an opportunity to serve the Attorney General as Independent Counsel. I wish Ken Starr the very best and will do everything I can to help him with a speedy and orderly transition."

As August wore on and we were preparing to depart for Olive Branch, Mississippi, David Hale called and said that he and Sue would be allowed to join us for an over-night stay. We reserved a room for them at the Holiday Inn and proceeded with our travel. At the time the Hales were to arrive I went to the hotel lobby to greet them. When they did not arrive on time I was concerned. The circumstances under which they had been living were unpredictable, to say the least. My vigil in the lobby continued for an uncomfortably long time until they arrived, and when they arrived it was instantly apparent that there were big changes in their lives. In front of the hotel is a large circle fed by streets from the West, South, and North. As I watched the circle for arriving vehicles a small, older model pickup truck, with Arkansas plates, drew to a stop in front of the hotel. In it were David and Sue Hale, alone. It was the week of August 22, 1994. I walked out to meet them and told them where to park. it was difficult to resist a barrage of questions, but restraint got the better of me and I waited until they got settled in their room. I would learn soon enough.

David and Sue stopped by our room and he suggested that we leave Peggy and Sue to catch up on families and friends. Outside the room, he nervously indicated that he did not want to talk. We went outside and began walking toward a nearby lake. Well away from the hotel, David stopped and began to tell me about the series of events leading to his arrival in a pickup truck. He was clearly frightened and unsure of himself. Even then, he spoke in a whisper. He related to me that soon after the announcement that Kenneth Starr was to replace Robert Fiske the atmosphere had changed, and not for the better, in his view. Soon a "high ranking" person from the Justice Department in Washington had arrived. He and Sue immediately saw a change in attitude toward them by their protectors. He told me that they had become rude to Sue and had reduced her to tears on several occasions. They had been led to believe that they would be escorted to Olive Branch, but when it came time to leave they were told, to their astonishment, to "just go." That was the reason they were late because they couldn't "just go" without a car. They had to borrow the truck from a friend and that had taken some time. He said that he had no idea what would happen when he returned the next day. He was to call his protective detail as he was leaving and meet them back in Little Rock.

Peggy and I took them to dinner that night in Germantown, Tennessee, and did our best to cheer them up. They managed to keep a brave facade, behind which one can only imagine the torment. We remained in Olive Branch for many more days of genuine pleasure with our friends and then returned home. Soon after we arrived back in Virginia, we learned that David and Sue had been relocated in Shreveport, Louisiana. It was not common knowledge at that time. They were still required to inform their protective detail of significant movements, but otherwise, they were alone and on their own.

1994 was an eventful year in many ways. Parker Dozhier's father died on February 6, 1994. It was Parker's sad duty to make funeral arrangements. His mother had passed away just over a year earlier. Now Parker was the only one left. He made arrangements to have his father interred at a nearby cemetery in Hot Springs, Arkansas. Parker made those arrangements with the assistance of a funeral home employee, Caryn Mann. A friend of mine often says that when one door closes another opens. In Parker's case, that would prove to be true. Several weeks after his father had been laid to rest, a visitor showed up at his bait shop, unannounced. It was Caryn Mann, the funeral home employee who had assisted him during his grief. Parker was surprised that Caryn had come to see him, though he seemed to be pleased. She continued to appear at his bait shop and soon they were seeing each other frequently. Over the July fourth weekend, Caryn and her thirteen-year-old son, Joshua, moved into Parker's mobile home. I can't recall just when Steve and I first met Caryn, whether it was before or after she came to live with Parker, but we did see her each time that we visited with Parker after that fourth of July, 1994. The environment at Dozhier's seemed to be all that a thirteen-year-old boy could want. Boats, fish, and unlimited bucolic days on the shore of a beautiful river. There was no doubt in our minds that Parker was pleased with the new arrangement, at least for a time. On several occasions, while Parker and Caryn were together, Steve and I took them out to dinner in Hot Springs.

Thirteen-year-old boys were not the only ones who could enjoy Dozhier's. Fifty-plus-year-old boys could as well. It has been well established that I enjoy fishing and fortunately, when in Arkansas, I could get to Dozhier's. It was during one of those visits, in December 1993, when Steve Boynton, David Hale and I drove out to Lake Catherine to see Parker that we met a friend of Parker's and a frequent visitor, Jim Peck. Jim was an accomplished fisherman and Professor of Botany at the University of Arkansas at Little Rock. He had met Parker in 1981, soon after his arrival in Arkansas. Unfortunately, I never had the pleasure of his company on the water. Two months after we first met, he was side-swiped and forced off the road by a semi-truck, sustaining injuries that plague him to this day. That occurred following pizza at the closest place to Parker's that served food. Obviously named by a prosperous Hot Springs public relations firm, Beano's was the site of what could have been the last supper for Jim. Steve Boynton, Parker Dozhier and I had been his companions that evening as we, luckily, would be again. It was February 20, 1994. I did have the pleasure of his company on many occasions that didn't involve fishing and those experiences have enriched my life. Jim can be very entertaining with his sharp wit and facile mind, so being there when he was around was enjoyable. There were other attributes possessed by Professor Peck that I would come to know. In fact, I rank Jim in the top echelon of people who cherish and demonstrate integrity, sacrifice, service to mankind, duty and honor, coupled with an unmatched loyalty. Jim's role in this story is extraordinary and though I would derive great pleasure from telling it, his words and feelings are far more eloquent.

"Oh, yes, I remember it well." September 23nd, 1993, while reading the last remaining local Little Rock newspaper, I saw that our new US Attorney for Little Rock had been approved by the Senate last night. Paula Casey, another Casey at the bar, I quipped. Then I saw the shocker, a stunning headline, and story. A Little Rock municipal judge, David Hale, was soon to be indicted by a federal grand jury. Hale was now accusing the new Governor Jim Guy Tucker and the past Governor/new President of the United States, Bill Clinton of financial misadventure. This was NEWS!

"My first thoughts were of questions left unanswered by the truncated style employed by newspapers, making the story fit the space. Little David had certainly picked the biggest giants in the State Valley and in the Federal Valley. Players, operatives, and the "hydraulics of money" would be invoked, at the private, corporate, state, and federal level to remove, discredit, and punish this judge.

"Then I paused, took a deep breath, and pondered the deeper, darker realities about the story and the many questions that were left unanswered. Strange not to treat this investigation like the proverbial molasses jar on the Iowa dairy farm, in which the newly tangled flies died quietly, putrefied, and attracted another crop of victims. I could not remember any other high figure in the Arkansas political family being so publicly crucified, with the exception of Arkansas Attorney General Steve Clark. He politically threatened Bill Clinton and financially messed with that nursing home business of the Daddy Warbucks family of Arkansas who ran Stephens, Inc. My eyebrows raised at the implication of this thought.

"An investigated target that is hammered quickly and publicly will rarely provide much more for the prosecution. If taken down slowly enough, then the target may often want to help the prosecutor make the case against them and their fellow conspirators. They want to come clean as if they were in a confessional. There is a strange convergence between legal and clerical professions. Both require penitents. But, this was not to be the approach here. This was P. T. Barnum public... It was all out in the open, keeping The Others at bay. Questions kept on coming. The answers that seemed most likely were unsettling."

"Although a resident of the State of Arkansas for a dozen years, I am still a stranger in a land that is strange to me. You could sooner believe the newspapers advertisements than take as fact any news article about the political family. All one really could believe about these folks was learned from "street talk" and not the local newspapers, much less the fluff from "talking heads" on the tube. There were hundreds of pretenders who claimed to know what was going on, but few contenders actually knew."

"I was just a college professor, a country botanist of sorts, who studied the ferns of Arkansas. Being far removed from those in the political or business realms, I found it passing strange that the press stories were very different from the stories told at early morning coffee when connected or informed faculty "-splained" things in the manner of good old boy autocrats. Around the table sat professors and administrators with extensive Arkansas backgrounds in business, education, journalism, politics, history and economics. Many of them were native born "Arkies", a self-identifying term or "Arkansawyers", a term that separated common hill-folk from those with acquired pretense."

"The coffee crew included many who had been very active Young Democrats, some who had served in earlier administrations, some were still active party animals that loved the smell of a campaign, and a few were close friends to those with influence. The topics were current events: the ups-and-downs of specific legislation, the lethal pressures by lobbyists, and the ins-and-outs of people seeking influence for themselves or their ideas."

"Over the years I had concluded from these discussions that the state's political family was quirky and that state politics was not for sissies. It was commonly told that "rewarding friends and punishing enemies" was the starting point of Arkansas politics. But that it went further than that, and one needed to know that "during the campaign, attack one's enemies; after victory, attack one's friends." I guess that the fight was so strong 'cause the stakes were so small."

"I knew enough about this "one party state" and its "personality cults" to realize that Judge David Hale was in serious trouble. By implicating both "golden boys" of the Arkansas Democratic Party, Hale had not curried favor with his friends nor the Big Money of the state Oligarchy. He was now persona non grata, "blowing the whistle", and the newest leper in the colony. He would be considered a federal carpetbagger and vilified like no one else in Arkansas since post-reconstruction times. He would need new friends. The old ones either would shun him or claim that they could not "get involved" with him in public or private. I remember that I actually wished I could meet him, get my few questions answered, and slip away before his personal doom descended."

"How little did I know about making wishes in Arkansas. Now it is too late. Now it is but to laugh. In short order, I was introduced to Judge David Hale and noted that his former business associates were not real friends and that "friends absent" were making things very difficult. Then a semi-tractor trailer rig in the left lane on a four-lane interstate signaled right, sideswiped me, and ran me off the road, totaling my car and finished my capability to conduct field studies on the Arkansas flora. It took six months to be rid of the constant pain. Meanwhile, while I was at a loss as how to continue my professional research, I dedicated myself to community service, and with a sense of civic duty and compassion, I began to provide, with the approval of Starr's agents, various forms of assistance and service to help David Hale and his family ensure their privacy interests and rights."

"Out of a sense of duty to authority, developed twenty years earlier while serving in the U.S. Army, I did this for the convenience of the FBI agents assigned to the Office of Independent Counsel in Little Rock. Specifically, for two years (1994-1996) I facilitated Hale's movements to and from Little Rock to meet with federal authorities or with the court. When required, convenient, and permitted, he stayed overnight at my residence in Little Rock. During the first Whitewater trial in 1996, David Hale remained in town at my residence. For nine days I transported him to Court where he testified. I then picked him up and transported him back to my residence for sanctuary at the end of each day. This saved the prosecution considerable personnel, labor, time and money. Hale decompressed in a home setting rather than stare at bare motel walls and security personnel."

"First out of duty, and then out of compassion, a friendship commenced. Over those three years (1994, 1995 and 1996) we spent a great deal of time together and did the talking cure. Through it all, we became friends and then Friends. David told me stories about Arkansas history, politics, business, finance and government. The stories often were total send-ups and howls. Most had a point about why and how people came together to get things done and to help each other."

"My favorite is one where Jim McDougal and another Young Democrat were out in the August summer heat and humidity doing duties as campaign advance men. In the countryside, McDougal would keep the windows of the car rolled down to bring in the cooling breezes. But when they approached a town, McDougal rolled up the windows. The Young Democrat was dying from the sweltering heat with the windows down, and could not for the life of him comprehend why a sane person would roll up the windows in towns and the breezes would lessen, but rolling up the windows was not the solution. The Young Democrat finally could stand it no longer, turned to McDougal, and begged him not to roll up the windows. Diamond Jim McDougal smiled, and with his best imitation of FDR's voice, told the campaign neophyte, "With the windows rolled up, The People will think that we have a car with air conditioning, a rare and expensive thing out here. If two little no-account people in this god-forsaken campaign have a car with air conditioning, then this is a well-heeled campaign. The True Believers will know enough to note the name of our candidate and will vote for him in this primary as this must be the sponsored campaign, the one with the backing of the Big Money. We are on the winning side." What made this exceptionally hilarious to me is that the Young Democrat is now a three-piece suit Arkansas Republican, occupying such a high and public office, that he could be embarrassed to have this story told about his adventures and to acknowledge the likes of Jim MacDougal as an early mentor. And there are hundreds of such stories about Arkansas politics, politicians, and people in high places who got there, not by merit, but with the help of friends."

"In turn, I kept David apprised of the news and opinion in local and national media...and little of it was good news and a surprising amount of it was vicious, incomplete, and inaccurate. This went far beyond gladiator blood sports. It was beyond the pale of a simple "falling out" among associates. Many had been David's Friends, fraternity brothers, fellow lawyers, and close business associates. He had worked their campaigns and served them well in good times and bad."

"David Hale needed Friends to replace those he lost or those who no longer could come forward. He still had civil rights and privacy interests that warranted a bubble of protection. He cooperated fully with Special Counsel Fiske and Independent Counsel Starr. It was an honor and privilege to be of service for the Office of Independent Counsel. After the Whitewater trial, I continued to provide assistance to David Hale and his family, things any friend would do. In Little Rock, I reduced their unnecessary exposure to press intrusions by picking up their medical prescriptions at the pharmacy and the mail at the postal box. These were forwarded to them. I moved documents to their accountant, lawyers, and doctors. Sometimes, a sealed message was taken to federal authorities. I relayed phone requests from old friends who wanted to express their concern and prayers. I did not forward the many threatening phone calls nor bother David with their enumeration; they (the callers) were probably paid with WOM, walking around money. I never charged him for meals or use of my phone...nor have I charged anyone else who was welcome in my home during that stressful period in Arkansas. And I facilitated the anniversary, holiday, and Mother's Day rose from David to Sue to ensure that the Hale family traditions continued even when David could not do so under federal wraps. But we are all even, as Sue paid me in brownies...oh, Heavens! What brownies...all the time telling me I needed to diet harder."

"David Hale kept his agreements with Special Counsel Fiske and then-Independent Counsel Kenneth Starr. He testified extensively, completely and waived his fifth amendment rights, leaving 1600 pages of federal testimony in the record, and it was used against him. As promised, he cooperated with federal authorities. He was incarcerated in May 1996. He served his time. He continued to cooperate fully with the OIC."

"I visited Judge Hale twice at the medical prison at Fort Worth, Texas, where he was evaluated for assignment in the Bureau of Prisons facilities. After Judge Hale was transferred from Federal Prison in Fort Worth, Texas, to the Federal Prison Camp outside of Texarkana, Texas, I commuted from Little Rock each weekend and visited for 3 - 4 hours during normal permitted visiting hours."

"Early 1998 David was released from Texarkana. He entered the City of Faith halfway house in Little Rock located but a few blocks from my home. I drove David from the Halfway House to his work site where he was a receptionist at a law firm. At the end of the day, I drove him back to the halfway house. I had to sign him out and sign him in each time. I was with David Hale and his family when Judge Reasoner changed his last month at the halfway house to one-month home detention. As that home detention had to be in the district of the Little Rock Court, he could not be home with family, but stayed at my house in home detention for one month. We had calls in the middle of each night to see if we were really at home and not elsewhere."

"As of July 1996, malicious state charges were filed on Hale, even as he sat in prison with a letter of federal immunity that no one would enforce and had lost his fifth amendment rights in the process of testifying in the Whitewater trial. There is no way to mount or assist in one's defense against state charges while in federal prison in another state. There was no law library in Texas prisons useful for the pertinent Arkansas charges. There were no case files. There was no way to go out and get the documents that are exculpatory to get the goods on those who bear false witness, and on those who give false testimony in depositions."

"Then I converted much of my home into a law library, law office, law conference room, and law files storage area to enable David Hale to build a legal defense against these retaliatory state charges. David was not going to plead guilty to something he did not do. I located a former biology student who had been to law school. He was now a practicing Arkansas defense lawyer. He worked pro bono on Hale's case. I worked as a quasi-paralegal fetching and copying items from the local law library and sending them to Hale. I constructed case files. I obtained FOI documents. I obtained public record documents. I constructed a chronology. I kept a newspaper clip file. I developed a library of reference indices and news-opinion media tapes. I read federal, state, regulatory, and other documents. I tried to keep the accreting mass of paper organized."

"I took David Hale to Little Rock hospitals twice for life-threatening heart disorders. In my home, I witnessed the life-giving charge of the pacemaker-defibrillator jolt David four times to reset his heart rhythms. His remaining health was lost in prison. He was 100% disabled. But Hale's once friends now political enemies just laughed with glee, being the mean-spirited wretches that they are. These sorry past friends wished Jim Guy Tucker well. Tucker never spent a single day in prison, and he has still a lot of other people's money in his pockets. And then we lost Jim McDougal to medical misadventure in prison in March 1998. David Hale had pleaded with the OIC not to imprison Jim McDougal, as Hale had barely made it through, and we all knew that Jim McDougal was in far worse shape. Now Tucker is healthy with a brand new liver, but he still will not darken a cell."

"And then it got real strange. On January 26, 1998, Bill Clinton denied Monica three times, wagging his finger for emphasis. The following day Hillary invoked the dogs of war against a vast right wing conspiracy. Eight months later I drove David Hale and myself to Fort Smith, Arkansas to answer fully and truthfully any and all questions of the Office of Special Review and the Grand Jury empaneled to investigate false accusations about journalists who covered Whitewater, the Office of Independent Counsel in Little Rock, David Hale's credibility, and my character. I told them what, why, and how I helped David Hale and his family. In preparation, I hired no lawyer. I was not subpoenaed but was asked and went voluntarily, not requiring mileage nor witness fees for my testimony. It was an honor and privilege to experience the Grand Jury System and found it to be so much better than the slimy inquisition by media that preceded it. When this story, inflated by opinion-porn panderers such as Geraldo and Salon e-magazine, was fully figured out, it too opened like Al Capone's vault in Chicago, and was found empty."

"In my opinion, the whole affair was contrived by a West-wing conspiracy of Hale's enemies to tamper with a federal witness, to retaliate against David Hale, to ruin his health, and to poison the jury pool, while the state conducted that jury trial to send him to the state prison farm and end his life in some cotton patch without heart medication. Reward friends and punish enemies."

"The prosecutors and jury queried my motivation. I told them I did not do this for money, not for quid pro quo, not for some trivial or jejune MICE [Investigators assume it must be for Money, Ideology, Conscience or Ego], nor for fifteen minutes of fame or more likely, infamy. My service started out as duty, honor, loyalty and compassion. But the reprisals, retaliation, and plain meanness of Hale's former friends had angered me, and I just got determined in sustaining my service. This is called "Iowa Stubborn", a character trait made famous in the musical, Music Man. This all has become personal, very personal."

"Let me explain. Most of us are not Good Samaritans, but just fellow travelers who are also in the ditch, set upon by our personal thieves of choice. We strangers and neighbors just decided to help each other get out of the ditch so that we all could just go on our way. We do good acts not out of pride for having done them. We do not want thanks. We just want out of the ditch we are now in, and we are very determined to do it. That is the basis of my sustained compassion. No matter how hard it is for some to comprehend, motivations can also include faith, belief, duty, honor, and service."

"It is ironical to me that while the Whitewater scandal was headline news in Little Rock, my then-Governor Jim Guy Tucker, and my local university Chancellor were encouraging faculty to become involved in community service programs. Probably, my particular community service program was not exactly what the Chancellor nor what Governor Tucker had in mind. So it goes."

"Lastly, Mea Culpa. I voted for Bill Clinton in every Arkansas gubernatorial election he was in since 1981. Ten years later, in the hot summer of 1991, I sought and obtained a promising message of encouragement for an endorsement from the Story County (Iowa) Democratic Party chair couple. They are old friends of mine. in Iowa, that county plays a bell weather role in determining which Democrat will win state endorsement. I personally gave Bill Clinton that message with a phone number to call and to collect their endorsement. I shook his hand. This odd exchange was noticed by the press. It occurred at a public event held at the opening of a biotechnology facility at Redfield, Arkansas. In retrospect, I hope my old friends will forgive me, as Bill Clinton did not turn out to be the president we imagined nor for whom we hoped."

[The above came from a personal conversation with Professor Peck. (2000-2001) I chose to use his own words rather than my memory of the conversation.]

CHAPTER FOURTEEN ~
COMING HOME, GOING AWAY

Grandchildren bring new hope and great joy, and for two days, January 31, 1997, and February 1, 1997, Peggy and I were experiencing both. Then, late in the afternoon of Jonathan Taylor Kelly's second day of life, a new emotion replaced hope and joy. It was fear, enduring and smothering fear. Jonathan had been deemed a healthy baby boy, all nine pounds, six ounces, by his pediatrician. His mother, Marcail Henderson Kelly had had a difficult labor, and after twenty hours a caesarean birth was performed. Ron Kelly, our son-in-law, had scrubbed and donned surgical clothing in order that he could be with his wife and baby. It was an omen of great bravery to come.

On Saturday we were visiting in the Alexandria, Virginia, hospital where Jonathan had been born the previous day. He had not yet mastered the task of breastfeeding so a nurse brought nutrition in a bottle. With some expert guidance, Jonathan was able to ingest his first meal. Then trouble began big trouble, the life and death kind.

My friend and associate, Rex Armistead, had been visiting with us at the hospital that day and had held Jonathan for a photograph. Rex and I then left the hospital for coffee and conversation. Since Rex had attended the wedding of our daughter and son-in-law the previous year, he was pleased to have met the new arrival. We were not gone very long and when I returned alone to the hospital room the baby was gone. The nurse had suddenly taken the baby from the room and said that she would be right back. It had already been several minutes since she left the room with Jonathan, and everyone there was on edge.

Someone came to the room and briefly explained that he had experienced an increase in his pulse rate and was under observation in pediatric intensive care. Marki and Ron suggested that Peggy and I go home and get some sleep. We did, reluctantly, because we didn't know when or what would come and we needed to conserve our strength. Not long after we arrived home we had a call from Marki. She and the baby were being moved to nearby Children's Hospital in Washington,

D.C.

There was a possibility that he would require a heart transplant and Children's was the closest hospital with that capability. Marki promised a call as soon as she knew what the situation at Children's would be and again insisted that we not come to the hospital. Sleep had become impossible as the hours wore on without a call, then, in the early morning hours, the call came. Jonathan was in very serious trouble, in the intensive care unit at Children's hospital. The preliminary prognosis was not good for Jonathan. He had severe heart defects which had not been detected by sonograms prior to his birth. He would require a series of heart surgeries, providing he could live long enough.

The following days brought more information about Jonathan's condition and it was not good news. His heart condition had a name, hypoplastic left heart. One of the worst possible conditions for an infant starting a new life. His heart would have to be rebuilt, literally. All of the things that had taken place earlier in my life seemed insignificant by comparison. The most compelling priority now was the survival of our baby. We knew that our lives would change, dramatically and that we must make whatever sacrifice necessary to give him a fighting chance. It soon became evident that it would require full-time support and that would place an impossible strain on Ron and Marki. Peggy and I talked with them about the task ahead and asked them to come and live with us so that we could share the coming burdens. Our modest home was already being shared with Peggy's elderly mother, her dog, and our dog. Soon we had added two cats, a baby, and his parents.

Jonathan had passed his first hurdle by improving enough to come home and we quickly fell into a schedule. My shift usually came at 3:00 a.m. and like the others, it required medication, regular temperature takings, diapering, and vigilance. He was in a delicate balancing act between hope and despair. His periods of sleep became my periods of reflection. I still had to keep up my work and my family, more now than ever.

Steve Boynton and I had continued our work and the travel required for it since late 1993. After the arrival of Kenneth Starr as independent counsel we were able to continue seeing and talking with David Hale, only now he was living in Shreveport, Louisiana and had a telephone. On several occasions between late August 1994, and late May 1996, we had seen David. A few of those times had been at Parker Dozhier's and once, as we sat in the back of that federal court in Little Rock, hearing the testimonials to him from the investigators with whom he had been cooperating. Then, his sentence. We did not talk with him that day. He was allowed to remain free long enough to appear as a witness for 9 days in the stand in the trial of Governor Jim Guy Tucker and Jim and Susan McDougal. After the trial, he returned to Shreveport to prepare himself and his family for leave-taking.

Those last few days before reporting to Federal Prison were gut-wrenching days. I know, because I spoke almost daily with both David and Sue. We had known each other for many years and had been friendly. By then we had become friends. I had come to admire both David and Sue for their bravery and resolute behavior in the face of overwhelming circumstances. In addition to friendship, I was also observing, for history, an important human story. My wish at the time was that the story could be told at some point in the future by *The American Spectator. Fate did not allow for that, so this book will do it.*

As the days drew short for the goodbye to come in the Hale family, David called me and shared his feelings. He told me that Sue, and their daughter, Amy, wanted to go with him to Fort Worth, and he did not want them to. He was considering their feelings and deeply believed that it would be an ignoble experience for them and surely, the humiliation would accompany them. I asked David to think of their point of view. Certainly, it was their love and loyalty that dictated their wishes. Then, I offered a compromise. I suggested that I come and accompany them from Shreveport to the prison, and after their goodbyes, I would see Sue and Amy safely home. More quickly than I would have imagined, David agreed. David did not ask me to do that, but I was glad when he accepted my offer. I talked with Steve Boynton and he agreed that he, too, would join us. We met David, Sue, and Amy at the residence provided to them by the United States Government around 7:00 a. m. on a morning in May 1996. David did not have to report to the prison until 1:00 p.m. that day, but we had a reason to leave as early as we did. Having a press and public relations background, I was determined to allow the Hale's one last small pleasure. For more than two years they had endured the vilest and unceasing public attacks imaginable. Other felons, such as the McDougals, Jim Guy Tucker, and Webster Hubble had gushing testimonials from FOB's (Friends of Bill) both in the administration and in some quarters of the media. They, after all, had remained mum about what they knew and to many, that was a noble and praiseworthy position to take. Their venom was reserved for David, and he had to watch where he stepped.

There was no doubt in my mind that hands in Washington were being rubbed in glee because they would earn a double prize that day. They would have a convict for future testimony and would be amused that evening by network news film of David Hale, their most despised villain, walking into federal prison. One could imagine the celebrations being readied all over Washington and other enlightened places. We, meanwhile, were about to do the unthinkable. Who, in their right mind, wants to go to prison early?

We made a pass by the prison entrance just to reconnoiter. David was out of sight in the back seat, while Sue and Amy sat upright. I was driving and Steve was in the front passenger seat. There was one automobile stationed directly across from the entrance to the prison and in it was one reporter talking into a cell phone. She, no doubt, was from a local television station and had arrived to try to get a leg up on the mob. We moved by without slowing and in a circuitous route, stopped at a fast food restaurant where Steve and I could while away some time over coffee. According to plan, we shook hands with David, and wishing him well, took our leave. It was time for family.

Little more than an hour later, Sue and Amy returned in sad triumph. As David lay on the back seat, the car that had once passed the press sentry with two men and two women in it, went unnoticed through the gate with two women in it. It was 11:00 a.m.

CHAPTER FIFTEEN ~
TELEPHONE CHANGE

Steve Boynton, Sue, Amy and I stopped at a Cracker Barrel Restaurant just off the interstate between Fort Worth and Dallas and had a quiet lunch. We then drove to the gigantic Dallas/Fort Worth airport to drop Steve. He would return to Washington, while I drove Sue and Amy back to Shreveport. It was a silent trip as each person was deep in thought.

I had told David to call me collect, at any time, and fully expected him to do so. Not knowing the rules and protocols of the Federal Bureau of Prisons, we had left it at that. When I did not hear from him during the following two weeks, I called Sue and expressed my concerns. Sue had not heard from him either and was to go for a visit that coming weekend. She had received an indoctrination when she and Amy had accompanied David when he reported to prison and following directions, had taken the necessary steps for the visitation. After her visit, I received a call and report from her. David was unable to make collect calls. He was also unable to receive visitors without the approval of the Federal Bureau of Prisons. In order for him to call or for me to visit, certain forms must be filed and signed by each of us. With regard to the calls, he could make them and they would be charged to an account maintained by each inmate. If they wanted cigarettes or a candy bar, for instance, it would come out of the account.

I sent a personal check to Sue Hale and asked her to place it in David's account so that he could call both Steve and me. It was for $200.00 and I asked Sue to tell me when it needed to be replaced. I told Steve about it in passing and he insisted that it be covered by funds provided by *The American Spectator*. The significance of this action is noteworthy since *The American Spectator* was accused of paying David Hale, when in fact, all we were doing was providing a method of communication between Hale and ourselves. If it had been possible for him to place collect calls, it would have been handled in that manner. I would later send another $200.00 check to Sue for the account that would not be charged to *The American Spectator*. Since I had told news organizations or others had, on my behalf, that there was only $200.00 given to the Hale phone account, I must apologize. It was not until we were forced into an investigation that I discovered the second check for $200.00. It was written on my personal account in December 1996. The same rules apply to phone calls, and visits. Sue gave me the necessary information. In order to visit or take phone calls from David, I would have to request the necessary forms from the prison, fill them out, and return them. They would, in turn, depending on whether I answered the questionnaire in the affirmative, allow David to call me, and me to visit him. Both Steve Boynton and I followed the procedures, indicating that each of us would take calls from David and that each of us wanted to visit him.

The Federal Bureau of Prisons is an arm of the United States Department of Justice, part of the President's executive branch. Thus, we became marked men. All phone calls made by inmates are recorded by the prison. All visits are monitored and controlled. Nonetheless, Steve and I visited David at the federal prison in Fort Worth and later, in Texarkana where he had been reassigned after months of medical evaluation. Each time we were in Texarkana we would see the steady and ever loyal, Jim Peck.

From May 1996 until January 31, 1997, Steve and I had visited David three times at Fort Worth, and at least five times in Texarkana. Following the birth of Jonathan, I was only able to visit one more time. We would talk many more times after the last visit, each time the conversation was predominantly about my grandson. David demonstrated an admirable compassion and subordinated his concerns in deference to mine.

CHAPTER SIXTEEN ~
A HOUSE DIVIDED

In early fall, 1996 and shortly before a board meeting of *The American Spectator* Ron Burr, the publisher reminded me that it was time to consider compensation of the magazine's staff. I had been selected by the board previously to serve as chairman of the compensation committee. That committee had been established to recommend salary and bonuses for the top three people at the magazine, R. Emmett Tyrrell, Ronald E. Burr, and Wladyslaw Plesczynski. Editor-in-chief, Publisher, and Executive Editor, respectively. Also serving on that committee were Jerry Gerde, a Panama City, Florida attorney and longtime friend of both Bob Tyrrell and Ron Burr, and John Von Kannon, a former publisher of *The American Spectator*, then a vice president of the Heritage Foundation. I had been on the board for many years, and like most members of the board had trusted that the staff would do the right thing. For most of those years, the magazine had a small and loyal group of readers, hovering around 30,000 subscribers.

Our board meetings, as a rule, consisted of listening to Ron Burr and Bob Tyrrell give their reports. There was always gentle encouragement for what they were doing, and spirited conversation about national and world affairs. Those meetings were generally over by noon and were followed by a lunch during which luminaries on the board, and there were several (among them Former Secretary of the Treasury, William E. Bill Simon, Former Ambassador to the United Nations Jeane Kirkpatrick, Jack Kemp, Former Professional Quarterback and member of congress, then candidate for Vice President, Frank Shakespeare, former Ambassador to the Vatican and General William C. Westmoreland) made enlightening observations for the benefit of themselves and their fellow board members. Some of those board members were very famous people. Not much was at stake, given the enormity of the daily concerns that many of them faced. In essence, it was paternalistic, and in the case of one member, maternalistic board. Few members of the board would have been there had their personal achievements not far exceeded those of the institute which they guided. Things were changing, though, and the magazine was achieving many of its goals. For most of its existence, the magazine was published in tabloid style and that had changed in recent years. It was now a glossy covered production that could sit nicely on a newsstand and often did. The circulation was growing, thanks to the content of the stories being covered. It was evident that the board members were taking more interest in their roles and consequentially, the compensation committee was born.

The financial picture of the magazine was improved, mainly the result of increased circulation, and there had been a rise in compensation for the staff. The year before had seen the rise of compensation for Bob, Ron, and Wlady, plus generous bonuses, elevating each of them to a respectable income level. Prior to that time, one presumes, those decisions had been made independently of the board. Therefore, I was in shock when I asked for and received from Ron Burr his suggestions about annual bonuses for himself, Bob and Wlady. He suggested $100,000.00 for each of them. That, in addition to the newly generous salaries that they were receiving. Burr wildly overstated salaries at the recently launched Weekly Standard in an attempt to justify his request. He also overlooked an important element of the comparison. The Weekly Standard was not a non-profit publication. There was no evidence that either Bob or Wlady were parties to Burr's memo to me. Indeed, when I discussed it with Bob, he was in total agreement with my thinking.

Ron's recommendation was couched in comparison to other publications, not all of them non-profit organizations, as was *The American Spectator*. The magazine had depended on the generosity of others for its very existence for more than twenty- five years. In view of that request, I demurred when asked for a report of the compensation committee, suggesting that a review would be conducted and a report would be forthcoming.

John Von Kannon, Jerry Gerde and I had several discussions about Ron's request and we conducted our own review of compensation at similar organizations. On January 6, 1997, in a conference call to the board of directors, I made our report to the board. While generous, our recommendations fell far short of Burr's expectations. It was soon after that time when a chill descended...brrrr.

Bob Tyrrell called me at home to discuss a matter unrelated to the decision of the compensation committee. He asked me if I would be willing to join the staff of *The American Spectator* and in the conversation gave me several reasons for his query. I told him that I would give it my consideration. Several other calls were received from Bob about the same subject. Since he was soon to go away on an extended business trip, I told him that I would meet with him on his return for a discussion about his offer.

Bob and I met upon his return and he reiterated his desire to have me join him at *The American Spectator.* I told him what I would require in order to accept. Salary was not the only consideration. I told Bob that I felt it would be necessary for Ron Burr to be in accord since we would be working as a team. I had witnessed some discord at the magazine previously, though I did not realize the extent of it. Bob soon reported that Ron was "on board' and that we should proceed with our plans. We would present our arrangement to the board of directors at the coming spring meeting. Subsequently, Bob called and asked me to meet with him, and Ron Burr at his home. Bob maintained an office in his home and spent most of his time there while writing. Writing occupied most of his time, so he was not at *The American Spectator* office's each day. Our discussion concerned a budget shortage in the funds earmarked for the project that Steve Boynton and I were working on. Ron indicated that roughly $130,000 more had been spent than had been received. Since I had played no role in accounting or disbursing funds for the project, I was of little use in the discussion, and Steve Boynton was out of the country. I suggested that the three of us arrange a meeting with Dick Larry to discuss the problem and to reach a resolution.

We soon had our meeting, which, as always, was a pleasant one. Dick Larry looked at the figures prepared by Ron Burr and said that the shortage could be the result of misallocation of the funds since portions of the funds had been spent within *The American Spectator* on items not directly related to our project. Dick said that in any case if there was a problem, it could be cleared up by future grants. The meeting ended on friendly terms, so I thought, and in my mind, the problem was resolved. I never questioned Dick's conclusion or the thoughtfulness of his approach to the issues raised.

Soon I was asked to meet again with Bob and Ron about the same subject. I expressed to them both that I was satisfied that the situation would be resolved in a satisfactory manner. Ron asked me about Steve's books and I told him that each time Steve went on an extended trip he would have me come to his office and show me the location of all of his files related to this project, and the ledger that he kept. It was a precaution prudently taken by Steve in the event something untoward happened to him. It hadn't been necessary for me to avail myself of his records in the past, but if there was a need, I could. I suggested that if Ron felt it would be helpful to him, I would get a copy of Steve's ledger for him. Ron said it would be appreciated, and I went by Steve's office and took the ledger to the magazine's offices, and copied it on their copy machine. I gave it to Ron as he and Bob Tyrrell came out of a meeting in his office. I specifically asked Ron to treat it as confidential information. Having never seen the contents of the ledger, I made no effort to read it or understand it prior to giving it to Ron. What I copied was each page of the ledger. I had no need to see it myself, for I had every reason to know that Steve Boynton would properly account for each dime of money in his care. Unfortunately, that act of helpfulness resulted in more friction.

Soon after Steve returned to the country he faxed to me a copy of a message that he had just received from Ron. In the message Ron said that he had "gotten Dave Henderson's version of an accounting" and it had been insufficient. He asked Steve for a full accounting. Steve asked me what this was all about and I told him about giving Ron his ledger. Steve immediately knew why Burr was disturbed. He told me that he kept disbursements in the ledger for things other than compensation to himself and me. Our compensation was contained elsewhere in his files. Steve had not been previously asked for that information, but he had, in his lawyerly way, prepared for that possibility. He said that he would immediately get the correct information to Ron. Steve was in no way put out by Burr's request, and I understood what Steve had just explained to me, but, it did not erase my annoyance at the tone of Ron's message. I Immediately faxed this message to Ron. "I did not give you my version of anything. What I gave you was Steve's ledger in hope that it would be helpful to you." I was steamed. Steve worked the remainder of the day and prepared an accounting, reflecting all expenditures, and sent it to Ron Burr. As a courtesy, he also sent a copy to Dick Larry. Dick replied to Steve that he didn't question his expenditures, but he wanted an accounting of the expenditures that had caused the shortage of funds being claimed by Burr. He was making no accusations, rather he was being careful, as always, that funds were spent in the manner for which they had been intended. His understanding of the issues involved would guide the foundation's future grants to *The American Spectator*.

Most of those events occurred during the early months of 1997, and while they were the harbinger of things to come, they were soon replaced by more important concerns.

Surgeons at Children's Hospital had been selected and our job was to keep Jonathan as healthy as possible under the circumstances. He had to have the first surgery in order to buy time for ones that were to follow.

The pediatrician caring for Jonathan decided to have him admitted to Fairfax Hospital for testing prior to surgery. He was placed on a regular pediatric ward and we were wary of that arrangement. Ron would spend the night in the room with his baby and I would arrive at 5:00 to relieve him and allow him to go to work. On one of those nights, I experienced my worst nightmare while fully awake. For reasons known only to God, I awakened at 2:00 A.M. immediately dressed and headed to the hospital. I was three hours early. Entering the room, I saw Ron, looking dazed and just awakening. I went directly to Jonathan and placed my hand on his skin. By then we all had developed an acute sense of his temperature ranges and he was hot. Dangerously hot. We summoned the nurse and she told us that she had just given him Tylenol and hadn't bothered to wake Ron. It was a call from Marki that had awakened him. She had called to say that I was on my way to the hospital. We quickly told the nurse that we had dealt with a high temperature in the past by sponge bathing Jonathan with cool water. Her superior knowledge informed us that Tylenol was what was called for.

That was when Ron and I took over. There was a sink in the room and we immediately began wetting towels and applying them to the baby. Simultaneously, we were calling for the resident on duty. Ron also placed a call to Jonathan's pediatrician who instructed the resident as to what she could and couldn't do. The resident, realizing the seriousness of the situation, called for a lab technician in an attempt to get an IV line in a vein. The lab technician made a couple of unsuccessful efforts to find a vein and only succeeded in hurting the baby. We immediately stopped that effort and demanded that a team of Pediatric Intensive Care personnel be dispatched to take him into their care. General George Patton would have been proud of us. After all, it was not a request.

Soon the room was filled by people who knew exactly what they were doing. We would get to know them very well in the coming two and one-half years. In short order, Jonathan was packed in ice and in the fabulous hands of Dr. Gary Fudderman, Intensivist, pediatrician, and magician. He was surrounded by the finest group of staff that one could imagine. Dr. Fudderman had already placed a call to an equally impressive pediatric cardiologist, Dr. Frank M. Galioto, Jr. and he was there in minutes, with an echo machine looking into Jonathan's heart. Dr. Fudderman explained that Jonathan's body was shutting down and it would be necessary to place a main line into his heart. This would require quick surgery and some risk. He added that he had done it many times and that he was very good at it. No brag. Just fact. And he was good at it. He sent us out for coffee to spare us the fear. He came to the cafeteria to tell us that it was done and he invited us back. It was explained to us as we stood and watched them work that if Jonathan was going to go to Children's Hospital for his heart surgery he would have to go soon.

In short order Jonathan's pediatrician was also at our side, followed by Peggy and Marki. He weighed what was going on and then both he and Dr. Fudderman told us our options. They were in agreement that anything that Children's Hospital could do could also be done at Fairfax Hospital. They made it clear that they were not in any way trying to interfere with his doctors at Children's Hospital. We were impressed to learn that Jonathan's pediatrician had once been head of pediatrics at Children's and Dr. Galioto had been head of pediatric cardiology there as well. We were told that one of the best pediatric heart surgeons in the world operated at Fairfax, Dr. Akl. And, odd as it seems, they all worked as a team. it was a decision to be made by Ron and Marki, but surely, it was a gift from God. It had the added benefit of being a fifteen-minute drive from our home.

Jonathan was stabilized enough for the lifesaving surgery performed by Dr. Akl, though his recovery was fraught with risk and heroics. He remained in the pediatric intensive care unit (PICU) at Fairfax hospital for many weeks. He was baptized on Easter Sunday in his bed in PICU, and no one was betting that he would survive. But he did.

CHAPTER SEVENTEEN ~
FRIENDLY FIRE?

In May 1997 the board of directors of *The American Spectator* met in New York. Sitting around the table was the usual collection of directors bantering back and forth in friendly recognition. The meeting was soon called to order and we began to address the agenda items. While we had been around the table for several minutes I had paid no attention to the agenda which had been placed there by the publisher, Ron Burr. My eyes followed down the list of items on the agenda and stopped abruptly at, "... approving the consultancy of Dave Henderson for one year..." Consultancy? I had been offered a permanent job as Vice President and had accepted it. I was white hot as it dawned on me what was at play here. Surely, Bob Tyrrell would not consider such an abrupt departure from our agreement without discussing it in advance and having my concurrence. No skilled executive would do something that crude, unless doing it intentionally in a blatant display of insubordination. In this case, Ron was clearly being insubordinate to Bob. Obviously, I could not remain there and participate in such a discussion since I was a board member. I excused myself with the observation that the agenda item was not my understanding that had been previously reached. Former Treasury Secretary, William E. Simon asked me, "What is the correct characterization?" I replied that I could not enter into the discussion, then turned to the Chairman of the Board, R. Emmett Tyrrell, Jr. and said, "Bob?" as I left the room. It was an invitation for an explanation that I would not hear.

I did not return for the remainder of the board meeting. One thing was for sure in my mind. Whatever was going on I would have no part in it. I certainly would not agree to a consultancy. As many say, "Been there, done that." My career had included many consultancies, from the White House to Fortune 500 companies. I had enjoyed working closely with corporate CEO's at some of this country's largest corporations and had never been shown the discourtesy I had just experienced. If Bob Tyrrell was willing to be duped by his subordinate, so be it. Later I would learn that certain directors had been told by Ron Burr that he was, in effect, CEO of *The American Spectator*. I presumed if it were so, that it was by fiat and not abdication. Also, during the many years that I had been on the board, I could not recall one instance where the board had been involved in a decision regarding the hiring of personnel.

Bob told me after the meeting that he had been blindsided and he was not informed that it would be on the agenda. A disturbing pattern was emerging, one that would erupt in the not too distant future.

Bob was reassuring and told me not to worry about it. He said that we would work it out. And he did. He was in his own mind, still in charge, though his authority would continue to be challenged by his longtime friend and co-worker, Ron Burr. Those challenges to Bob's authority would end on October 6, 1977.

One of the main reasons Bob wanted me to come to the magazine was to be a buffer, to prevent his having to deal with every problem. He felt that my presence there would have a moderating effect on the staff. I was to report to him, not the publisher.

Earlier in my consulting career, I had the honor of working for a fortune 500 company that bore the name of the founder. The founder, over the years of growing the company, had employed executives of the highest capabilities, a method shared by most visionaries. It is not uncommon for those talented employees to challenge their bosses, and often, it is encouraged, but it can get out of hand. The founder to whom I refer had taken an unusual dressing down in the presence of other executives by one of his top officers, whom he had placed in a sensitive and important position. The visionary founder, away from the view of those who had witnessed the arrogance of their colleague, had asked the offender to take a walk with him. They walked a few hundred feet away from the building that bore the name of the founder, all the while talking business. Then, the simple man, who had the drive, the idea, the willingness to take the risks necessary to create employment for thousands of people, turned toward the High Rise building that bore his name and gestured toward it.

It is not at all uncommon for smart men, or women, to work for others who they would consider their intellectual inferiors, however, they and most others cannot bridge that gap, crossed by the few, who make the difference in our world. And those who seek and find those special places unknown to most, are deserving of our respect. The rewards that they achieve are most often deserved, if not understood, by those who are closest to them. Their complex, and often misunderstood personalities, are a testament to their uniqueness. This simple question begs an answer. Has any race car driver, with their daring, skill, or fame, ever equaled the accomplishments of Henry Ford?

For the next few weeks, I continued to perform the tasks that I had been working on for some time. Bob, the visionary, continued to reassure me that he wanted me on board and told me that Ron was in agreement. Ron gave me a letter of resignation from the board of directors and I signed it. If I was to work at the magazine as an employee that was the correct course of action to take.

Bob informed me that he wanted me to report for duty on Monday, July 14, 1997. I arrived at *The American Spectator* and an office was made available to me. Bob gave me several assignments and I began to work on them. I had known the staff for many years and felt comfortable with them. All in all, they were a dedicated and hard working group, and always of good cheer. I was hopeful that a rapprochement with Ron could be achieved and that we could get the nastiness behind us and move on. Ron had been an important part of the magazine for many years, and until recently, had been cooperative and supporting. I had enjoyed a good relationship with him in the past. I was proud of my ability to get along with others and expected to be able to demonstrate that in these new circumstances. It was not to be.

Years earlier, when John Von Kannon was on *The American Spectator* staff as the publisher and principal fundraiser, he developed leukemia and was given ten days to live. It had been a shock to all of his friends and during treatment, which, fortunately, led to a full recovery, his absence left a great void at the magazine. I had been asked to take on some of his fundraising duties for the magazine during his absence. I did so and was happy to have done it. I was happier when the "Baron", as John was called, was able to return to work.

When Bob Tyrrell decided to move the magazine from Bloomington, Indiana, to Washington, D.C., Ron Burr called me and asked if I would serve as registered agent for the corporation in Virginia, until they could get *The American Spectator* established there. It was a modest request, requiring no sacrifice on my part, and I did it. Whenever I had been called on by Ron or Bob over the years I had helped in any way that I could.

When the move to Washington was completed, I made it my responsibility to introduce Ron Burr to as many corporate representatives, trade association executives and others in the opinion sector of Washington as possible. From that base, and with Bob's direction, Ron had skillfully created "The Washington Club", an important source of funding for the magazine. Ron had met and married a charming woman after relocating in Arlington, Virginia and they were blessed with three beautiful children, all possessing impeccable manners. His family was the center of his life. He was a dependable and hard working executive.

In view of our history, I was at a loss to explain his behavior. From the day that I arrived, he went out of his way to avoid me. He would not speak when we passed in the halls. He was sending petty memos to Bob almost daily telling him that he needed to do one or another thing. They were annoying Bob and distracting him from his writing for the magazine and the book that he was working on. Ron had gone out of his way, and entirely out of character, to insult the most loyal patron the magazine had ever had, the Scaife Foundations. He refused to add me to the payroll and he refused to follow any order given him by Bob. It was a dumbfounding performance. Why would someone with so many things going for him, place himself in such jeopardy? Did he still believe that he was the CEO?

It may be explained by the different roles played by both Ron and Bob over the years, as well as by their differing lifestyles. It could be argued, and has been by some, that Ron was just doing his job. However, some things are not permissible in an organization, be it the military, a business, or government. There is one leader of an organization, and in this case, it was R. Emmett Tyrrell, Jr. He had founded the organization, given it its identity and through his sheer force of will, had defined it. In the mid-1970's Bob had been widely recognized as a young leader to watch. Time magazine had listed him as one of fifty "Future Leaders of America." I had personally nominated him for The United States Jaycee's Ten Outstanding Young Men, an award given annually by the organization. It was a highly coveted award and it had a long history of identifying young leaders who were destined for greatness. The award is given to recipients not yet thirty-five years old. Bob was one of those chosen for the award during a ceremony in January 1977. He joined a small, but important group of previous recipients who had become household names. Richard Nixon, Nelson and David Rockefeller, Bobby Kennedy, Elvis Presley, Ralph Nader, and Dick Cheney were just a few of them. In a strange twist of fate, one of the ten young men chosen along with Bob Tyrrell that year was a newly-elected Congressman from Arkansas and a future Governor of that state, Jim Guy Tucker. Bob Tyrrell was viewed by the public, the board of directors and the subscribers as the personification of *The American Spectator*.

Bob was the show horse and Ron was a workhorse. Perhaps it had grown intolerable over the years. Bob was widely seen as a bit of a playboy, following his divorce, and for a time, he encouraged that image. He did not assert himself, rather he encouraged a collegial approach to the operation of the magazine. Bob had given many writers a start over the years and he had many loyal friends as a result. Ron, too, had his supporters. It was a dichotomy when viewed from the outside, that seemed to work smoothly.

Bob and Ron's relationship had deteriorated into open aggression by the summer of 1997. Bob was perplexed by the behavior that was being exhibited by Ron and he directed him to take a six-month paid leave of absence, to reflect on both the past and the future. Again, Ron was unyielding, and he simply ignored Bob's directive. It had become mutiny. Bob was placed in a position where he had two options, throw up his hands and concede authority, or fire his longtime friend and associate. Either course of action would be unpleasant, but one course of action was unthinkable.

Bob called a special board of directors meeting, not that he needed their permission, to explain to them why he had reached the decision to fire Ron. There was unanimous agreement that Bob had the authority, and most felt that the decision was justified. Each person agreed that there should be some monetary settlement. After all, Ron had been with the magazine since 1969, two years after the magazine began. The board established a committee to reach a settlement on severance pay for Ron. No one was happy that things had deteriorated in such a way as to force this action. There was also an agreement that the basis for a settlement would be mutual confidentiality. That was as much for Ron's benefit as it was for *The American Spectator*. Future employment opportunities for Ron were the leading factor in that decision. He was to be fired, not ruined. Ron was notified by letter, signed by the editor-in-chief, R. Emmett Tyrrell, Jr. that he was terminated on October 6, 1997.

The American Spectator has kept its part of the agreement and has not revealed the real story of Ron's departure. I have remained silent as well. Until now. When Bob presented Ron with his letter of termination, there was a flurry of activity in the office. First Ron pleaded with Bob to reconsider. He then made threats to take other staffers with him if he had to go. It was not pretty. I heard Ron, as did others, ask Bob how he thought this would look in the pages of The Washington Post. A threat, a promise, or a bargaining point?

Howard Kurtz, media writer for the Washington Post, soon obliged. His account of the story seemed to conform to Ron's point of view. That, in itself, was confirmation that the Magazine had remained silent about the full circumstances. Kurtz began what was to become a revisionist view of Ron Burr's employment history with *The American Spectator*. No doubt he took at face value what he was told.

The committee established to decide Ron's severance pay soon had a rude awakening. Ron brought to the table a conflict negotiator from Detroit, Michigan. They demanded $1.3 million from *The American Spectator*. Ron, knowing full well the financial condition of the magazine, was in effect, demanding the bankruptcy of the magazine and the resultant loss of jobs by all of his former staffers, some of whom had remained loyal to him. It was an impossible demand, not to be taken seriously. However, Ron continued his efforts, finally yielding to a generous, though much smaller settlement. It was a continuing pattern as it had been with bonuses. The agreed to amount in both cases, I can now see, were unwarranted.

It is sad to write about the dark side of human nature and I must take part of the blame. Ron saw me as a threat to himself and during that period had spoken to others of a take-over by Scaife, and in his mind, I was the instrument of that takeover. If only he knew. One of the questions posed to me by prosecutors during my grand jury appearances was, "Are you a close friend of Richard Mellon Scaife?" I answered, saying, "I like him, but guys like me don't get to be buddies with billionaires." That question was predicated on many news stories over the years erroneously claiming that I was a friend or "close" friend of Dick Scaife. I answered the question as succinctly and as honestly as I could. I would be honored if I were his friend, and I have enjoyed the limited time I have spent with him, which, if averaged over the thirty years that I have known him, maybe as much as six minutes per year. I am grateful for that relationship, but to call it a friendship is a loose definition of the word. No, Ron, it was not an attempted takeover. That was your department.

CHAPTER EIGHTEEN ~
CONTEMPTIBLE TRAITOR

In early January 1994, I placed a call to David Brock's home and heard this message. "I can't come to the phone right now. I'm either on another call, writing or out taking down a president." It was a pompous and intemperate message, soon to be removed by order of Bob Tyrrell after I advised him of its contents. This was barely two weeks after his famous 'Troopergate" story had appeared in the pages of *The American Spectator*.

David had had great success with his book, "The Real Anita Hill, an outgrowth of an earlier piece in *The American Spectator* and he had understandably become a "darling" of the conservative establishment. He had shown himself to be the equal of the left wing attack machine, and his Land Rover was a reminder of that. He was a very young man and already he was enjoying the trappings of success, which for most, come later in life. The salary that he received from *The American Spectator* dwarfed that of other writers. But taking down a president? Really!

No one knew at the time, but David's best work was behind him at *The American Spectator*. He would apply his considerable talents to influencing the less discerning illuminati at *The American Spectator*, and the few articles authored by him that appeared in the pages of the magazine began to lose their bite. He saved that for other publications. In a harbinger piece, published in Forbes Media Critic (17 June 1997) he sought to discredit the reporting of others, and though not expressly stated, it was clear to the careful reader that his criticism included his current employer. It appeared that he had already begun his long walk away from his old allies. Not just yet, mind you, because there was still money to be had and the cachet of his association with *The American Spectator* was a useful entree to the conservative book-buying public. It was also useful to have researchers, unlimited access to Lexus/Nexis, telephones and expense accounts. Those things were vital to a writer, especially to one with plans to write another book. They were also extremely expensive. It could be argued that those things used to build an organization, within reason, are permissible. But when used to damage that organization, they are contemptible. "In the land of the blind, the one-eyed man is king." David had become a star in a galaxy yet to be identified. He was treated gingerly at *The American Spectator*, and with great deference. He seemed to imprint his own sense of "journalistic ethics" on Ron Burr and Wlady Plesczynski. "We'll ask David," was a frequent refrain.

In the early months of 1994 Steve Boynton and I met often with Wlady upon our returns from Arkansas and other environs and we debriefed him on our findings. Usually, David Brock and other writers, seeming eager to hear what we had to say, would sit in on those meetings. Ron Burr had made it clear earlier that "he didn't want to know," because he had other things to do. It was a practice that would be suspended by both Steve and myself after it became clear that nothing was coming of those meetings.

Ron Burr solicited a memo from Wlady on "The Arkansas Project" and it was rendered on September 30, 1997, just days before he was fired. It would find its way to the media, along with dozens of other internal documents. In Wlady's memo, he characterized the efforts of Steve Boynton and me with these words, "...There always seemed to be a lot of hush-hush and heavy breathing, but it never amounted to anything concrete enough for a story." Wlady showed no interest in what we were doing, but the editor of one of the nation's largest newspapers, Robert (Bob) Bartley always found the time to visit whenever I was in New York. Heavy breathing may connote different things to different people. If one had grown up in the affluent confines of Santa Barbara, California, for instance. But to someone whose formative years were confined to the tobacco, corn and hay fields of Western Kentucky, heavy breathing was most often the result of hard work and heavy lifting. And that is exactly what Steve and I were doing. Perhaps David Brock had already prescribed what could and couldn't be "concrete enough for a story" in his Forbes Media Critic article. David eventually produced a book, "The Seduction of Hillary Rodham Clinton", and when it was completed, it revealed that he, too, had been seduced.

One news story about Burr's dismissal, quoted a "former board member" of The American Spectator, as, "A betrayal of Biblical Proportions." A comment like that could have come from someone in the Vatican who labored over Biblical perplexities. Self-betrayal, depending upon one's point of view, could apply equally in this case. Since so many years have passed since I wrote this account of "The Arkansas Project" I can, without shame, reveal the identity of that board member. It was Frank Shakespeare, the former ambassador to the Vatican.

Bob Bartley (editor of The Wall Street Journal) asked me if I believed that David Hale was telling the truth. David had already been sentenced but had not yet been sent to prison. I told him that I did believe David. Bob said that he would like to meet Hale and I told him I would arrange it. Soon after that, David had business in Washington and I asked Bob Bartley if he could come to Washington and meet David. He took an early shuttle flight from New York to Washington and met me at the hotel in Pentagon City where David was staying. I took him up to David's room and introduced them. I gave them privacy by going down to the Hotel's coffee shop. About thirty minutes later, Bob rejoined me and said, "He's telling the truth."

There was another incident which must be revealed that shaped my decision not to bother with confiding in the enigmatic Managing Editor. Bob Tyrrell had labored long and hard to acquire a story, write it and verify it. It had required an extensive review of sworn testimony from witnesses in federal court, books, interviews with scores of people, and the self-incrimination and confession of personal wrongdoing by a named source. That source had provided documentation to support his revelation. Others at the magazine had failed to involve themselves, or to study the vast amount of information available to them regarding the long history of nefarious activity at Mena, Arkansas. Both Bob and I had invested immense time and energy in an attempt to understand what had taken place there, and we had reasonable concerns. There was enough there to have inspired investigations by the congress, federal courts, The Arkansas State Police, the IRS, and other federal and state agencies. Many of those investigations were ongoing at the time. Bob asked me to meet him at the *TAS* office for a meeting. Bob was aware, and I was not, that he had hard resistance from the editorial staff regarding his article, and he wanted a witness to the blow-up that he anticipated. Bob called in Chris Caldwell, an editor, and asked him to line-edit the article. Incredibly, Caldwell refused to do so. Flabbergasted, Bob told him that he could either do it or leave. Chris strode out of the office and within minutes Wlady appeared and protested that if Chris Caldwell had to go, he too, would resign. To the credit of Chris Caldwell, regardless of the merit of his recalcitrance, he maintained his principle and did resign. Wlady did not follow him. It was then when I began to see anarchy within the institution. At that time, I was still a member of the board of directors and a more enlightened one. Mena, too, was apparently prescribed. The integrity of the magazine had to be saved from the founder and editor-in-chief, by usurpers, with moral certitude that rivaled Hillary Clinton's. Contrary to the current wisdom, neither Bob Tyrrell's story in *The American Spectator* nor his book, "Boy Clinton," accused President Clinton of drug running at Mena. Both, however, concluded that he knew about those activities.

Wlady's memo of September 30, 1997, continued, "In any event, I got the sense [that] Henderson spent most of his time with Bob when dealing with someone at the magazine, and Bob never asked me to pay any attention to Boynton and Henderson's work. He seemed completely content to have them all to himself." Honestly, I don't know if this was written more as ammo for Ron Burr or as a statement of incompetence.

"Bob never asked me to pay any attention..." Our work was funded by my and the magazines' friends at the Scaife Family Trusts in Pittsburgh, but it was entrusted to the Spectator. Was that not reason in and of itself for the managing Editor to take what we were doing, seriously?

Others' comments that we were wasting Scaife Foundation money apparently were unaware that Steve Boynton and I made frequent trips to Pittsburgh where we would spend a considerable amount time, at the Duquesne Club in Dick Scaife's private dining room. Both Dick Larry and Dick Scaife were supportive and very interested but they became perplexed that the magazine was not using what we were finding. The long years of support of *The American Spectator* came to a heated end when an article by John Corry appeared in the *Spectator.* Corry was a former New York Times writer and highly thought of at the Spectator. Bob Tyrrell was at the beach on the Outer Banks of North Carolina and did not know, nor had he read Corry's article that was highly critical of previous writings by Chris Ruddy regarding the death of Vince Foster. An angry Dick Scaife called Bob Tyrrell to complain and when Bob told him that he had not read the article if infuriated Scaife. He told Bob that his support of the *Spectator* was ended, Bob had apparently left editorial decisions to Wlady in his absence.

This concocted news reminds me of a dear friend, the one-time Chief Justice of the Supreme Court of a western state, who once told me a story of a lawyer appearing before his court. The lawyer spun a preposterous story and the Justice responded, "Spare me, I have been to town a few Saturday nights myself." I knew just what he meant, and I will not embarrass him by revealing either his name or his state. He is a Democrat and it would not help his reputation to be known as my friend.

I know that Wlady never expected me to see his memo and it may come as a surprise, but I have had considerable success in uncovering information not intended for my eyes.

One writer at *The American Spectator*, James Ring Adams, worked closely with us and had articles in most editions. Jim's experience differed from that of Wlady. But, naturally, they would. Jim Adams actually gave our leads careful consideration, and he was rewarded with stories that remain unchallenged after several years. Jim Adams is a professional, and I suspect that he, too, has been to town a few Saturday nights.

Terry Eastland accepted Bob Tyrrell's offer to become interim publisher of *The American Spectator* in the fall of 1997. Terry brought stature and ability to the magazine. He had spent many years as a reporter, and he had been editor of Forbes Media Critic. He had been a long time contributor to *The American Spectator* and was well known to the magazine's staff. Terry, the author of several books, had also served in the Department of Justice from 1983 until 1988. In addition, he had the cachet of being a Rhodes Scholar. It was a good choice for Bob and *The American Spectator*.

In November the board of directors met in Washington, and in view of the stir created by Burr over his "fraud audit' demands, the board ordered an internal audit. The board reached their decision well informed. They took the position that the notion of a fraud audit was inflammatory and pointedly observed that there was no suspicion that a fraud had been committed, but since the issue had arisen it should be undertaken by Terry Eastland as a matter of prudence.

Terry dutifully accepted that responsibility and it consumed much of his attention over several months. Outside auditors were retained for a preliminary audit and in the course of their work, both Steve Boynton and I submitted to their interviews. Terry meticulously continued, personally examining each receipt, each phone charge, each travel expense, ad infinitum. Since Terry had not been at the magazine during the period of those activities, I found myself more and more becoming an interpreter of events to him. When he would become confused over an item he would often ask me for an explanation and I was able to supply the information. It was helpful to both of us that I had maintained complete phone records from the beginning to the end of my involvement.

Another set of records that I had were even more important. I had exclusively used my gold American Express card in all of my travels, and I must praise the company. Gold card holders receive a year-end statement of all charges. It is arranged chronologically as well as categorically. Those year-end summaries from 1993-1996 were invaluable in placing me in certain places at certain times. They solved what might have been lingering riddles. Steve Boynton made all of his records available to Terry as well. It was a difficult project to complete, but in the end, it was clear that all money from "The Arkansas Project" was accounted for. That is, it was clear to us. Others would soon dispute those findings. *The American Spectator* absorbed the cost of its internal misallocation. Ron Burr had raised serious questions about how Steve Boynton had managed funds paid to him by *The American Spectator*. Burr's diversionary finger-pointing led to costly, and unnecessary trouble for The *American Spectator.* For his efforts, he received a salary of $180,000 each year, plus insurance for himself and family, for two years after he was fired. This from a manager who "Didn't want to know how the effort was being run."

CHAPTER NINETEEN ~
LOVE AND HATRED

Jonathan had thrived and had become a happy and well-adjusted little boy. It was heartbreaking to have to do what had to be done. He was in his twelfth month and it was time for the next surgery, this time, a complex and dangerous open heart procedure that would take hours to complete. We had known for almost a year that this time would come, but it didn't make it any easier when his mother and father had to take him from his warm bed at 5:00 a.m. and into the waiting arms of the surgical team in whose care his fate would be decided. This surgery would begin the rebuilding of Jonathan's heart. He would never have a fully functioning heart, so he was to have one designed surgically that would offer him the most hope. Ultimately, if all went well, he would have a functioning heart. But first, he had to make it through this one.

Watching the car disappear in the darkness, Peggy and I were crushed. It was Monday, January 26, 1998. There was nothing that we could do but get ourselves ready to go to the hospital for the long and anguishing wait. In the early afternoon his surgeon, Dr. Akl came to us in the waiting room. Those few seconds before he reached us were the most excruciating time of my life. But the news would be good. The surgery had been successful, Jonathan was already in PICU and we could soon see him. Elation and happy tears replaced the dread that had been with us for months. We knew that he was in the best place possible, PICU, where all of his "friends" were looking after him.

The next morning, I was in the Pediatric Intensive Care Unit (PICU) with Jonathan, so I missed Hillary's appearance on the Today show with Matt Lauer. Little did I know what forces were to be unleashed against me and others by that appearance. The months to follow were a direct threat to Jonathan as well as they were to me because he would continue to need the full support of all of his family. Things went well for Jonathan and he spent his first birthday, January 31, 1998, in the hospital. All of us were there with him as we had been in the previous days. We could see the end of his stay coming and we were excited about having him back home.

On Monday, February 2, 1998, Jonathan was released from the hospital and came home. By now all of the hospital staff were referring to him as the "miracle" baby. They had seen him clear hurdle after hurdle in a most remarkable way. There was great joy in our household and it carried over into the next day at the office. The staff was eager to hear the stories that I was telling them and I had a permanent smile all morning.

Around noon I received a phone call from someone who clearly did not want to talk about my grandson. The caller identified himself as Joe Conason with The New York Observer. As soon as I acknowledged that I was, indeed, Dave Henderson, he began asking questions. He wasn't waiting for answers, just asking questions, in rapid fire manner. Though I knew who he was, I had never met him. I had seen him on C-SPAN time after time defending the indefensible on matters pertaining to the President. And what made him memorable to me was the pain on his face. He had that acquired look of the morally superior most often found in left-wing zealots. Their burdens in ridding the world of injustice and Republicans leave them permanently in pain. Or so it seems to me. It is possible that drugs have that effect on people, but having no experience with drugs, it is more convenient for me to accept my own observation. I could tell that his was not a friendly call.

At the end of Conason's barrage of questions, I informed him that I had no intention of submitting to a telephone interview. "Gotcha journalism" was no stranger to me, and I had spent more than three years of my life helping General Westmoreland restore his besmirched reputation after he was blind-sided by Mike Wallace during a CBS interview. Now it was time to apply lessons learned. I told Joe that I would be willing to meet him personally for a discussion. He said that it was not possible since he was on deadline. Bingo. We would read his story the next day. Conason was persistent and knowing that he was on deadline, I suggested that I would consider answering his questions with conditions. I stated those conditions: Our conversation would be recorded and after his questions had been asked, I would have some questions for him. He was taken aback and replied that he had never had such a suggestion before. I reminded him that I, too, worked for a news organization and that my questions of him could be newsworthy. I reminded him that it was only something that I would consider. I was not then committed to that course of action. He finally relented, saying that he couldn't reveal his sources. That wouldn't be necessary. We would soon know the answer to that.

I told Conason that I would call him back later in the day to let him know of my decision. He told me what his deadline was and said that he would consider it a courtesy if I did call him. Nice manners. I told him that he would get a call, no matter what my decision would be.

Among the questions contained in Conason's litany was, "Do you know David Hale?" I had been expecting such a call, I just didn't know who it would be coming from. There were stories going out to certain Media folks, mostly on the Left, and their interest was aroused by information going to them from within *The American Spectator*. To David Brock and on to Sidney Blumenthal? It made sense to me.

I had quickly decided on a course of action with Conason. About five minutes before his deadline, I returned his call and informed him that I had decided not to answer his questions, with one exception. I did answer one of his questions. Yes, I did know David Hale and had known him for a very long time.

On Wednesday morning, February 4, 1998, the article appeared and it seemed that Conason had a partner. Sharing the by-line with Conason was Murray Waas. Now, that name was familiar to me. A reporter had revealed to me a conversation he had overheard between Waas and unnamed others. Waas had stated that he had proof that Jerry Falwell had been secretly funding David Hale. I knew that to be preposterous, but fully expected to read about it somewhere. David Hale was then in prison, but I did alert Sue Hale to the possibility of such a story. I will not forget Sue's response. She was working for minimum wage and barely getting by at the time. She said, "I had better go out in the backyard and start digging. David never told me about that and I could sure use the money." I could hear the smile in her voice. So, the opportunistic Waas was on the case.

Joe Conason accurately reported that I had declined to be interviewed on the phone except to say that I had known Hale for more than twenty-five years. The rest of the article did not reflect the same degree of accuracy, but it was a straight forward, if inflammatory, story of intrigue at *The American Spectator*, supposedly based on information supplied by current and former staffers. It also introduced Dick Scaife. The headline read, "Richard Scaife Paid for Dirt On Clinton in Arkansas Project," followed by two sub-heads. "Bill's Billionaire Foe Funneled Loads of Money to American Spectator" and "Can You Say "Right-wing Conspiracy?" Did that make you smile, Hillary?

This was not the first time that Dick Scaife had been singled out as a villain. Clinton's spin machine went after him with a vengeance. Scaife had funded the conservative establishment for decades and that had earned him the undying enmity of the left. His support had denied them many victories. From the early seventies, he had helped to create an infrastructure that had gradually been able to compete with the far more heavily subsidized left-wing. Foremost among them was the Heritage Foundation.

It is a myth that conservative money equals that of the liberal establishment. The combined wealth of conservative foundations does not equal that of the Ford Foundation. And Ford is one of many massive foundations that lavish money on left-wing causes. But Scaife money had allowed competing ideas to emerge, and the mainstreaming of those ideas had led to the election of Ronald Reagan. Is it any wonder then, that Richard M. Scaife was a foe to be destroyed, by any means possible?

Throughout history, American presidents had been defined by their leadership in the face of great challenges and obstacles. George Washington defeated the British and established a great nation. Abraham Lincoln faced the anguishing task of healing a divided country, and he died before the healing. Wars were fought and won under the leadership of other presidents. FDR had many worthy foes; Hitler, Stalin, Tojo, and Mussolini. Harry Truman inherited the same enemies and they were vanquished. Ronald Reagan faced down the "Evil Empire" and it imploded. Under George Bush, the Berlin Wall came down and Desert Storm restored order in Kuwait.

William Jefferson Clinton was the first modern President of the United States who came to office without a worthy enemy. Something had to be done about that. He had to create a new "demon." The "right-wing" became a mantra of his administration and its rallying cry. All of his shortcomings were dismissed as the result of the "right-wing." One of the first wars to be waged by the new administration occurred in Waco, Texas. Those "right-wing" crazies, led by David Koresh, were a threat to America and they had guns. Later Bill Clinton's political career would be revived by the heinous bombing of a federal building in Oklahoma City. Many innocent people, including children, died there. Another act committed by a "right-wing crazy," Timothy McVeigh, the convicted bomber. Clinton and his advisors clearly had not missed the moving and genuine display of sadness by Ronald Reagan, when the bodies of marines had been returned from Beirut after their barracks had been bombed. President Reagan had joined the families of those marines. Americans were moved and inspired as they watched The President embrace and console each of the grieving family members in that hanger at Dover Air Force Base.

Bill Clinton duplicated Ronald Reagan's actions when he met with families of the victims of the bombing in Oklahoma City. That occasion marked the turnaround in his flagging political fortunes. It did not matter that these acts were committed by cultists and emotionally disturbed individuals. It was convenient to the Clinton administration's story, and the story trumps all facts, to suggest that the right-wing had inspired those events.

And so, Dick Scaife became the "Titular leader of the vast right-wing conspiracy." In a strange twist of fate, a Scaife hater came to pay a visit to the "Clinton hater," a term invented to define Scaife and others. Steve Kangas, a man who published vicious diatribes against Dick Scaife on a website in Las Vegas, boarded a bus for a trip to Pittsburgh. He had in his possession a 9mm automatic handgun. According to his family, he knew no one in Pittsburgh and had never visited there. Apparently, though, he had no trouble locating his destination. He took his gun and a bottle of Jack Daniels into a public restroom there. An article in The Tribune-Review, a newspaper owned by Scaife, reported the story, but few others did.

It would be a one-way trip. Almost immediately after arriving on Feb. 8 [1999], Kangas went to One Oxford Center. He walked around inside the towering office complex for a time, then hid out in a public restroom on the 39th floor. Nine hours later, drunk to the point of incoherence, Kangas shot and killed himself in the restroom, on the same floor as the offices of Richard M. Scaife, publisher of the Tribune-Review and a nationally known backer of conservative causes.

The location was no accident. Kangas, 37, was obsessed with Scaife's politics; apparently, he traveled to Pittsburgh to confront, and possibly to kill, the man he believed to be evil incarnate. And he came close to completing whatever bizarre mission he was on. Scaife was in his office for much of that afternoon, but he never ran into Kangas. Late that night, Kangas turned the gun on himself moments after a maintenance worker found him semi-conscious in the men's room, according to a police report. He was carrying a box of ammunition when he died. The pistol was brand new; he had obtained a permit for it shortly before leaving Nevada..."

You don't have to be conservative to be crazy. Take note, James Carville's endless televised rants against Dick Scaife sent this would be assassin on his mission, and to his death. According to the news account, six days before he died, Kangas posted a message with an Internet discussion group blaming Scaife for all of President Clinton's legal troubles. "Clinton is, in my mind, a moderate Republican, and it is only the insanity of Richard Mellon Scaife that is causing them to go after this man."

Later in the article, the following demonstration of class appeared. "Scaife's lawyer, Yale Gutnick, on Saturday issued a statement on the incident: On behalf of Mr. Scaife, who is out of town, and the Scaife Foundations, we are profoundly saddened and sorry for Mr.

Kangas and his family and we offer our sincere condolences. We are pleased that no one else was injured, but this was a tragedy."

James Carville had done more than any other person to demonize Dick Scaife. Carville's spittle could have revived acres of dying plants, but most of it fell on camera lenses. Until Harris Wolford, a candidate for United States Senate from Pennsylvania came along, Carville and his partner, Paul Begala, were losers in the realm of political consultants. Carville was known to curl up in a fetal position at the first sign of trouble and he whiled away his frequent periods of under-employment watching Andy Griffith reruns. But he found a winner in Harris Wolford.

In a special election to fill an open senate seat in 1991, created by the tragic death of United States Senator John Heinz, in a helicopter accident in Philadelphia, Wolford ran on an issue that resonated with the voters, health care reform, and he defeated former Attorney General Richard Thornburg for the Senate seat. Victory for Democrats in senate contests had become a rarity in those days and Wolford's triumph had been sweet for the party. Carville had saved his flagging career, and he took it on the road. It was not surprising that he landed in the Clinton presidential campaign, and that the campaign would parrot the Wolford issue of health care reform. Apparently, someone had found a holy grail.

After Bill and Hillary had become president, she continued to flog the health care reform issue until it exposed itself as a land mine and blew up in her face. Her health care bill was planned without her party, in secret, a conspiracy some said. Wolford, too, would fade away as the voters grew tired of him, and he was defeated soundly in his first bid for reelection.

In spite of those unfortunate setbacks, Carville's rocket had been ignited and it was fueled by his mouth. Carville and Clinton would become a tag team to be envied by the World Wrestling Entertainment. The president would administer a gentle shove and James would go for the crotch. Occasionally, they switched roles. Carville's comic visage and bombastic demeanor made him a natural for the television sound bite.

The only thing missing from his act was the banjo. Not only did he provide entertainment, he could fill a full twenty-seven minutes with his evasions and creations. The label on his back, no doubt, read, "Made by television for television." One positive thing can be said about Carville. He made no effort to hide his ignorance or his sometimes brilliance. It was there, in living color, for the world to see.

CHAPTER TWENTY ~
THE SCRIPT

Joe Conason had rung the dinner bell with his New York Observer article and the swill attracted the usual bottom feeders. It would be hard to blame them had they not been so scripted. Like a children's puppet show, little figures were running about, while the strings that controlled them led to 1600 Pennsylvania Avenue. The puppet master, in this case, seemed to be Sidney Blumenthal, but he, too, was connected to strings. This story was too valuable to the puppeteers to allow it to be a twenty-four-hour story, so it would be nursed slowly into its fullness.

Every White House has its "go to" reporters and that would be seen here. And, this wasn't an entirely new story. It had taken just two weeks from the firing of Ron Burr on Monday, October 6, 1997, until Monday, October 20, 1997, when The Washington Post's media writer, Howard Kurtz, had written about it in the Style Section, but that was different. Now Hillary Rodham Clinton had spoken and her subjects were marching resolutely to war. A week had already passed and surely she was becoming impatient. Pundits were beginning to chuckle about her vast right wing conspiracy comments on the Today show, but she had other notions, as Jeffrey Toobin, a staff writer at The New Yorker and legal analyst at ABC News helpfully pointed out in his subsequent book, A Vast Conspiracy. Toobin described the following on page 258. "...Mrs. Clinton was still flush from her triumph in New York when she returned on Tuesday afternoon to join Harry Thomason's vigil in the solarium. "I guess that will teach them to f--- with us." the first lady said..." Jeffrey, First or otherwise, that was no lady. That was a czarina, out to do whatever was necessary and to whom. If her co-president was so reckless as to jeopardize her power, she would show him a thing or two.

Four days later, on February 8, 1998, United States Senator Robert Torricelli, a Democrat from New Jersey, appeared on ABC's This Week with Sam and Cokie. Torricelli blew on the embers of Conason's New York Observer article. Appearing with him was William Bennett, of

Empower America and brother of Robert Bennett, the President's lawyer in the Paula Jones case. Bennett was the author of the "Book of Virtues," but the subject of that segment was not rectitude. It was a discussion of the President's relationship with Monica Lewinski. This topic had to be uncomfortable for Torricelli, but he had a Joker up his sleeve. In a revealing move, Torricelli tried to change the subject.

TORRICELLI: "I think you're going to miss the story of the week. The New York Observer story this week suggesting that Richard Scaife supplied six hundred thousand dollars in the Arkansas project, which (gibberish)...was washed through a paper called The Spectator, may have influenced or changed testimony, which indeed Mr. Starr may have known about, is an interesting part of where Mr. Starr runs into problems."

BENNETT: (Gibberish)...on national TV, I sit on Mr., Scaife's Board. Let me tell you what we did this last time: We gave money to some abstinence (?) programs in Pittsburgh, we gave some money for some environmental projects in Montana. We gave money to the American Enterprise Institute and God forgive us, to the Philosophy Department of Miami University of Ohio."

TORRICELLI: "Then why did you give money to witnesses in the Paula Jones case?"

BENNETT: We didn't give money to witnesses."

TORRICELLI: "Well, apparently Mr. Hale received money, which comes very close to witness tampering..."

BENNETT: "If you're going to look for vast right-wing conspiracies in foundations, let me suggest you look at the Ford Foundation, at the MacArthur Foundation. Those are left wing Foundations."

TORRICELLI: "I don't think they gave money to witnesses in a case...I'm sorry you're on these Boards because my guess is that before the week is out...my guess is that Mr. Scaife and his Boards are going to receive visits by the Justice Department and the FBI. Because here are the allegations in The New York Observer: First, uh..."

SAM DONALDSON: "Do you believe them?"

TORRICELLI: "I do from what I read. They haven't been refuted and apparently around this table we believe anything that's not been refuted..."

DONALDSON: "But when... you say it's come close to witness-tampering and that is a crime..."

TORRICELLI: "Well, it appears in the New York Observer that Mr. Hale and one of those troopers for the Arkansas State Police received money and may have changed their testimony. That is a serious federal crime."

BENNETT: (Harrumph)

DONALDSON: "...we should have two hours, not one hour. (Looks at Bennett and says:) You get the last word"

BENNETT: "...that the Justice Department look at whatever is appropriate. The Scaife Foundation. Let people look at the Starr leaks, but by all means, let us look at the Office of the President of The United States. Let justice be done in all these places. And the President needs to stop stonewalling. I'll bet you the foundations won't stonewall like the President."

The transcript of that exchange is from ABC TV. Right down to the gibberish. Now, let's examine it.

In the first statement by Torricelli, he said the article in The New York Observer suggested that money from *The American Spectator* may have influenced or changed testimony, which indeed Mr. Starr may have known about, is an interesting part of where Mr. Starr runs into problems.

The New York Observer article by Joe Conason referred to by Senator Torricelli, had said that Steve Boynton denied that he had given money to Hale. In the twisted logic of Torricelli, presumably, that denial was a suggestion of the opposite. Some reporter's, in arriving at a preferred point of view, use the technique of asking an accusatory question, getting a straight forward negative answer, then couching it as a denial. The use of the word denial is a much more powerful word than if, for instance, the actual response had been a straightforward no. There was no mention in the article about influencing or changing testimony. There was no mention of Ken Starr knowing about it. Here the Senator, in his excitement, got ahead of the script. That story had not yet been written. But it would be. Apparently, to borrow the Senator's language, he knew that the story would be written. When the curtain rises, each actor follows the script, but in this instance, Torricelli had stepped on someone else's line. The Senator's jack-boot suggestion that the Justice Department and the FBI would soon appear speaks, ominously, for itself.

In a remarkable coincidence, the following morning I met a friend for breakfast at the Four Seasons Hotel on Pennsylvania Avenue in Washington. My favorite description of coincidence is God's way of remaining anonymous. Maybe He did have a role in this. I had not seen my friend for some time and we always tried to get together whenever he returned from London, where he was living. Shortly after we were shown to our table, George Will, an ABC regular on This Week with Sam and Cokie, was delivered to the table adjacent to ours. He sat there alone for a few minutes, reading a paper. He was joined by United States Senator Robert Torricelli. Torricelli was so close to me that I could almost feel his breath. Neither Will nor Torricelli knew who I was. Torricelli had something to sell. I was in a position to hear his sales pitch. Regrettably, my distraction was embarrassing. I was torn between listening to my friend, who was unaware of the Washington ritual taking place at the next table, and listening to Will and Torricelli. Sam Donaldson's wish for two hours, rather than one, was coming true.

That week Torricelli injected a speech into the congressional record.

The strongest hint of the coming strategy was signaled during Torricelli's reference to the Independent Counsel, Ken Starr. Their plan was to implicate him as a willing facilitator of alleged criminal behavior by his principal witness, David Hale. We will see just how that was done.

It was to be a busy week for both Senator Torricelli and another member of congress, John Conyers, Democrat of Michigan, and ranking member of the House Judiciary committee. Conyers was as dependable as anyone in the cast. He would perform in the current production, but reserve his starring role for the coming impeachment hearings. That week both Conyers and Torricelli would send letters to the Attorney General, Janet Reno, asking her for a federal investigation of the allegations outlined in Conason's article in the New York Observer. Conyers couriered a letter to Dick Scaife on Wednesday, February 11, 1998, demanding answers to the several questions contained in therein.

All that was missing in our circus ring was the sword-swallower. In another ring was The Show, the one that the show's producers were trying to prevent the audience from seeing. It was billed as the President and the Intern. It was more compelling and had a cast of two.

CHAPTER TWENTY-ONE ~
GULLO-BLE

A writer for the Associated Press, Karen Gullo, began calling everyone associated with the story about the "Arkansas Project" and after a few days, her questions revealed that she had a new source. I was not one of the people who talked to her, although she tried. Karen Gullo was good enough to reveal her source to us.   One of her colleagues at the Associated Press, Pete Yost, had written many stories about Whitewater, and it was well known to the AP that Yost had David Hale's ear. Gullo imposed upon Pete Yost to run interference for her with Hale. Yost called Hale and conveyed Gullo's request for an interview. David declined the interview even though he trusted Yost and had talked with him on many occasions. Yost was skeptical of the allegations being thrown at us. He had the advantage of someone who had been on the beat for a long time and he had done his homework. After being told by Yost that Hale would not talk to her, Karen Gullo again sought to employ Yost as a go-between. She asked that he present a list of questions, written by her, to Hale. She would settle for a response to the written questionnaire. He read her questions but didn't respond.

People who are wise in the ways of the media will often talk to a reporter knowing that they stand to find out the direction of a story from the questions asked. David Hale didn't have to talk to the reporter to gain valuable information. Karen Gullo's questionnaire revealed far more than one would usually find in an interview. The questions, faxed to David, identified Gullo's source as certainly as if she had spoken the name. The questions were specific about David's visits with Parker Dozhier. They were so specific as to make a positive identification when Gullo's questions identified the source as a woman. Caryn Mann was the only "she" who could possibly be her source. Realizing who Gullo was relying on for her information provided a bit of comic relief. I identified Caryn Mann earlier, but I only revealed a small clue as to her awesome powers. In addition to her knowledge of the whereabouts of the body of Jimmie Hoffa, she boasted that she could start or stop rain.

She had, as an employee of the CIA, directed troops during Desert Storm, telepathically. Karen had worked as a telephone psychic. She read Tarot cards at an off-beat Hot Springs bookstore. She drew hex signs and burned candles on Dozhier's dock.

The lady was weird, though in many ways she was a sympathetic figure. She was one of those poor souls with a child to raise and never enough money to raise him well. She seemed to rely upon the largess of men, whose bed's she shared, to help her stretch her meager income. Her hard edges were understandable given the life that she led. Survival is a strong instinct and often leads to expediency over trustworthiness. For women like Caryn, trailers are as familiar as nannies for yuppies and Beamers for boomers. When James Carville spoke disparagingly of dragging hundred dollar bills through trailer parks, he was speaking from his own experience. What he failed to mention was the importance of $100 to the desperate mother. For the experienced survivor, misleading the willing is second nature. And she had a certain charm, at least to Parker Dozhier. A visitor could easily see, during that summer of 1994, that there was affection between them and Parker had even started taking them to church. I had not heard him mention that he was a church goer until after the arrival of Caryn Mann and her son, Josh Rand. It appeared that Parker was about to become a family man.

Parker found out that raising a thirteen-year-old boy was not an easy job. He would, on occasion, talk about Josh's difficulties by day at school and at night with gangs. Parker was getting a quick lesson in modern teen rebellion. He was troubled about it. Caryn and Josh lived with Parker for the better part of two years until the accumulating tensions resulted in Caryn's departure from the relationship. But if Parker Dozhier thought he had heard the last of Caryn Mann and Josh Rand, he had a big surprise coming 18 months after they left.

Gullo's Associated Press story surfaced on Thursday, March 5, 1998. Unlike Joe Conason's earlier article in The New York Observer, this story had the imprimatur of a mainstream news organization, unhindered by the baggage carried by Conason. No one could accuse Conason of being an unbiased reporter. I do not suggest in this case that

Karen Gullo was or was not biased. That I do not know. The point is, The Associated Press has long been a trusted source of news. Hence, the appearance of Gullo's story carried far more weight than did the Conason piece. Her story would command attention without the support of United States Senators and other partisans. But they were taking no chances. The ever dependable Senator Torricelli reacted, according to another Associated Press account two days later on March 7, 1998, by asking Attorney General Janet Reno to "investigate whether independent counsel Kenneth W. Starr was aware of a link between a key witness and a businessman receiving money from a conservative magazine." Mr. Torricelli said an article by the Associated Press raises serious concerns about whether the Whitewater prosecutor is conducting an objective investigation." This March 7, 1998, AP story was unsigned, but to this reader, it sounded like anonymous self-congratulation.

The article further pointed out that, "Mr. Torricelli had made earlier requests to Miss Reno to look into the relationship between Hale and political conservatives at odds with President Clinton. It is certainly possible that Gullo was fed and directed to this story by Sidney Blumenthal. It is also possible that Senator Torricelli was simply following White House instructions. But that is beside the point, for the story had become a legitimate news story. Other stories would follow, but no one bothered to verify that the source was credible.

Karen Gullo broke some new ground in the story, mainly because she had Caryn Mann as a source. Several of Caryn Mann's observations contained in Gullo's article were true. She had correctly placed David Hale at Parker Dozhier's, as well as Steve Boynton and me. Gullo had a few things wrong, such as this passage, "Magazine officials said they paid about $200 to federal prison officials that allowed Hale to make phone calls to Boynton and others at the Spectator while Hale served a 20-month sentence for mail fraud and conspiracy." This bit of information caused Karen Gullo and The Associated Press to draw a sharp and sudden rebuke from the Department of Prisons. The $200 had not been paid to the Federal Prison officials, as I noted in an earlier chapter.

But, Gullo had reached another reader. On March 9, 1998, The White House Bulletin, a condensation of news stories, had this gem. "Time reported that "for a public troubled by the image of an embattled President distracted by a consuming scandal, the reality is even worse than the fears." Although aides say Clinton "will not be sidetracked," he "calls his lawyers constantly, the intense voice unmistakable. What surprises his lawyers at the other end of the line is the way Clinton jumps into the conversation as if in mid-sentence: Explaining the latest piece to emerge from the grand jury or the deposition, putting it in context, dissecting its implication." Last Thursday, Clinton was "hyperventilating about a minor" AP story that suggested a "Whitewater witness might be financially connected" to Richard Mellon Scaife. A defense lawyer on the case said: "The President is completely and totally obsessed with the case." Another lawyer "put it more bluntly," saying: "Sure he's paying attention to this. It's life and death."

I am still perplexed even after two years by what Karen Gullo did not write in her article and why she did not write it. She obviously had access to Caryn Mann as she prepared her story. Yet, Caryn would add many things to the story in later renditions told to and reported by Murray Waas and Jonathan Broder in SALON magazine. My perplexity will, no doubt, continue since I sincerely doubt that either Karen or Caryn will ever address these questions: Did Caryn Mann tell the same story to Gullo that she would later tell to Waas and Broder? If so, did Karen Gullo use restraint in writing her story knowing the weakness of her source? Did Caryn Mann invent the stories told to Waas? Or was she fed the story by Waas or others? Caryn Mann's testimony changed over time. Who influenced her and how? It would be important to have answers to those questions. If Gullo was privy to the stories yet to come and used sound journalistic judgment in her own restraint, she is to be complimented. At the very least, she is to be thanked for giving advance notice of her source's identity. I know that Karen Gullo would prefer not to have received my thanks and I can understand that; however, it was an honest, if sloppy mistake. Hopefully, she will take comfort in the fact that the next person to reveal sources had a far more sinister and calculating motive, as we will see.

CHAPTER TWENTY-TWO ~
TWO FOOLS FOR SCANDAL

A side show was building in Arkansas as a result of Karen Gullo's Associated Press article. Parker Dozhier's Rainbow Landing was about to become inundated by the inquiring minds of the press and media. The Arkansas Democrat-Gazette had featured Gullo's AP article prominently. Not to be outdone, they assigned a writer to burnish the story with local color. Dozhier was being saturated with calls from media. He called me in Washington for guidance. I told him that it was his call whether or not he granted interviews. If he did, to just tell the truth. He had nothing to hide, nor did we. Joe Stumpe of the Arkansas Democrat-Gazette got the jump on the competition. His story received prominent placement in the paper. It also contained a picture of Dozhier's Bait Shop with Parker's dog Maggie front and center. Stumpe had interviewed Dozhier and laced his article with quotes.

Another writer for The Arkansas Democrat-Gazette, Gene Lyons, had been laboring for years as an apologist for Bill Clinton. In the eye of Lyons, Clinton could do no wrong, and Clinton critics could do no right. He usually reserved his harshest diatribes for the Independent Counsel, but in this story, he would find a bone that he continues to chew to this day. While accepting the story of Caryn Mann enthusiastically, he actually had the audacity to write these words later the next day

"Here we go again: Yet another accuser has stepped, been *pushed or dragged* forward to make *unverified and unverifiable charges* of sexual misbehavior against President Clinton. "Still another heavy-breathing (There's that phrase again) media freak out is under way. The pack thinks it's finally got the slippery SOB cornered."

"Once again, despite clear signs that former White House assistant Kathleen Willey's appearance on "60 Minutes" was carefully timed for maximum impact among Kenneth Starr, CBS News, and the Paula Jones legal team, *nobody's expected to notice the choreography.*"
"Instead, the public is encouraged to *play mind reader*. It's a nationwide parlor game, like *fiddling with a Ouija board or dialing the Psychic*

Friends Network..." [Emphasis added]

Imagine, this Lyons opinion piece appeared exactly one day after The "Arkansas Project" had its debut on Salon magazine which had as its star "witness", a mind reader, a Psychic friends network wannabe, and a Tarot card and tea leaf reader. And nobody's expected to notice the choreography of The White House, The Justice Department, Sidney Blumenthal, James Carville, Paul Begala, Lanny Davis, Bill Press of CNN, Al Hunt of The Wall Street Journal, Salon Magazine, David Talbot, Murray Waas, Jonathan Broder, Joe Conason, Gene Lyons, Geraldo Rivera, Susan McDougal and her lawyer, Mark Geragos, Senator Torricelli, Congressman John Conyers, Hillary Clinton, possibly Karen Gullo, David Brock, and a couple of disgruntled *American Spectator* has beens. This list of dung beetles is far from complete, but you get the idea. Sweet irony. I couldn't have made this up. Indeed, as I write on this day, March 18, 2000, precisely two years later, Gene Lyons and Joe Conason are hawking their new book, "The Hunting of The President," a reprise of Lyon's book, "Fools for Scandal." As a serialization, this new book could easily have been named "Fools for Scandal II" or better still, "Two Fools for Scandal."

On a Saturday in March 1998, much like this Saturday, I returned from a trip to the local Giant food store and had a message from Danny Wattenburg. I had not heard from Danny in a long time but had come to know him when he was writing for *The American Spectator* in 1993 and 1994. It is my habit to return calls, even to bill collectors, and I soon had Danny Wattenburg on the phone. Danny asked if I knew Murray Waas. I did not, but knew of him. Danny told me that he had been talking with Waas. Waas told him that he had a video of David Hale, L. D. Brown, Parker Dozhier, Steve Boynton and me, taken in a hotel room in Little Rock. I informed Danny that it would be impossible for Waas or anyone else to have such a video. Danny asked if I would talk to Waas. Without hesitation, I told Danny that I would not. That was no deterrent to Waas. Less than five minutes after my conversation with Wattenburg, a call came in and I answered it. The unfamiliar voice asked for Dave Henderson. I answered that I was he.

The caller identified himself as Murray Waas and before he could say another word, I said, "I told Danny Wattenburg that I would not talk to you and now I am telling you the same. Goodbye!" I then hung up. In time I learned that lying, the ploy with the video, was a trademark approach used by Waas. He would use similar stories, so outrageous that one could hardly resist talking with him, just to tear down the lie, not realizing that he would twist their words into other meanings. If this writer would lie to talk to someone, I would leave that pleasure for others to experience. Lying to get a person to talk is almost as repugnant as plagiarism in the journalistic canon of ethics. Do one; do both. The best journalists will never misquote sources. I was confident that Waas would do so intentionally.

Waas and his co-writer, Jonathan Broder [not related to David Broder] launched their broadside on March 17, 1998, in Salon magazine, and the article, with some high-powered help, would make Salon magazine semi-famous. That article would be followed by a long series of stories, and some of them would identify Gene Lyons and Joe Conason as collaborators. That relationship lasted for over two years, and Waas said he was writing a book...but Conason and Lyons left him off the cover; relying on his efforts through their book.

The article, "The Road to Hale" had this headline, "KEY WHITEWATER WITNESS DAVID HALE RECEIVED SECRET CASH PAYMENTS FROM ANTI-CLINTON BILLIONAIRE RICHARD MELLON SCAIFE." There was nothing equivocal about that banner. The headline writer had committed Salon to a course of action that was fraught with peril and exposed them and others to libel action. The article by Jonathan Broder and Murray Waas had a dateline of Bentonville, Arkansas.

Let's have a look. The article, which named Caryn Mann and her son Josh Rand as eyewitnesses, and unnamed, "knowledgeable", and anonymous sources began.

"David Hale, the key witness against President Clinton in Kenneth Starr's Whitewater investigation, received numerous cash payments from a clandestine anti-Clinton campaign funded by conservative Billionaire Richard Mellon Scaife, two eyewitnesses told

Salon."

"It is not known exactly how much money Hale received, but the eyewitnesses, Caryn Mann and her son Joshua Rand, (both) said the payments occurred regularly over a two-year period, from 1994 to 1996, after Hale became a federal witness in Starr's Whitewater investigation. The payments ranged from as little as $40 to as much as $500, according to Mann and Rand." Two other sources familiar with Scaife's campaign independently confirmed the effort to funnel money to Hale. These sources spoke to Salon on condition of anonymity."

"...Hale's payments came from representatives of the so-called Arkansas Project, a $2.4 million campaign to investigate Clinton and his associates between 1993 and 1997, according to sources familiar with the arrangement. These sources told Salon that Scaife, who has underwritten a wide variety of anti-Clinton legal and media efforts, funded the Arkansas Project through several tax-exempt foundations which he controls."

"Under the scheme, two of Scaife's charitable foundations transferred as much as $600,000 a year to a third charitable foundation which owns the conservative *American Spectator* magazine, knowledgeable sources at the magazine said. *The American Spectator* then transferred most of the funds to Stephen S. Boynton, an attorney and conservative political activist with long-standing ties to Scaife. Boynton then used the money to pay private investigators to unearth damaging details about the president, First Lady Hillary Clinton, and their associates."

"...Parker would receive money from Boynton," Rand told Salon. "He would essentially put that in his right pocket, and then he'd pull money out of his left pocket and give it to David Hale." Rand said on several occasions, Dozhier instructed him to take money out of the bait shop cash register for Hale."

"Contacted by telephone, Dozhier called the allegations that he had given money to Hale "bulls---," adding, "I never made any payments to David Hale in my life...Not a dime." Dozhier then abruptly hung up.

"Rand, however, provided eyewitness details of the payments.

"I saw him give money to David Hale," Rand said. "A couple of times, Parker asked me to go out to the bait shop and get $120 in twenties, tens, usually small bills. I'd bring it into the house, and Parker and David Hale would be sitting there, and I'd see Parker give it to David Hale."

"Sometimes it was only $40, 60, or 80 dollars at a time, but other times it was $120 or $240 or $500," Rand said. "If Hale needed to pay a $200 bill Parker would give him the money, plus an extra $100 or $120 for his pocket. It depended on how many times he came to town."

"Contacted a second time by telephone, Dozhier said Rand was destined to be a chalk outline somewhere."

Whoa. Let's stop here for a minute and get our breath. Parker Dozhier's colorful language would be wrapped around his neck, big time. Parker's observation was based on two years of witnessing the wayward, truant activities engaged in by Josh. He was describing a troubled juvenile delinquent on the path to ruin, but it would be turned into a "death threat" and things would get even more bizarre. Shall we proceed?

"...Rand, who often minded the bait shop for Dozhier, said he recorded how much money the shop had earned and spent each day and placed a written record of those transactions in a bank bag at closing time. "Sometimes, it just wouldn't add up," he said. "Sometimes, my little pieces of paper would be missing, or the amounts written on them would be changed. It would always be different from the amount I put in the bag."

"Mann said that Dozhier was well-compensated for his role in the scheme. She said she kept Dozhier's books and kept track of regular incoming checks from Boynton and his associate, David Henderson, the Vice President of *The American Spectator* Educational Foundation and a longtime associate of Scaife. Mann, who now lives in the western Arkansas town of Bentonville, said the checks began arriving sporadically in 1994 but by 1995, checks for $1,000 were arriving monthly. She also said Boynton and Henderson showed up frequently to speak with Hale and Dozhier, and after they left, there was "always an abundance of cash."

"After one such visit, she said, she looked inside the safe that Dozhier kept in their bedroom. "There were stacks of money, 100s, 50s and 20s," she told Salon."

"Since the cash was not recorded in the bait shop's books, Mann said she could not assess how much Dozhier received from Boynton and Henderson, but she said it was enough to allow Dozhier to pay off $60,000 in back taxes and to pay his bills on six credit cards, each one totaling $15,000 to $20,000."

"Mann said Dozhier first began receiving and disbursing the money in 1994. At that time, "there were discussions about giving David cash," she said. "Parker told me that Steve Boynton and Dave Henderson had asked him if he could help Hale, Mann said. Dozhier himself began receiving checks and cash from Boynton and Henderson."

"Mann also said Dozhier and Hale met with Boynton and Henderson twice in 1995, once in Washington, D.C. and a second time at a resort in Biloxi, Mississippi. In January 1996, the men met again in Washington. At those meetings, Mann said, "They kept saying they weren't getting enough money, and every time they complained to Steve (Boynton) and Dave (Henderson), they got more money.""

"Two former executives of *The American Spectator*, speaking on condition of anonymity, independently corroborated a key portion of Mann's story: that funds from the Arkansas Project went to David Hale. One of the former executives said that Henderson had told him that he was trying to assist Hale in 1995 - the same time period that Mann and her son said they had seen Dozhier make cash payments to Hale."

"Henderson told me that David Hale's family needed to be taken care of, and they had a way of doing that," the former *The American Spectator* executive said. "There was a mechanism.""

In an interview, the second former *The American Spectator* executive, also speaking on condition of anonymity, corroborated this account.

"...After the New York Observer first disclosed the existence of the Arkansas Project last month, *The American Spectator's* board of directors ordered an internal analysis of how the funds to Boynton were spent..."

Those were the highlights of the first Salon article. To rephrase Gene Lyons, here we go again: Yet another accuser has stepped, been pushed or dragged forward to make unverified and unverifiable charges of criminal conduct against critics of President Clinton.

CHAPTER TWENTY-THREE ~
RED WORMS, BILOXI AND MISSISSIPPI MUD

Like red worms in the manure bed beside Parker Dozhier's bait shop, the Salon Magazine article would spawn many offspring. To carry the analogy further, the uninformed, slightly informed, and misinformed thought they had hooked the big fish. Now they had to land him. The claims by the various sources in Waas' and Broder's article were the equivalent of throwing dynamite in the water as a substitute for bait. Both cause great damage. Sometimes the charge goes off in the hand of the thrower.

An article from the Associated Press on Sunday, March 29, 1998, again, with no by-line, had this information. "A U.S. attorney in Arkansas appointed by President Clinton sent FBI agents to interview a woman familiar with key Whitewater witness David Hale's ties to conservative activists, the woman says."

"...Mann said the FBI visited her after a reporter for the Salon Internet magazine contacted former Senator David H. Pryor, D-Ark., on her behalf for assistance in getting the attention of law enforcement officials in Arkansas."

"David Talbot, the editor of the magazine, said Saturday that "Salon decided to contact law enforcement officials about Caryn Mann...because she was very concerned about her safety and that of her teenage son."

"In addition, Talbot said Dozhier made a threat on the son during a conversation with a Salon reporter and that under these circumstances the magazine felt a "civic and humanitarian obligation to help Mann and her son."

"He said Pryor was contacted only after attempts to provide the information about alleged threats to five federal and local law enforcement agencies."

"Pryor, who runs Clinton's new legal defense fund, could not be reached for comment."

Well, there it is, in black and white. After five federal and local law enforcement agencies recognized no threat, the next, and preferred course of action, was to go to a politician. This "threat" had been concocted by Waas to make things appear even more left-handed or sinister. Waas would claim later that he had received death threats! And what is a former United States Senator to do? Raising money for this president's legal defense fund didn't occupy all of his time, though the potential was there for a full-time job.

After the protective umbrella of the FBI had been raised, a new layer of protection was afforded to Caryn Mann. An attorney, and Friend of Bill, David Matthews became her lawyer. Since neither The Rutherford Institute nor Dick Scaife was paying Matthews bills, no one bothered to ask who was. Mark that one off as an oversight by the ever vigilant press. Matthews, no doubt, gave some valuable advice to Caryn Mann, i.e., lying to federal investigators is a big time no-no. She suddenly had a change of vision after the Waas and Broder piece. Her new position was that she didn't personally see any of this supposed hanky-panky of money changing hands; it was her son, who was thirteen and fourteen years old during the timeframe of those allegations. Let the juvenile take the heat. There was no retraction, just a shift in direction. Now that we have had a break, let's go back to that story with one eye-witness less.

We could start anywhere, but let's go with something light and work our way up. "Mann also said Dozhier and Hale met with Boynton and Henderson twice in 1995, once in Washington, D.C. and once in Biloxi, Mississippi..." Greg Gordon of the Minneapolis Star Tribune called me after this story appeared in Salon for some follow-up questions. I had previously given an interview to Greg and had talked with both him and his colleague, Tom Hamburger by phone. I can only remember one of the questions that Greg asked me. It was, "Did you meet with David Hale and Parker Dozhier in Biloxi, Mississippi?" I said no. Greg then asked if I had met with Hale and Dozhier in a suburb of Biloxi, and again I said no. I told Greg that while I was in the Air Force I had been stationed at Kessler Air Force Base in Biloxi, Mississippi and that if I had been there, I would have recognized it. Greg followed up with this question.

"Then, are you denying that you met Hale and Dozhier in Olive Branch, Mississippi? I almost fell out of my chair laughing. When I regained control, I asked Greg if he had any idea where Olive Branch, Mississippi was? He said he didn't. I told him that it was about twenty minutes south of Memphis, Tennessee, and indeed, I had met with Hale and Dozhier there in August of 1995.

As I have previously related, each summer, Peggy and I attend an annual reunion with our old Jaycee friends. That year Parker and David had driven over to spend part of a day with me in Olive Branch. I had taken them to my favorite eatery in Olive Branch, The Oasis Grill and Shoe Shine Parlor, for a lunch of fresh vegetables, sweet iced tea and corn bread. If you are ever in Olive Branch, I would highly recommend it.

Greg Gordon said, "You are helping yourself with these answers." What? How was I helping myself, Greg? It seemed more likely that I was helping him understand geography. Biloxi, Mississippi is on the Gulf Coast, and Olive Branch is in the northern-most county of the state. And now, I am worried that Caryn may have directed some of our Desert Storm troops to the Sudan or Jordan. I hope they made it back.

Murray Waas would report the Biloxi meeting in an article later that summer. He reported on the grand jury appearance of Caryn Mann. "Mann told the grand jury of trips that Boynton and Henderson had made to Hot Springs to meet with Hale and Dozhier, and also a "covert meeting" that they had at a "resort" in Biloxi." This is priceless. Waas had added, "covert meeting and a "resort" to the telling.

As to the wads of cash that always appeared in Dozhier's safe after Steve Boynton and I visited, were it so I would have been writing this book in a federal prison cell, and I can assure you that I am presently writing at home.

With respect to the "corroboration by former *American Spectator* executives to the part of the story about helping the Hale family, I can report that they were partially correct. In 1994, I was saddened to see my friends, David and Sue Hale lose their home in order to pay legal fees. I gave some thought to trying to get the United States

Jaycees to establish a Legal Defense Fund for David, and I still have my notes on the subject written on a legal pad. When we were in Olive Branch in the summer of 1994, I discussed it with some of my old friends. In the end, the consensus was that it would not work. It had been too many years since David had been national president and the organization had shrunk to a shadow of its old self. And it was a fact, realized by each of us, no matter what lofty positions we once held in the organization, we were like yesterday's newspaper, consigned to the bottom of the bird cage. I am sorry to say that the effort was abandoned before it began.

Another passage in the article stating that the board of directors of *The American Spectator* ordered an internal analysis of how the funds to Boynton were spent, stated as fact that it was done "After the New York Observer first disclosed the existence of the Arkansas Project." That is the work of dishonest "journalists" trying to imply guilt. The board made that decision in November of the preceding year. I believe that I have fully reported that action and the reasons for it in a previous chapter, and that nothing was misspent by The Arkansas Project.

Reference was made to "Dozhier receiving checks from Boynton and Henderson sporadically in 1994 and then regularly in 1995." Steve Boynton wrote all checks, at all times. He wrote a monthly check to Parker Dozhier every month for approximately 48 months. They were $1000 each. And Caryn, there was nothing sporadic about it. I sent no money to Dozhier or anyone else from those funds. I submitted my expenses to Steve Boynton and I received my monthly retainer from him. I was reimbursed for the $200 personal check that I sent to Sue Hale for David's prison account. To repeat myself, I sent an additional $200 to Sue for the same purpose and I did not seek reimbursement for it.

"...Stephen S. Boynton, an attorney and conservative political activist with long-standing ties to Scaife." That oft-repeated phrase is particularly galling to me because it is so patently false. Steve Boynton was introduced to Richard Larry, President of the Sarah Scaife Foundation, by me, in the fall of 1993. It was me, not Steve Boynton, who had long-standing ties to Scaife. As to the conservative political activist part, perhaps United States Senator Ernest "Fritz" Hollings, D-S.C. could be consulted. He had employed Steve as his legislative assistant.

I could go on, but there is no further need to give examples. After all, the grand jury has already heard them. There is probably nothing that could be more disillusioning to the dung beetles, but Steve Boynton and I are pretty normal people, if normal defines honesty, integrity, duty, honor, and trust. The very last thing that either of us would do is abuse a trust. We didn't, we have not, and we will not.

Some of the spawn from this article attempted to paint Steve and me as profligate. An example can be found in an article in the New York Times by Neil Lewis. Mr. Lewis, (one must be formal when referring to the New York Times) suggested that Steve and I had paid ourselves exorbitant fees and once chartered an airplane to visit David Hale while he was in prison in Texarkana, Texas. Wrong on both counts, Neil. We paid ourselves nothing. Our compensation was set by *The American Spectator* and a bill was submitted each month by Steve Boynton. After he received payment, he would write a check to himself and to me.

Where he got the aircraft *chartering* story is beyond me. Obviously, much of it was conjecture on his part. And may I add, conjecture doesn't make "All the news that's fit to print," the proud motto of the New York Times. Not even close. (In hindsight now in 2016 it is clear where he got the impression. Ron Burr salted our expense records to the media with the help of other former Spectator personnel. I'm sure that we paid Rex Armistead for the cost of operating his private aircraft on that round trip between Clarksdale, MS and Fort Smith, Arkansas. I'll bet it must have been a couple of hundred dollars, a net savings since we didn't use our commercial tickets for the leg between Memphis and Fort Smith.

The real story? Why not? Steve Boynton and I had flown to Memphis, Tennessee, and rented a car to drive to Lulu, Mississippi, to meet a private investigator who worked on assignments for us. Our plan was to return to Memphis and then fly to Texarkana for a visit with David

Hale. The drive from Memphis to Lulu, Mississippi, is about one and one-half hours. After we had arrived at the home of Rex Armistead, a violent storm system enveloped the mid-south region. Rex said that it would pass through the area during the night. He volunteered to fly us in his single engine, two-seater Cessna to Texarkana. His airplane was in Clarksdale, Mississippi, only a few minutes' drive from his home.

Steve and I considered the options, with me opting to fly commercially. I hate and fear small aircraft in bad weather. Rex suggested that we wait to see what the morning would bring and then decide. The following morning was bright and clear. The storm had passed as Rex had said it would. Aviators know about those things or they perish. It was a pleasant flight at low altitude, the enjoyable kind of flight if one likes to observe the terrain below. And I do. A train headed westbound, was spotted just as we crossed the Mississippi River. For a few minutes I amused myself counting the cars, then I resumed the more rewarding topographical study.

It is certainly possible that someone on the ground saw our arrival and departure and passed that information along. I can't imagine that it would have made a bit of difference to anyone who was not monitoring our movements.

Rex Armistead has received slanderous diatribes by Lyons, Waas, and others. If you really want to know the man, look elsewhere. I would suggest, "Mississippi Mud" from Simon and Schuster's Pocket books. It is a book, first published in 1995, and written by Pulitzer Prize-winning Journalist, Edward Humes. It is also a *True Story, soon to become a major motion picture.*

Tony Snow, a columnist for the Detroit News wrote the most succinct paragraph to come from this sorry mess. "...According to press reports, Murray Waas--who co-wrote the Salon story--contacted David Pryor, former U.S Senator and Arkansas governor who now heads the Clinton legal defense fund. He informed Pryor of the bombshell involving the worm baron, the entrail reader, and the chalk outline."

CHAPTER TWENTY-FOUR ~
ACT TWO

It took just two days from publication of the Broder and Waas Salon article, "The Road To Hale" for the celebration to begin. It was some affair, as reported by William Powers in the National Journal.

"Around the beginning of March, the invitations began arriving for yet another media party. This was not your ordinary Washington invite, however, but an attempt at humor: a gag on the theme of Kenneth Starr. "Salon commands Your Appearance at a Starr-Studded Evening," it read. "You are hereby subpoenaed to appear before Salon's party tribunal. Be prepared to reveal personal as well as professional details of your life, the more sordid the better."

Powers continued," The sponsor of the party, a daily on-line magazine called Salon that's based in San Francisco was no household name here. The magazine is widely known among the Web-literate for publishing some of the sharpest on-line writing, by an extremely diverse crew of writers that has included Clintonista James Carville, right-winger David Horowitz, and feminist troublemaker Camille Paglia."

The article made reference to the March 17 Broder and Waas story in Salon and briefly summarized it. Continuing, Powers wrote, "Any reader with a basic understanding of the Whitewater case instantly recognized this as a serious allegation. "If true--and it's not clear yet whether it is--it could have major consequences for Starr's Whitewater investigation. Not incidentally, the story also has the potential to make Bill and Hillary Clinton look more like victims of the "Vast right-wing conspiracy" that the First lady has identified as the source of all their problems.

"So it seems fitting that at Salon's Washington bash on March 19, among those in attendance was Sidney Blumenthal, a former journalist, and current Clinton aide, as well as chief steward and propagator of the vast-right-wing conspiracy theory. But it is slightly surprising to learn that Blumenthal went so far as to invite Salon staffers to swing by the White House the next day, to meet Hillary Clinton at a reception for the White House fellows program (which Blumenthal's wife, Jacqueline, heads). And more surprising still is that halfway through the reception the president himself appeared and was introduced to the four guests from Salon: editor David Talbot, executive editor Gary Kamiya, managing editor Andrew Ross, and Broder, the magazine's Washington bureau chief. According to Talbot, the President spoke about Salon's Whitewater story with evident excitement, in what Talbot described as a "holy sh-t" tone: "Wow, this David Hale thing." Clinton said. "I didn't know that!" (Talbot told me: "I think Sid had given him the printout.")

Slate magazine, an online rival of Salon and founded by Microsoft's Bill Gates, had this to say about the party, as reported in the Washington Times Inside Politics column:

"The following item appeared in the "Chatterbox" column, edited by Mickey Kaus, in the on-line magazine Slate.

"True love: An excellent conspiratorial moment at a recent Washington, D.C., party given for Salon magazine. Present were: presidential aide Sidney Blumenthal, newscaster Jim Leher, columnist Molly Ivins, journalist Christopher Hitchens, stuntman David Brock, and Murray Waas, the oddball investigative reporter who has been chronicling the machinations of the Vast Right Wing Conspiracy for Salon and the New York Observer. At one point, Waas, looking around the room as if to make sure no one was following him, snuck out the rear door into the unlit backyard. A few seconds later, Blumenthal slipped out the same back door to join Waas. They could then be seen having a brief, but intense, tete-a-tete in the darkness."

The president's personal attorney, David Kendall, had previously asked the White House staff to cooperate with David Brock, saying that he had had a metamorphosis. Again? First, it had been from little David into Giant Goliath, and now from a worm into a butterfly. He had, after all, publicly apologized to the president, in an article in Esquire magazine, for all the trouble his "Troopergate" story in The American Spectator had caused. Brock had posed for a picture, the additional thousand words to the Esquire article, stripped to the waist, bound to a tree and surrounded by an unlit bonfire, a modern-day Joan of Arc.

The stories continued in Salon magazine in rapid fire sequence, each one striving to out-do the others. They became so legendary in the White House, in a period of one month, that the President of The United States, appearing at the White House Correspondent's Dinner, singled them out in his opening remarks.

"...Seriously, I have been looking so much forward to seeing all of you this weekend. I just wanted to know one thing: how come there's no table for Salon Magazine?" His comment was supposed to draw laughter, but few of the sophisticates in the ballroom accommodated him and he continued. "That was supposed to be funny. Don't take yourselves so seriously. You'll see the light, don't worry about it, loosen up." The puppeteer had revealed himself to the audience.

The president's remarks were intended to accomplish several goals, and no doubt some of them were achieved. The elite of the nation's media were a captive audience, and he was giving weight to Salon's reporting, nudging them toward acceptance of the content of that reporting. In a subtle way, they were being chided. The unspoken message was; you have not been doing your job. When Hillary said that my troubles were the consequence of the vast right-wing conspiracy, she was right, and it took an enterprising online magazine to get the story that all of you have missed. Now, I want to see more reporting by all of you on this story. Not so subtle were his words, "You'll see the light, don't worry about it..." Here, he knew exactly what was going on behind the scenes. April had been a very busy month, and even though the press was still focused on the Monica Lewinski story, he was determined to refocus their attention.

Activities during the last few days in March and up until the April 25 White House Correspondent's Dinner, had given rise to hope in the embattled White House. If the independent counsel could be shown to be embroiled in illicit activities, nothing that he could say regarding the president and the Intern would be taken seriously. The White House attack apparatus had been in unrelenting pursuit of Kenneth Starr since his August 1994, appointment, and it had succeeded remarkably well.

Kenneth Starr had his supporters and detractors. In that regard, I was both. He had a tin ear for politics. Politics has a gravity that held him close to the ground. The law moves like a glacier while politics is an avalanche. The Attorney General placed another helping on his plate each time he was prepared to clean up the kitchen. He was cut by a thousand lashes, administered by the highly effective attack machine employed by the Clinton Administration, and in some cases, by himself. In any other administration, the whole gang would have broken rocks for obstruction of justice, but in the age of Clinton, James Carville simply amused the host of a major television network when he declared "waah" on the independent counsel and threatened to break his kneecaps.

A confident Independent Counsel would have had him before a court as fast as Janet Reno, but by then Kenneth Starr had been defeated, and he knew it. In a sad and sickening way, the President and his henchmen had flouted the law, lied to grand juries, thrown endless roadblocks before the courts, and all the while they were receiving the applause of the American people. This is what happens when the public gives an unlimited budget to the government and allows them to use it to deceive their benefactors. Remember the campaign phrase in 1992, "It's the economy stupid." In 1996 it should have been, "It's the cash, stupid." We got what the gulled citizenry asked for. We will continue to pay for a long, long time.

CHAPTER TWENTY-FIVE ~
POWER INTIMIDATED

Little Rock, Arkansas is ground zero for investigations concerning Whitewater. Passions run deep there. Much of that passion is fueled by self-interest. In some cases, that self-interest could mean money and jobs, and in others, avoiding getting crushed by the investigation, or perhaps, by the Clinton machine.

Little Rock's newspaper, The Arkansas Democrat-Gazette has two extraordinary writers. One writes a regular column, which appears each Wednesday on the op-ed page, and he is extraordinary for his tunnel-vision. If you doubt that description of him and have access to the Internet, connect to www.ardemgaz.com/ on any Wednesday and look for Gene Lyons in the editorial section. The other is editor of the editorial page, Paul Greenberg, and he is extraordinarily good. He has a Pulitzer Prize to attest to his greatness, but you wouldn't have to know that to recognize him as one of the best writers in America. You would know that as soon as you read one of his editorials or columns.

Gene Lyons, on Wednesday, March 25, 1998, "...Absent Hale, Starr hasn't even the pretense of a case against the president." [Lyons now writes mainly for the Arkansas Times, a weekly alternative freebie; worth the price.]

"Accompanied by FBI agents under Starr's control, we now learn, Hale made regular visits to a fishing camp owned by a Hot Springs Clinton-hater named Parker Dozhier. There he met regularly with American Spectator lawyer Steve Boynton and a second "Arkansas Project" operative named David Henderson."

Let me be as clear as I possibly can. Gene Lyons is practicing yellow journalism here. What he is trying to do is connect Kenneth Starr to Steve Boynton and me. You may remember that I described earlier the five times that I met with David Hale while he was under the protective custody of the FBI. Each of those five times, the agents were those of Robert Fiske who was employed by the Department of Justice. Lyons is not ignorant, and he knew this. There was not one time that I ever saw David Hale in the company of FBI agents while he was cooperating with Kenneth Starr. Lyons is simply a propagandist. He intentionally wrote those words. Robert Fiske was no longer of concern to Lyons or his patrons, but Independent Counsel Starr was. This lie would be a constant refrain, used to inflame public opinion against Starr. Earlier, Tom Oliphant, writing in the Sunday Boston Globe, was able to get that bit (Starr's FBI) of disinformation in twice in a five-hundred-word article. I owe Gene Lyons nothing less than my contempt and I intend to continue exposing his lies.

Lyons regurgitated the Waas and Broder story, based on Caryn Mann's "eye-witness" account, and then threw in this bit, "Equally important, sources at *The American Spectator*, which apparently has a few honorable conservative journalists on its staff, confirm the payments." But which payments? Apparently, Gene? You just can't bring yourself to offer an unequivocal word of praise to conservatives even if they are weasels like yourself.

One of the items that Caryn Mann took with her when she left Dozhier's was a fax sent by Parker to an aide of United States Senator Lauch Faircloth. Once again, the Minneapolis Star- Tribune played a role in surfacing this "major story." The fax raised a firestorm in Little Rock, and here is the way the classy Paul Greenberg handled it.

"What's this, The Hon. Henry Woods complaining about a sinister plot against him? That's right: Henry Woods, he of the old McMath administration and highway audit, the friend and then foe of Orval Faubus, the long-time Democratic political operative elevated to Grand Old Man of the federal bench in Arkansas, the outspoken judge with a leprechaun's sense of humor...Now that same Henry Woods is complaining about "an effort to intimidate me," and he wants it investigated."

"Intimidate Henry Woods? You might as well try to intimidate a grizzly. Besides, few citizens are so well equipped to handle anyone out to intimidate them as one with all the powers of a federal judge, an office that comes as close to absolute monarch as our Constitution allows. And what is His Honor's evidence for this, to lapse into

Hillaryspeak, vast-right-wing conspiracy against him? Well, it seems *The American Spectator.* the bible of the country's Clintonphobes, once did some opposition research on the judge, among other associates of the Clintons. This is supposed to be a big deal."

"Wait. That's not all. Get this, all you conspiracy theorists out there: Remember David Bossie? He's the scandal-hunter who used to work for the Republican (and therefore naturally suspect) Senator Lauch Faircloth of North Carolina. And this aide once requested Judge Wood's financial disclosure statement."

"Shocking. Here's a public record actually being made available to a member of the public. Some of us naïfs in the press might have thought that this was just why judges are required to file such statements--so the public can see them if it wishes. Shows you how much we knew."

"...Except for Clinton apologists, who must now rank as one of the country's larger industries, the rest of the country seems to have greeted this Big Story with one enormous yawn."

Greenberg's article continued on in that vein at some length, and while it would be interesting to read the entire article, I want to share just two more paragraphs.

"However amusing all these fun and games, the bashing of the independent counsel may tend to overlook one detail that used to be considered of some importance in the administration of justice, namely Justice."

"Despite the badmouthing he gets, let it be remembered that Kenneth Starr's team has caught some crooks in high places. One was in the Governor's Mansion (and it wasn't easy prying him loose) and another was the third-ranking official in this administration's, yes, Justice Department. Despite outward appearances, this isn't a banana republic yet. Justice does get done on occasion."

Greg Gordon and Tom Hamburger had been the two writers for the Minneapolis Star-Tribune who had written the Judge Henry Woods shocker. While they were writing it, I got a call from them for my reaction. I told them that in my opinion, any citizen was perfectly within his rights to communicate with elected congressional officials and their offices. I also mentioned an obscure document, the Constitution, which, if memory serves me correctly, guarantees that right. When told by them that Judge Woods said that he felt intimidated, it was hard to suppress a laugh. (Greg Gordon had that effect on me.) I said that I doubted that he was intimidated and that he was a very powerful man. I was quoted to that effect in the article. What Judge Henry Woods was doing in saying that he had been intimidated, was intimidating.

CHAPTER TWENTY-SIX ~
HALFWAY HOUSE

Then, things got just plain nasty. At the weekly press briefing of the Attorney General, Janet Reno, on Thursday, April 2, 1998, she said, "I think it must be pursued, and I want to make a determination as to how it should be pursued. It is on my desk."

She was, of course, responding to a question from a member of the assembled press with reference to the Arkansas Project.

This was reported the following day by...The Minneapolis Star-Tribune's Greg Gordon and Tom Hamburger.

"...Hale's attorney and the conservatives alleged to have been his benefactors vehemently denied that Hale received money. Yet, allegations from a woman and her son in Bentonville, Arkansas, are of interest to Justice Department officials."

"...Caryn Mann is Dozhier's former girlfriend and was an active Clinton supporter in 1992..."

Deep in the story Mann, "...said she had no knowledge of whether Dozhier or the visitors attempted to sway Hale's testimony."

"They were in an out at crucial times," she recalled. "If you checked the flight schedule and the testimony, you'll see that they coincide."

It is time for a reality check. A statement by David Hale, without corroborating evidence, would be useless in a court of law. Therefore, for anyone to suggest that someone was trying to get him to change his story is ludicrous on its face because to do so, Hale would have exposed himself to more serious consequences by lying to the Independent Counsel. Then there is the matter of the grand jury testimony. Caryn Mann and others had no way of knowing, but David Hale, in spite of news stories to the contrary, spent just two days before the Whitewater Grand Jury. I was not aware of that fact at the time either. Whether or not I happened to have been in Arkansas and saw Hale before he gave his grand jury testimony is still a mystery to me. I don't know the dates that he actually addressed the grand jury. Caryn Mann, with her supernatural powers, may very well be able to penetrate the secrecy of grand juries, but few others can. Perhaps what she meant to say was that I was there on occasions before David had meetings with the staff of the Independent Counsel, Kenneth Starr. If that was her intention, I can confirm that. We must also recognize that her story was woven partly from what she had personally experienced, and from reporter's questions which suggested obstruction of justice, witness tampering, and other criminal conduct. Those questions came directly from the script. A lot of people had the same script.

Those intrepid reporters, in the same article, had this to say about David Hale. "He served about twenty months of a 28-month term at a federal halfway house in Little Rock, then was released after prosecutors said he should be rewarded for his "substantial and ongoing" assistance in Starr's investigation. Tom Hamburger, himself a former Arkansas reporter, perhaps was just continuing to bend to power.

What pathetic reporting. Pardon the pun, but they made hamburger of the truth. Their facts would surprise the guards at Fort Worth Federal Prison and the ones at Texarkana Federal Prison, who handcuffed and put Hale in chains each time he was moved. Surprised too, would be the doctors from the Mayo clinic who treated him while he lay chained to his bed, and who placed a life-saving defibrillator in his body. Jim Peck would also be surprised after visiting him dutifully each weekend in the Federal Prison in Texarkana. And tell me, Greg Gordon and Tom Hamburger. You both know full well that I always took your calls and answered your questions directly. Tell me that my visits to Fort Worth and Texarkana were to halfway houses. And finally, you should apologize in the pages of the Minneapolis Star-Tribune to Sue and Amy Hale. Both of them recall, in vivid detail, their visits to federal prisons, not halfway houses. Then try to remember that you owe your best efforts, at both honesty and accuracy, to your readers. After that, locate just one federal halfway house. Never mind, for then and now they are all operated by private and church organizations.

The media can be frustrating when they begin choosing sides and in this particular case, after the sides had been chosen, it was like the Yankees against a sandlot team. After all, we were conservatives and were to be given short shrift. The avalanche coming was aimed at our little valley, and specifically, at a tiny village. Its only inhabitants were Dick Scaife, Dick Larry, Steve Boynton, Parker Dozhier, David Hale, myself, our families, and the village news, *The American Spectator*. Kenneth Starr was intended as an ancillary target.

The media see a bird with one wing, flying around the political landscape. The laws of nature, of course, prohibit that. On the other side, apparently unseen is a wing flapping happily away in its obscurity. It is the right-wing that is seen by the media while the invisible left-wing helps keep the bird in flight. Imagine the boom in the aviation industry if they could duplicate the media model. They would save $billions in construction costs. But would the editor of The New York Times fly on it?

I have ambivalent feelings about the media. They both inform and infuriate me. And God bless them, for without them our nation would be the poorer. Few things can inspire the better nature of mankind than the well-written prose of those who make it their life's work to explore and dig for stories in the public interest. Unfortunately, those talents can have the obverse effect. In many cases, the gifts of writers are used to conceal, rather than illuminate. To inflame, rather than enlighten. And it is my conclusion that it cannot be prevented. It is the duty of the reader and viewer to distinguish the real from the phony, the self-interest from the public interest.

Television news is media's fast food equivalent. And, like fast food, too many Americans decide to go there for their quick fix. Television news malnourishes the intellect like fast food malnourishes the body. Sadly, most viewers choose not to add to the flimsy sound bites and shallow reporting. Reading books and newspapers is old fashioned.

Network news has fallen on hard times in the age of cable television and the Internet, although some of their competition in cable television does little more than prostitute itself for one or another political cause. Of that genre, one host stands out above all the others.

Geraldo Rivera is the perfect example of what networks, NBC in this case, should not do. Granted, his program is mercifully seen by a minuscule number of people. To illustrate, an audience fifty times larger than Geraldo's, gets more news, and better quality, from Charles McCord, on Imus in the morning. Many of them also get to see McCord deliver the news, because, in this strange world, Don Imus's radio program is also seen on MSNBC, the cable creation of Microsoft and NBC. Radio looks better on the screen than a lot of MSNBC's other programming.

Having added Geraldo Rivera to my list of dung-beetles almost makes me want to apologize to the other dung beetles, but not quite. They go on his program to find their sustenance.

In the age of the Internet, it is unimaginable that a reader or a TV show host cannot get to the truth if they want to. With a push of a button or the click of a mouse we can ask our browsers to locate information on any topic, and it is ours in the bat of an eye. The best librarian could not equal those searches in a lifetime. There are websites that allow us to read the daily news from most cities in the world, and if we know what we are looking for, we will know it before the morning newspaper reports it. These things are exciting for the people and troubling for the media.

CHAPTER TWENTY-SEVEN ~
WHOSE JUSTICE?

It was crystal clear by early April 1998 that there would be a Federal investigation of "The Arkansas Project." That is, it was crystal clear to those who were paying attention to the script. It had been the intention of those driving the story all along. Now all that had to be decided was who would do the investigating. Under the law governing the Independent Counsel, it was clear that Kenneth Starr had jurisdiction. Anyone with an appreciation of the inner workings of the Clinton Justice Department could see that they did not want Starr to conduct this investigation. There was too much political gain to be had from this affair to allow it to fall under the control of an independent authority.

One need only look at unfolding events in the first spring of the new millennium to be reminded of the role Janet Reno's Justice Department has employed in protecting the Clinton's. The recent revelations of The LaBella memo, long suppressed, and unavailable to the congress, finally made available by the Los Angeles Times. Charles LaBella had been hired by the Justice Department to conduct an investigation of the 1996 fund-raising abuses of the Clinton/Gore reelection campaign and when he, joined by FBI director Louis Freeh, had recommended the appointment of an independent counsel, he was sacked by Reno. Justice had directly run interference with the California United States Attorney through justice aide, Lee Radek. We learned through this story that the same cast of characters who had recommended against the LaBella and Freeh conclusions had been the same ones that strongly pushed an investigation into the supernatural ranting of an Arkansas/Chicago/Fort Lauderdale psychic. Janet Reno, Eric Holder, and Lee Radek comprise The Department of Injustice at The Department of Justice.

The ink was barely dry on the LaBella/Freeh story when another, and potentially more serious, story emerged from the efforts of Judicial Watch, the public interest watchdog agency that has doggedly pursued its investigation of the Filegate affair. During depositions of contract employees working on White House computers, it was learned that tens of thousands, (Some say nearly a million) e-mail messages received by the White House had, through a "glitch," been lost. Those e-mail messages which had been under subpoena by various congressional committees, including the impeachment committee, were not turned over to those committees, even though we now know that the White House was aware of their existence. Worse, the contract employees had, according to their testimony, been threatened with jail if they revealed to anyone just what they knew about their little secret. One wonders how many times and in how many situations have those or similar threats been used to contain damaging testimony. I certainly have my own insights.

It is March 25, 2000, as I am writing, and yet another Saturday. We were informed yesterday in the New York Times and the Washington Post that the Department of Justice, and not a Special Counsel, had begun a criminal investigation of the missing e-mail. How very convenient.

What can be expected to happen, if past performance is any guide, is that justice will drag out its investigation until after the November elections? Some in the media will reread Howard Kurtz's book, "Spin Cycle" in amused appreciation of this administration's great ability to bamboozle the American electorate, then proceed to help them achieve their objectives. There is no reason to expect any other course of action and little reason to hope otherwise. The federal courts are the only institutions remaining in this country where the powerful Clintonistas have a chance of being held accountable. It has been demonstrated, in a small way, by Judge Susan Webber Wright, the federal judge in Arkansas, who imposed a fine on president Clinton for lying to her court. Judge Royce Lamberth, a federal judge in the District of Columbia who supervises the Judicial Watch lawsuit on behalf of former Bush administration employees whose FBI files were illegally obtained, is in a similar position. He has proved himself to be tough-minded, and no doubt he is feared by the White House, but I would wager that he is the only one feared by the White House in this case.

It is, then, against that backdrop that we view the actions of the Justice Department regarding the "Arkansas Project." The law was clear; Justice would have to turn this case over to the Independent Counsel. While the law was clear, politics was a greater force, and it was employed in all its sheer, brute clarity.

On April 9, 1998, and after Janet Reno had decided to refer the matter to the Independent Counsel, The Deputy Attorney General, Eric H. Holder, Jr, who, along with the head of Justice's Office of Professional Responsibility, Lee Radek, had helped Reno to decide not to follow LaBella and Freeh's recommendations earlier, sent this letter to Kenneth Starr:

Dear Judge Starr:

As you are aware, the United States Attorney's office for the Western District of Arkansas was recently provided with information suggesting that David Hale, who we understand is a witness in various matters under your jurisdiction, may have received cash and other gratuities from individuals seeking to discredit the President during a time when Hale was actively cooperating with your investigation. In addition to being possible criminal witness-tampering, see, e.g., 18 U. S. C. 201(b) (3-4), (2-3), 18 U. S. C. 1512 (b), this information may be of a sort that you have an affirmative obligation to disclose to parties matters being handled by your office, and may, of course influence your future deliberations on the various matters still pending under your jurisdiction. We are also concerned that if he was quoted accurately by the press, one of the participants in these alleged payments has made what could reasonably be interpreted as a threat against a witness. After confirming that information, it is our view that you have investigative and prosecutorial jurisdiction over these allegations because your jurisdiction specifically encompasses obstruction and warranted further investigation, we are therefore providing you with all information on this matter in our possession at this time.

witness tampering matters arising out of your investigation, which this does. Since the matter appears to us to be within your jurisdiction and given these unique facts, the Department lacks jurisdiction to investigate it. 28 U. S. C. 597 (a).

In the course of your exploration of these allegations, however, should you develop any evidence of misconduct by any member of your staff, including FBI agents assigned to assist you, the office of Professional Responsibility (OPR) is prepared to take appropriate action. In light of the Department's potential supervisory role in this matter, please inform OPR of the results of your investigation of these allegations. I am also forwarding a copy of this letter to OPR. This will help to assure the public that these allegations were properly handled by those with appropriate jurisdiction over them.

Section 597 (a) permits an independent counsel to refer matters, in writing, back to the Department of Justice. There have been suggestions that your office would have a conflict of interest, or the appearance of a conflict, in looking into this matter, because of the importance of Hale to your investigation and because the payments allegedly came from funds provided by Richard Scaife. Should you believe that this matter would be better investigated by the Department of Justice, we would be prepared to accept a referral from you.

If you have any questions or concerns about this referral, please feel free to contact me.

Sincerely,

Eric H. Holder, Jr.

When Holder made that available to the media, it spoke volumes about The Department of Justice's war with the Independent Counsel, and with Justice.

The ball had been served, with enough spin on it to intimidate the best of players. The audience and cast would watch to see how their opponent in the far court would handle it. It was clear to all that the Salon reporting had been taken as fact by the Justice Department. An investigation would only be a procedural nicety, after which the culprits would be found guilty as charged by the unbiased reporters and editors covering the story. Resultantly, having been discredited, the Independent Counsel would close up shop and go home, allowing Bill and Hillary to live happily ever after. In their make-believe world, even the "happily ever after" was taken as fact. The vast right-wing conspiracy would be exposed and it would pay for its sins accordingly. And just to make sure, Justice had given an out to the Independent Counsel. So that he could save face and not be the one to dispatch himself, they would be happy, no, eager, to do it for him. Finally, if he refused their offer, he had an obligation to share his findings with the Office of Professional Responsibility so they could leak his information and blame the leaks on him.

If any of this sounds far-fetched, just try to live long enough to read the history of this period. I hope you will enjoy good health as you wait.

[It is 6:31 a.m. August 16, 2016, as I read those words written fifteen years ago. A lot of my friends did not live long enough to see what that brief period of history led us to, but it is here in full force and it is undeniable. History does repeat itself.]

CHAPTER TWENTY-EIGHT ~
STARR GAZING

The audience roared its approval as the actors appeared and spoke their lines. The following day Karen Gullo of the Associated Press reported the Justice Department's Eric Holder Letter to Kenneth Starr. Other than a rehash of the letter, affirming the most salient parts which had been written for the benefit of the press, she added these useful tidbits.

"American Spectator publisher Terry Eastland said no money was ever given to Hale. Hale's lawyer said he is not aware of any payments."

"Mann's attorney, David Matthews, said she would cooperate with Starr. But he said, "To avoid even the appearance of a conflict, Mr. Starr should refer this back to the Justice Department for review."

Greg Gordon and Tom Hamburger of the Minneapolis Star-Tribune beneath the headline,

"Starr asked to investigate possible payments to his own witness..."

"...But Deputy Attorney General Eric Holder cautioned Starr that he might have a conflict of interest investigating payments to David Hale and Holder invited the independent counsel to refer the matter back to the Justice Department."

"...The allegations of cash payments, though vehemently denied by those alleged to have made them, threaten to throw a wrench in Starr's four-year-old investigation of Clinton's Whitewater real estate investment."

"Within hours of the Justice Department decision, a lawyer for Susan McDougal said that he had found new witnesses who knew of payments to Hale--and that he would seek to have his client released immediately from a federal prison in California."

"...Susan McDougal's lawyer, Mark Geragos, said from Little Rock Thursday that two witnesses at *The American Spectator* - one former employee and one current employee...have told him, through an intermediary, "that money was routed to Hale.""

"It was being accounted for in a false fashion," Geragos said. "David Hale was bought and paid for." [Your intermediary Mark? Waas, Broder, Talbot, Blumenthal?] Public lying by attorneys is OK? Geragos later made charges on CNN that *The American Spectator* had given 2 or more million dollars to Hale and that the New York times had paid Jim McDougal for his Whitewater stories.

"...U.S. District Judge Henry Woods of Arkansas, who presided over an early phase of the Whitewater trial, said Thursday that it would be "outrageous" if Starr were to head such an inquiry because of his possible conflicts."

Richard Larry, an officer at the two Scaife foundations that funded the Arkansas project, said this week that he has "checked with all those involved" and that Hale got no money from the project. He rejected as "nonsense" allegations of a Starr-Scaife relationship. "No one in this office, from Mr. Scaife on down, has ever met, corresponded [with], had a telephone conversation with Judge Starr," he said.

April 10 was a busy day. The President's personal lawyer, David Kendall, wrote his own five-page letter to Starr, in which he made his and the president's point of view known. "I do not think you or your office can creditably or appropriately conduct this investigation." He suggested that by handing the investigation back to the Justice Department it would "increase public confidence in the outcome of the investigation, whatever it is." Helping to destroy *public confidence* in the Independent Counsel had, after all, been one of his duties as the President's lawyer.

And so it went. Geragos and his client Susan McDougal would become fixtures on the evening news, and particularly, on the Geraldo Rivera shows. She did look pretty in that orange jumpsuit, but the chains were a bit too much. Geragos had the look of an old western movie villain, tying the widow to the railroad tracks.

Caryn Mann would be given her fifteen minutes of fame on CNN, and of course, Rivera Live. Even I would make numerous appearances on Geraldo's programs, after a fashion. My appearances and those of Steve Boynton came to be after we each received a hand-delivered letter from Charles Thompson, a producer for Geraldo. In his letters to us, which were identical, he asked for our cooperation in obtaining video footage of each of us. He made it clear that he would get it, one way or another but said that he would prefer that it be given voluntarily. He did not want to stake us out.

I read it as a reasonable and courteous request. Thompson had left his phone number with the letter, which he had personally delivered. After talking with Steve Boynton and telling him that I was inclined to be cooperative, with limits imposed, he agreed. I called Thompson and had a friendly conversation with him. When I asked him how he planned to use the video (he had identified himself as being with NBC) he was evasive, but under my further questions, he admitted that Geraldo had asked him to get it. That told me all I needed to know. I told Charles Thompson that both Steve Boynton and I had Labrador Retrievers and that Steve walked his dogs each morning around 7:00 a.m. He could come to Steve's home at that time on an agreed day and film the walk. He would not, however, be permitted to talk to us or get any verbal response from us.

Thompson accepted our offer and our restrictions. He arrived on the appointed morning with a cameraman in tow and they followed us on our walk. I had not brought my own dog, rather I walked one of Steve's young and untrained dogs. It was hilarious. The dog kept walking in front of me and I was on the verge of tripping over it for the entire walk. That keystone-cops video played over and over on Geraldo's daily broadcasts as he would exhort his viewers to remember these men's names, "Steve Boynton" and "Dave Henderson." We became his villains de jour. Thompson was a gentleman, and he kept his word. How sad it must be to have to work for someone like Rivera.

Down in Arkansas, on Lake Catherine, the "Gravel-Voiced Bag Man", Parker Dozhier, withstood his own press onslaught. Once the great man himself, Geraldo Riviera, having been refused an interview by Parker, stood in front of Dozhier's bait shop and worm barony, microphone in hand, while he intoned the opener for his show. It was reminiscent of Bernard Shaw in Baghdad, or Rather, Brokow, and

Jennings being blown about by a hurricane. A great time was had by all.

The joy was short-lived, however, when the independent counsel returned the serve in a hand-delivered letter to Attorney General Janet Reno on April 16, 1998.

"Dear Attorney General Reno:

This is in response to Deputy Attorney General Holder's letter of April 9, 1998, referring to the Office of the Independent Counsel ("OIC") certain allegations that David Hale, a witness who has been cooperating with our office, may have received cash and other gratuities from individual's seeking to discredit the President. While noting that our jurisdiction explicitly includes obstruction of justice and witness tampering in connection with our investigation, Mr. Holder suggests that the OIC "would have a conflict of interest, or the appearance of a conflict, in looking into this matter."

Preliminary information indicates that most if not all of the alleged FBI-supervised contacts between David Hale and Parker Dozhier occurred prior to August 1994. i.e., while the investigation was being conducted under the auspices of the Department of Justice. To the extent that any activity of potential investigative interest may have taken place, it thus appears- - at least initially - - that it occurred almost entirely before the point at which I became Independent Counsel.

Nonetheless, after reviewing the allegations that have been made regarding Mr. Hale, we have concluded that any investigation of these allegations may involve at most the appearance of a conflict of interest on the part of the OIC. We also note, however, that the Department of Justice may have not only an appearance problem but multiple actual conflicts of interest in connection with an investigation of Mr. Hale, including (1) a conflict potentially arising from the fact that the Department of Justice, which under the Ethics in Government Act is statutorily precluded from investigation the matters that the OIC is currently looking into, would itself be investigating the OIC, (2) a conflict potentially arising from the fact that Mr. Hale has provided information that is damaging to the President of the United States, and a conflict arising from the fact that, because the alleged FBI-supervised contacts between David Hale and Parker Dozhier appear largely to have been prior to August of 1994, any activity of investigative interest that may have occurred took place primarily during the time that the investigation was being conducted on behalf of the Department of Justice.

We are deeply concerned that the above considerations would create actual conflict of interest problems in any investigation of these allegations by the Department of Justice, particularly when viewed in combination with the positions that the Department has taken on the various testimonial privileges that are hindering our investigation.

To address these important issues, the OIC has developed several proposed alternate mechanisms for investigating this matter in a manner that comports fully with our respective obligations and with the public's interest in the proper and honest administration of justice. We believe it is appropriate for the OIC and the Department of Justice to attempt to reach agreement on which of these mechanisms should be implemented, to assure public confidence in the discharge of our responsibilities in our respective investigative jurisdictions. I look forward to the opportunity to meet with you, at your earliest convenience, to discuss these alternate mechanisms and our mutual interest in a complete, thorough, and unbiased investigation.

Sincerely,

Kenneth W. Starr

Volley returned, and impressively. Most certainly the Department of Justice had been surprised and disappointed that the OIC had not rolled over. And he didn't even copy Eric Holder. Starr's letter made reference to actions of the Justice Department "that are hindering our investigation." Then he threw the biggest challenge imaginable back to Justice, "...a complete, thorough, and unbiased investigation."

169

CHAPTER TWENTY-NINE ~
GOOD FELONS:BAD FELONS

There was no question that there would be an investigation. What was unclear to all parties involved, the press, The Justice Department, the Independent Counsel and of course, those of us who had been publicly accused of criminal wrongdoing, was just what the process would be and under whose guidance it would be conducted. The prudent used this time to locate attorneys and plan for the coming fireworks. Our committed opponents continued to stir the pot and do whatever they could to further inflame their partisans, who reacted predictably and virulently.

Salon magazine continued to churn out article after repetitive article, each one containing more bile than fact. They would choose individuals whom they could connect to imaginary roles in the vast-right-wing conspiracy. Salon's targets were pretty much left to their own devices.

One of their targets and one who they missed by a mile was Ted Olson. They had conflated Olson's friendship with Kenneth Starr, his brief representation of David Hale, and his friendship with and later service to *The American Spectator* as a member of the Board of Directors, into something of greater significance than the facts, would dictate. What the President's kamikaze legions would or could not bring themselves to accept is that conservatives, like liberals, tend to know and relate to each other. If they do not know someone personally, an introduction can usually be arranged through a mutual friend or acquaintance. That had been true of my meeting with Ted Olson. By anyone's reckoning, Ted Olson is a gifted and formidable adversary as much as he is a generous and loyal friend to those who are close to him. Ted had suffered his own investigation and persecution when, as a member of the Reagan Administration's Justice Department he was accused of misleading congress, investigated for 3 years by an Independent Counsel, and no evidence of a crime was ever found. I sought a meeting with Ted in either late 1994 or early 1995 and through the auspices of someone who knew him, I was able to meet him. I liked him instantly and was impressed by his reassuring manner and his friendliness.

Ted Olson made an attractive target for the dung beetles, because he so clearly outclassed them, and they feared that he may once again rise to a position of importance in a future Republican administration. No doubt he will. Bob Tyrrell and I started discussing sometime in 1994, how valuable it would be to have him on the board of *The American Spectator*. Eventually, Ted did join the Board, but he was strongly resisted by Ron Burr. Ron had a visceral dislike of lawyers, often expressed, and he was coming to the realization that an active Board of Directors was a threat to his power. Burr's memory, according to numerous press accounts and Salon stories was of having been in the same meeting with Ted Olson that I was the first time we met. That may be so, although I have no memory of it. Some of the false accounts of that first meeting have been extrapolated into the myth that Ted was a "godfather" of the Arkansas Project. Ted Olson did not participate, nor was he asked to participate in either the planning or conduct of the Project. In truth, there was no planning. We just went where the story took us.

As predicted, Ted Olson did continue his rise, but also experienced great tragedy on 9/11, 2001 when the plane carrying his wife, Barbara Olson, crashed into the Pentagon killing all passengers. He argued the case of Bush v Gore before the Supreme Court and later was nominated for Solicitor General of the Supreme Court by President George W. Bush. Ironically, from this author's point of view, the supreme Court hearing in Bush v. Gore reinforced my Forrest Gump-like ways since the opposing attorney David Boies had been the attorney for CBS in the CBS v Westmoreland case. David had deposed me in that case, and we had both spent many days in the Courtroom of Federal courtroom of Judge Pierre Leval in Manhattan. David was a partner in the powerhouse New York firm of Cravath, Swaine, and Moore. He was unquestionably a great lawyer but bested by Ted Olson.

Naturally, the hearing before the Senate Judiciary Committee was laced with accusatory questioning by the Democrat Chairman of the committee, Senator Patrick Leahy, regarding the Arkansas Project. Also note that David Brock, and Ron Burr, former staff of *The American Spectator* had registered their disapproval to the committee and both Steve Boynton and I had done the opposite. After a lengthy and contentious hearing, Ted was approved. See Congressional Record Senate S5578 May 24, 2001.

I must say that things get weirder and weirder. Gene Lyons just repeated in his column today, March 29, 2000, that Ted Olson "...oversaw both the founding and the aftermath of the Spectator's Richard Mellon Scaife-funded Arkansas project." Now, get this Lyons! When Steve Boynton and I traveled to Little Rock, Arkansas on November 19, 1993, to meet with David Hale and his attorney, Randy Coleman, neither Steve nor I knew Ted Olson. Now, may I ask you a question? Is it just possible that you were too eager to hear something that you wanted to hear when you cite Ron Burr as the source describing a meeting in Ted Olson's office, a meeting that I also acknowledge? Look at the timeline. Isn't that what you "journalists" do by rote?

Here is what did happen. When the Senate banking committee, chaired by former US senator Al D'Amato began conducting its Whitewater hearings in 1995, it was assumed that David Hale would be called as a witness before the committee. He and his attorney, Randy Coleman were both aware that David would need Washington Counsel to guide him through the pitfalls unique to the moods and whims of the highly partisan committee. David Hale asked me if I would introduce him to someone of stature in Washington who could be counted on guide him through the process. I agreed to do so, and Ted Olson was first on my list. Another friend arranged for a meeting between David Hale and Fred Fielding, former Deputy White House counsel in the Reagan administration. I accompanied David to both meetings. He was impressed by both Ted and Fred, and he would have been well represented by either. It happened that when the time came to make a decision, David settled on asking Ted first, and if that didn't work out, he would turn to Fred Fielding with the same request.

Some few months passed from the time of the introductory meetings with Ted Olson and Fred Fielding, while the nation watched the rancorous senate banking committee hearings each week on C-SPAN. Senators of both parties strutted before the cameras and jumped at the slightest opportunity to reinforce their position before television. Ironically, senators of both parties wanted David Hale to come before the committee. The Democrats wanted him there to make him look bad. The Republicans wanted him there to make them look good. Ted Olson was not interested in either proposition, just in looking after his client's best interest. Good lawyers still do that in Washington. Ted was successful in keeping David Hale away from that circus to his everlasting credit, but he probably angered some of his senate friends.

The Clintonistas in the press reported that Ted Olson donated his legal services to David Hale. That is untrue. They reached an agreement, whereby David would pay Ted for his representation. I suspect that it is still one of the many obligations borne by David Hale. In 1995 it was not unreasonable to expect that David would have a future left after his ordeal was over, but that was not to be. Only felons approved by the administration, like felons Jim Guy Tucker, Webster Hubbell, and Susan McDougal are permitted to resume their lives after prison. They even have legions of public relations operatives burnishing their reputations and their celebrity, while favor seeking foreigners make cash available in astounding amounts. While David Hale's legal
representation and his payment arrangements were pursued all the way to a grand jury, I don't recall ever reading or hearing of an inquiry into who paid Susan McDougal's bills. We do know, of course, that Webb Hubbell received at least $750,000, and he was supposed to be a cooperating witness with the independent counsel. Fairness? Ethics? Equal before the law? Don't wager your future on it.

[Here I sit on this early morning in August 2016 not believing my own words written so long ago. "while favor seeking foreigners make cash available in astounding amounts."]

CHAPTER THIRTY ~
CHARACTER

Sam Dealy was an exceptionally bright and engaging young intern at *The American Spectator*. I particularly liked the young Texan and expect that he will have a brilliant future. One day in early summer, 1998 Sam walked into my office and asked, "Did you give money to David Hale?" I could tell by his expression and demeanor that asking the question was painful for him. Over a lifetime I have been both mentor and mentored and I know that trust is a necessary character trait for a mentor. Though I did not consider myself a mentor to Sam, he and I had shared many conversations. I was always interested in what he had to say. I suspect that he was troubled by talk that he heard and felt that he would hear the truth from me. I didn't hesitate in telling him that I had not given anything to David other than money for phone calls to me from prison, and even then, it was not given directly to him, but to his wife. I sincerely hope that Sam believed me. Given the stories that were being written, he had every right to ask.

I would be less than truthful if I didn't say that I was deeply troubled by how those untrue stories affected my friends and our friendships. It concerned me to think that friends and acquaintances of a lifetime probably had the same questions in their minds and hearts that Sam Dealy did. There were also my elderly parents and Peggy's mother to consider, as well as my brothers and sister. Anyone who has been a parent knows that moms and dads never stop being concerned for their children and they yearn for their well-being. My first urge had been to go on a press crusade and set the record straight, but after reflection based on my own experiences, I had concluded that such an effort would take years. Not only could I not defend myself, even if I made the effort, there were thirty or forty spokesmen who seemed to be on call for the White House. They would fan out after my appearances to smear me and anything that I may have said. Sadly, I concluded that the only way to be exonerated was in a court of law or a thorough investigation. David Hale had reached the same conclusion.

He had written to the Attorney General, Janet Reno, to the Independent Counsel, Kenneth Starr, and to the United States Attorney for the western district of Arkansas, P.K. Holmes, III, asking each of them to investigate the allegations. It would have been an act of sheer lunacy for David Hale to have done such a thing had the allegations been in the least bit true. I agreed with and applauded David's decision.

The greatest agony that I felt was not knowing if Dick Scaife and Richard Larry believed me. After all, Steve Boynton and I had expended a great deal of the money that had been given to *The American Spectator*. I had known for thirty years that money from the Scaife Foundations didn't come with strings attached. The fact that Richard M. Scaife and Richard M. Larry would be pulled into the coming investigation was embarrassing to me, especially in view of the fact that Steve Boynton and I had been given considerable latitude in the conduct of our work by *The American Spectator*, it could easily have been interpreted, based on the news stories, that he and I had criminally mismanaged the effort. Compounding these possible misunderstandings was the advice of our various attorneys prohibiting each of us from discussing with the other any of the issues in question. Indeed, they didn't want us to even treat each other as friends. Such is the nature of our legal system. It is as ugly as it is practical. Strong, real friendships can survive it, but not many others do. The total disruption of lives is the usual result of these tragedies and those cherished relationships are the greatest loss of all. There could only be one way to resolve these issues, and the opportunity would soon be at our doorsteps.

There was also considerable anxiety at *The American Spectator* because there were first amendment considerations to be taken into account. Were they to be dragged into an examination of how they spent their money and conducted their journalistic enterprises? Any news organization worthy of the name would automatically resist such an intrusion. One could imagine the wagons being circled from Paducah to Portland if The Washington Post or The New York Times were even mildly considered for such an investigation. Yet, there was a very real possibility that the outcome for *The American Spectator* would be different. I was entitled to legal representation by *The American Spectator* as an employee, but Steve Boynton was not. It became clear to me that my legal representation would extend only so far as it did not diverge from the interests of the magazine. In other words, if *The American Spectator's* interests and mine differed, my interest would be subordinate to theirs and I would be obliged to find my own counsel.

Lastly, my tenure at the magazine was finite since I had been employed under a one-year grant, and that would expire at the end of July 1998.

The end result was that while a modicum of first amendment protection was given to *The American Spectator*, it did not extend to either Steve or me. That suited me just fine. I did not want to have a sullied reputation for the remainder of my life under the protection of the first amendment.

By now everyone had learned that anything touching Bill and Hillary Clinton was radioactive. The great story for anyone who wants to dig for it is the vast west-wing conspiracy against those who would investigate or write about the corruption and deceit of the co-presidents and their equally corrupt acolytes. Janet Reno was not exempt, nor was the law.

Underscoring all of this, I just received a phone call this afternoon, March 31, 2000, from our old friends Marge and Jim McCauley. They were leaving their home in Atlanta and driving to their weekend retreat in the mountains of northern Georgia. Jim's started with a question, "Did you watch the Today Show with Matt Lauer this morning?" I told him that I had not. He said, "A couple of guys were on the show...", and I completed his sentence, Conason, and Lyons, "Yes, they were talking about a book, something about hunting." I said it is their book, "The Hunting of The President" and Jim said they were talking about "these characters who were paid by Richard Scaife to go down to Arkansas..." Jim told me that he turned to Marge and said, "Hey, they are talking about one of our best friends, and they are calling him a character." Jim did say that Matt Lauer asked how anyone could believe them since they were clearly biased in favor of the President. They said that they could document everything that they had written. We will see about that. I have the book and have read two paragraphs pertaining to Steve Boynton and me. There were about six clear lies in those two paragraphs. We will explore that book in some depth for it contains most of the Clintons' charges about The Arkansas Project, all easily refuted. But first, I want to finish telling my story while my character is intact.

CHAPTER THIRTY-ONE ~
OFFICE OF SPECIAL REVIEW

Eventually, Janet Reno and Kenneth Starr split the baby, in Solomon-like harmony. Neither of them would conduct the investigation that Reno wanted and Starr did not. The task fell to the recently-retired head of the Department of Justice's Office of Professional Responsibility, Michael J. Shaheen, Jr. Shaheen was a man of stature and he enjoyed a sterling reputation in legal circles. He would establish an Office of Special Investigation and report to three retired federal judges. Once his investigation was concluded, his findings would be submitted to the judges who would have great latitude in making determinations about a course of action. Ultimately, though, the final report would be submitted to the Independent Counsel, thus complying with the Independent Counsel law. It was the first week in June 1998.

Shaheen staffed his new operation with Assistant United States Attorneys, FBI, and IRS agents. It was an interesting fact that each of the Assistant US attorneys worked for United States Attorneys who had been appointed by Bill Clinton. It was also an unavoidable fact because every United States Attorney in the country had been appointed by President Clinton immediately after his election as president in 1992. Had that been remarkable foresight or a foreseen necessity? Whatever the reason, it was a marvelous way for a president to dispense favors and punish his enemies.

The Assistant US attorneys were from New Orleans, Oklahoma City, Chicago, and Washington, D.C. Shaheen himself, was a Mississippi native but had spent his professional life mostly in Washington.

The Judges that Shaheen reported to were Charles Renfrew, a federal judge and Deputy Attorney General during the Carter administration, and Arlin Adams, another federal judge who had himself been an Independent Counsel investigating the HUD scandal during the Reagan administration. Judge Renfrew, under the arrangement, was to pick a third judge to fill out the panel.

The American Spectator had retained Richard Leon, a partner in the law firm Baker and Hostettler and I went with Terry Eastland to meet him. Another partner in the firm was a friend of mine and he was there during the introduction, then he left the room. Richard Leon, Terry and I reviewed the situation. I described the activities that Steve Boynton and I had been involved in. Richard explained to me that he could represent me as well as the magazine. It was a decision for me to make. Good Washington lawyers are very expensive. Dick Leon was a good Washington lawyer. His fees would be paid by *The American Spectator.* Considering that I would be unemployed during the duration of the investigation, it was an easy decision.

The end of July was fast approaching. My grant at *The American Spectator* would expire then. I decided to ride out the investigation on my own. This was an entirely new experience for me. I knew that demands on my time would be enormous. It was also clear to me that prospective employers in my area of expertise would not want to be exposed or involved with someone accused of crimes and under a federal investigation. I was on my own, whether I wanted to be or not. Further, I did not want to impose on friends and cause them grief because of me. I was not, however, prepared for the isolation that would come.

Each person involved had their own lawyer. Each lawyer uniformly advised their client to refrain from communication with the others. To do otherwise could lead to suspicions that rehearsal was underway among the parties. The limited contact that I had with other parties was intentionally devoid of any mention of the case and its particulars. I was saddened that I had to forsake normal contact with lifelong friends. Going into this exercise I was satisfied that the innocence of all parties would ultimately trump the motivations of the accusers, but I will accept the observation that I am one naive country boy. In reality, the deck was stacked against us in every respect but two. First was truth, and the other was the grand jury. Grand Juries are a five-hundred-year-old tradition, begun in England and incorporated in the United States Constitution in the fifth amendment. They were established to prevent politically motivated prosecutions from unjustly indicting and trying citizens. Grand juries are made up of ordinary citizens, and unlike trial jurors, they are in charge. They do not decide guilt or innocence, rather, they decide if prosecutors have sufficient evidence to indict subjects.

Grand juries have enormous powers. They must be obeyed. They act in total secrecy. Violation of that secrecy is itself a crime. Only those who testify before a grand jury can reveal what they testified to. (Unscrupulous prosecutors can reveal what a subject is likely to testify to before a grand jury based upon interviews and questions that they will ask before the grand juries. It happens.) There are both federal and state grand juries, but for this case, we are describing federal grand juries.

Federal grand juries meet or (sit) one or two days a month unless called by prosecutors for special circumstances and they serve eighteen months. The courts can extend the time that a grand jury is convened in six-month increments. They can issue subpoenas for appearances of witnesses, the production of documents, or both. Usually, the prosecutors prepare the subpoenas and the grand jurors approve them.

It has been often said that a prosecutor can get a grand jury to indict a ham sandwich. No talking head on television forgets to quote that line. Some grand juries ignore prosecutors. They exercise their constitutional powers, and for those acts of defiance, they are dubbed "runaway grand juries." Some cheek, those grand jurors.

Persons appearing before grand juries must answer all questions truthfully or invoke their fifth amendment rights. Witnesses and subjects must appear before the grand jury without their lawyers. The lawyers must remain outside the grand jury chambers. A witness may ask for the opportunity to confer with their attorney, in which case they are permitted to leave the chambers for that purpose. Prosecutors usually ask most of the questions of a witness or subject; however, grand jurors have the right to question witnesses and subjects as well. Up to twenty-three jurors make up a federal grand jury. One of them serves as jury foreman and that person swears in the witness. I do not recommend to the average citizen that he become as familiar with the grand jury process as I have become. However, my personal experience with the grand jury, sitting in Fort Smith, Arkansas, was not at all unpleasant. It is easy for the innocent, and it takes few words to speak the truth. Speaking the truth, however, required many hours, and I left nothing unsaid in response to the questions asked.

CHAPTER THIRTY-TWO ~
GRAND JURY, ROUND ONE

Dick Leon and I had met in his office prior to our cab ride to the Office of Special Review. We spent a few minutes discussing activities that I would likely be questioned about by the investigative team. Then it was show time. I asked your indulgence in chapter one that I be allowed to explain some personal history to show how we arrived at this point, and I hope my explanation has been sufficient. Storytelling is as old as mankind, and still useful in a world of instant analysis by an assortment of Monday morning quarterbacks. Those who have lived and participated in events of significance generally know the details that they personally witnessed or influenced. Others may speculate about those events; however, it is a fool's errand to pretend to know the unknowable. What is in your heart or your mind or your experience will remain a mystery to others, unless you choose, or are compelled, to share it. Many of the events described here were shaped by the actions of Steve Boynton and myself. Now, they would be weighed and analyzed by the passionate and the dispassionate.

Dick knew just where to go since he had had previous meetings with the prosecutors. One by one he introduced me to the investigators as we entered their offices. The introductions were polite, and not unlike a business meeting. We convened in their conference room. There were assistant US Attorneys and an FBI agent. The agent participated in the questioning and he took notes. Dick Leon sat to my right. He spoke freely whenever he felt the need to do so. At times he gave me advice and even prompted me to address particular things. We spent several hours that day, Wednesday, July 29, 1998. For the most part, the investigators remained friendly and polite. I didn't get the impression that they were out to wear me down, but Dick Leon would tell me after the interview, "These guys are not going to become your buddies." He was right, of course, and friendliness is certainly one of the arrows in the investigator's quiver. My peace of mind, nonetheless, was enhanced by their civil behavior. They had a job to do, and perhaps they were not too much happier than I was with that prospect. I did not pretend to be able to get into their minds or to intuit their motives. Up front, I made it clear that I held no personal animus toward them. Life had dealt them a hand and they had to play it as surely as I had to play the one dealt to me. They were not the force that had driven us to that point, just the instruments of that force.

I learned that a subpoena had already been prepared, commanding my appearance before a Federal Grand Jury in Fort Smith, Arkansas, the following week. Dick Leon had accepted it on my behalf and had it in his briefcase. I assume that it had been presented to him after our arrival at the Office of Special Review. It was dated July 30, 1998, the following day.

Missing from the meeting that day was Michael J. Shaheen, Jr. I see no need to name the others who were there. I would see and hear from them several times in the coming months. That day I answered all of their questions to the best of my ability and I was instructed to make available all documents required by the subpoena. There would be many more documents turned over to the investigators than those initially required by the subpoena. Those documents were extremely helpful to me and to my friends. I had my personal and complete bank and telephone records for the entire period. With those documents, we were able to establish many things. I volunteered to make my home computer available to the investigators. They did not accept that offer. There was nothing that needed to be hidden; indeed, the more that was revealed to them, the stronger our position became.

Steve Boynton would go through the same process the following day, Thursday, July 30, 1998.

Friday, July 31, 1998, I completed my last day at *The American Spectator*. There was a brief send-off by the staff and I remember making the remark that both the President of The United States and I were to appear before grand juries in the coming days. I would be open and truthful to my grand jury. Predictably, the President was neither of those to the grand jury nor to the country. In fact, he wasn't even truthful to his friends and flacks. In this context, would it be reasonable to assume that he would be willing to lie to another grand jury, about other matters? Say, his role in the loan to Susan McDougal?

We didn't have much advance notice of the grand jury appearance. Dick Leon and I had to get cracking to make travel arrangements. Dick will not fly on small commuter airplanes, and I am not too fond of them either. To get to Fort Smith, we would have had to fly to Dallas and take a commuter plane back to Fort Smith. Dick asked me what was nearby that we could fly directly to and rent a car for the drive to Fort Smith. I told him that Tulsa, Oklahoma, would be the closest and would require about a two-hour drive. Dick had never been to Tulsa. Of course, I had lived there for three years while serving on the headquarters staff of The United States Jaycees. I suggested that we travel to Tulsa on Monday, August 3, 1998, and spend the night there. My appearance before the grand jury was scheduled for 9:00 A.M. on August 4. That would require that we leave Tulsa very early the following morning. I had no intention of being late for that appointment.

Dick Leon and I departed Tulsa at 6:00 A.M. on Tuesday, August 4, 1998. I drove; Dick reviewed his files. My subpoena commanded that I appear at the Judge Isaac C. Parker Federal Building in Fort Smith, Arkansas. From 1875 until 1891, Judge Isaac C. Parker was the most feared man on the frontier. The Indian Territories lay to the west of Fort Smith in Oklahoma. There was no law in the territories at that time. As a consequence, it provided refuge to outlaws of all stripes. It was a dangerous place to be. Judge Parker sent many rugged and burly men into the territories to recover outlaws by hook or by crook. When outlaws were forcibly returned to Fort Smith, they usually faced a quick trial, and often the gallows. Who can forget the great John Wayne, as "Rooster Cogburn" in his movie 'True Grit", riding off into the territories accompanied by Kim Darby as the cheeky "Matty Ross", "... from Yell County, (the home of David Hale nearly a century later) near Dardinelle, Arkansas." Matty had paid Rooster Cogburn to find the killer of her father and bring him to Judge Parker to be hanged. Other movies and books chronicled the twenty-one years that Judge Isaac C. Parker had presided over the court in Fort Smith. As many as 160 men were hanged by Judge Parker's order. For most of those years, there was no appeal from Judge Parker's sentences.

Dick Leon and I were heading southeast, through the territories of eastern Oklahoma to Fort Smith, seeking our own justice. Times certainly had changed. Though I was riding along the same path to Judge Parker's court, this time, the burly and rugged man riding next to me was there for my protection.

Passing the exit for Muscogee, Oklahoma brought fond memories racing back. Sam Powell, outdoor writer for the Tulsa Tribune and Tulsa World was from Muscogee. Sam and I had duck hunted together many times in that region. I quietly hummed Merle Haggard's, "Okie from Muscogee" as we continued on our way.

Both Dick and I expected to run a gauntlet of cameras entering the federal building, but the streets of Fort Smith were eerily quiet. Few cars were out. The town reminded me of the 1940s. There were no news cameras nor reporters awaiting our arrival. Maybe this grand jury secrecy was working?

Inside, security was tight. A metal detector was overseen by two marshals. They were friendly, in the manner of people from that part of the world. We passed through and were directed to the room that we were to report to. We were met by one of the Assistant U. S. attorneys who had participated in my interview in Washington. He politely told me what to expect inside the grand jury chambers. He would conduct the questioning before the grand jury. He then left Dick Leon and me in a small, windowless room. Dick reminded me that if I felt the need to discuss any of my answers to questions asked of me, I should leave the room and find him. He would remain nearby.

Momentarily, the Assistant U. S. Attorney came to get me and he escorted me into the grand jury chambers. It was a small room. At one end was a dais and one man was sitting there. Next to him was an empty chair and a small table with a microphone sitting on it. That was for my use. The man sitting next to the empty chair was the grand jury foreman, and he rose and beckoned me to join him on the dais. He then swore me in. The Assistant U. S. Attorney then instructed me in the procedures of the grand jury. He told me what rights I had and what I could not do. I could refuse to answer any or all questions by invoking my fifth amendment rights. I could leave the room for discussions with my attorney. I was told of the secrecy surrounding the process. He asked if I understood. When I said that I did, the questions began.

I was facing the grand jurors and the assistant U.S. Attorney stood near the wall, diagonally to my right, behind a microphone. A stenographer sat just below me. Dick Leon had told me that I would have to decide whether to address the grand jury or the assistant U.S. Attorney in responding to the questions. He told me that some grand juries liked to be involved and some did not. So, like a public speaker, it was necessary to read the audience.

The men and women who made up the grand jury seemed relaxed and engaged. For the four hours that I was asked and had answered questions, they remained attentive. My reading of them was that they were taking their duty seriously. A few of the grand jurors asked questions. They were well-informed questions. My decision about how to address the answers was to take in the entire room as I responded, making eye contact with each person in the room. They looked like the kind of people who would make good neighbors.

We recessed for lunch. Dick Leon and I walked to the nearest restaurant, located in a Holiday Inn, two blocks from the federal building. There were familiar faces in the restaurant; Parker Dozhier was there with his attorney and so were Steve Boynton and his lawyer. It was awkward because Dick Leon insisted that we sit alone and across the room. Steve Boynton, himself a lawyer, walked by our table and said hello as he passed. It was his way of saying he understood. I understood too, but it didn't make me like it.

After lunch, I returned to the grand jury where the questions continued. When they were concluded, I was instructed that I remained under subpoena and may be required to return at a later date. I was pleased to have been able to answer all questions without once conferring with my attorney. It had not been my worst experience. I had been through far more difficult situations in my life, and I faced more still.

Many of the questions, and my answers, related to hunting and fishing. It was a necessary part of the story, as you have seen, so I was pleasantly surprised to be approached by one of the grand jurors after our session concluded. He said that I should come to Arkansas and go duck hunting.

Steve Boynton followed my appearance before the grand jury that afternoon, and Dick Leon and I left immediately for the drive back to the "territories" and our flight to Washington.

CHAPTER THIRTY-THREE ~
GRAND JURY: ROUND TWO

August of 1998 was a historic month. Monica's blue dress, first revealed by Linda Tripp, had proven to be the dripping gun. After FBI analysis, the President's DNA, carefully stored on a GAP dress, caused great heartburn to the forces of virtue and simultaneously put to the lie their protestations of a decade, denying the randy nature of their idol. It also presented them with the opportunity to once and forever demonstrate their well-honed skills of personal destruction. Linda Tripp was toast.

Personal destruction has been a constant with the sham enterprise known as the Clinton Administration. The truth is devastating to those who must operate in darkness.

Not long after returning from Fort Smith I was called back for another interview (interrogation) at the Office of Special Review. This time, things were more contentious than they had been earlier. I could sense some frustration on the part of the investigators. They obviously were finding dry holes at the end of their explorations, and at least some of them seemed to believe something was there that they had been unable to uncover. They got a little testy with me when I repeatedly told them that David Hale had never asked for anything and had never been given anything. One of the Assistant U.S. Attorneys and an FBI agent questioned me for another two or three hours and concluded that they just could not believe what I was telling them, regardless of the lack of evidence to support their suspicions.

That session ended with the announcement that I had to return to Fort Smith once again to appear before the Grand Jury. I told them to give me the time and date and I would be there. Dick Leon was less than enthusiastic about the return trip, and I would have been as happy staying at home. But since we had to go, I had something to show Dick in Tulsa. He had been a Lacrosse player in college and had commented to me when we were driving through Oklahoma on our previous trip that he had once seen a painting of Indians playing Lacrosse. I had a vague memory of that portrait and thought it could possibly be in the

Gilcrease Museum in Tulsa. Gilcrease has a treasure in western art, and it features 18 of Frederic Remington's 22 bronzes. Many of Charles M. Russell's magnificent paintings are also featured.

We would arrange our travel, this time, to allow for a couple of hours in the museum. During our last visit, Dick had wanted to see Southern Hills Country Club. He had hoped to buy some things in their pro shop. We drove by the Country Club on our return from Fort Smith. The pro shop and course were closed. This time, we would do better. We took an early flight to Tulsa, arriving there in the afternoon. I was scheduled to appear in Fort Smith at 10:00 A.M. on Thursday, September 24, 1998. Someone was already before the grand jury when we arrived that day. I was next in line.

Dick Leon and I were waiting in the same small room that we had used before, an Assistant U.S. Attorney asked me out into the hallway leading to grand jury chambers. There he introduced me to Michael J. Shaheen who was most gracious and said that he was sorry that we had to meet under such circumstances. I was surprised to see him, but shouldn't have been. When I went into chambers and was sworn in by the grand jury foreman, I could see that the whole Office of Special Review team was in place. This was to be the main event because Dick Scaife himself was to appear, and so was Dick Larry. Steve Boynton had been called back. He also would do an encore.

The grand jurors seemed to all be there, too. They must have been expecting a big show that day. It is not every day that the average person will sit a few feet away from a billionaire, and be able to ask him questions as well. Questions that he must answer. I'll wager that they were totally taken off guard by Dick Scaife. I did not see either Dick Scaife or Dick Larry that day, because as soon as I was finished, Dick Leon and I immediately left for Tulsa. I was told that the elusive bankroller of the vast-right-wing conspiracy wore a golf shirt that day. If they were expecting to see the evil man of White House myth, their expectations were not realized. It would have been fun to have been the proverbial fly on the wall.

But I get ahead of myself. A different Assistant U.S. Attorney was asking the questions of me that day. He was the one who had not been satisfied with my explanation of certain events involving David Hale. While his boss and colleagues watched, he performed. I must confess, he was good. He must have found fifty different ways to ask me the same question. The questions started out matter of factly, but as I consistently answered his many iterations of the same question, he began to drip sarcasm as he re-worded his questions. Whether good or bad, I have a low tolerance for bad manners. I began to match the tone of his questions with my answers. Finally, my patience wore thin. I turned and addressed the grand jurors directly. I will never forget the words or the cold passion with which I spoke them. "I am fully aware that I appear before you and I answer you under penalty of perjury. I am also aware what those penalties entail." Then, I turned to address the Assistant U.S. Attorney, calling him by name, with these words. "I cannot give you the answer that your questions elicit because it didn't happen. Nothing was asked for, and nothing was given." At that point, and before he could respond, I did what I was entitled to, but had not done before. I rose and said, "And now, I will go and see my attorney." Hearing no objection, I walked out of the room and told Dick Leon what had just happened. Dick was far more objective in his analysis of what I described to him than I was. He was also familiar with the ways of lawyers. He told me that what I saw as a personal affront, may have been designed for another purpose. He did express his pleasure with my brief statement to the grand jury.

I returned to the grand jury and the Office of Special Review team of Michael J. Shaheen, Jr. There was a noticeable difference in the room. My previous inquisitor was then silent. Another Assistant U.S. Attorney asked a question or two in a friendlier tone, and it went around the room. Other Assistant U. S. Attorneys either asked a question or demurred. Two or three grand jurors asked questions. None of the questions were in any way related to the previous line of questioning. Then Shaheen asked a question. He asked it in a most gentle and seemingly helpful manner and I answered it quickly, too quickly. Even though I had given him a truthful answer, I would realize an hour or two later that it was a loaded question, and had I answered it any other way it would have caused me much grief. My testimony ended. The grand jury took their lunch break. I don't remember being reminded that I remained under subpoena. It may have happened, although that would be my last appearance before the grand jury.

Dick Leon and I had lunch at the Holiday Inn before returning to Tulsa. The dining room was full of the now familiar faces of the grand jurors. We ate quickly. Dick Leon remembered that he had left his Wall Street Journal in the federal building so he left to retrieve it, while I settled the lunch tab. Our rental car was parked in a public parking garage across the street and Dick would meet me there.

The Holiday Inn in Fort Smith has an atrium, from which all rooms face the center, including the public rooms. The dining room is sunken a couple of feet below the lobby level. There is an abundance of tropical plants ringing the dining room at lobby level. Leaving the dining room en route to the main lobby entrance, something caught my eye and instantly aroused my curiosity. A television camera was placed behind one of the tropical plants. When I saw it I was maybe six feet away from it. Two of the waitresses in the dining room spotted the camera about the same time that I did. Reflecting the age that we live in, they made a bee-line for it. They began to ask the camera man questions. "Are we going to be on TV? Did you get our picture? What station are you from? When will this be shown?" Their broad smiles reflected their pleasure at the prospect of them and their friends sharing this momentary celebrity. The cameraman's answers, however, told me that the object of his attention was not the working girls. He told them, as I stood transfixed, that he had been filming from the fourth floor for the past hour and he had just moved to the lobby area. He didn't know where the film was destined for; he had only been told to go and film the restaurant during lunch.

My experience narrowed the possibilities to two. Either the Office of Special Review had assigned the camera man to record who was seeing and talking to whom during lunch, or the much more likely possibility that it was a network feed, planned to embarrass the super villain, Richard Mellon Scaife, on the evening news. Anyone leaving the Isaac C. Parker federal building for lunch was likely to be there. Which of the two possibilities was the authentic one remains a mystery, but it was for naught. Dick Scaife did not dine at the Holiday Inn that day. Maybe he packed his lunch before he left Pittsburgh or the galley on his custom built DC-9 was filled with gourmet delights.

Earlier, when explaining how Karen Gullo, of the Associated press, had given away the identity of her source, Caryn Mann, I promised to explain how another reporter had outdone her. Now is the time.

The malodorous Murry Waas (literally, as well as figuratively, I am told) was working overtime to try to get information about the grand jury and those who had appeared before it. In a strange way, his efforts in that respect were a compliment to the secrecy being maintained by the Shaheen team. Twice in October, Waas had phoned Steve Boynton's lawyer, Frank W. Dunham, Jr., of the firm Cohen, Gettings & Durham in Arlington, Virginia. He had pressed Frank Dunham for information about whether Steve Boynton had been before the grand jury. In his first call, Waas had told Dunham of documentation in his possession from *The American Spectator* and he had tried to trade that information for more information about Steve's grand jury appearance.

In the second call, on October 16, 1998, Waas pressed Dunham for confirmation, either affirmatively or negatively, that Steve had or had not appeared before the grand jury. Waas was making the assumption that Steve Boynton had not appeared before the grand jury, for if he were innocent, he would have done so and would have provided the grand jury with anything that they wanted to know. Of course, Steve Boynton had cooperated with the grand jury as only an innocent person would. but Frank Dunham would neither confirm or deny his appearance to Waas. Dunham did, however, remind Waas about his earlier promise to send documents to him and that he had not done so. Dunham left the door open for reconsideration if Waas would make good his offer to supply the documents. Waas expressed concern that the documents would reveal his sources at *The American Spectator*.

Of course, a review of the documents could help Dunham better understand what the investigation was all about.

In a blink, Murray Waas chose the expedient over the ethical, packaged the "goods", and sent them to Frank. And they did give away the sources. I don't suggest that Murray had received the material directly from the sources because those materials found their way into many hands. Who got them first is unimportant. Where they originated was clear, as was the motive driving their disclosure.

Murray Waas didn't send everything that he had. But, there was one piece of information that could only have come from one source. But don't worry, Murray; Geraldo Rivera used it on one of his programs. It was the hand-written ledger of Steve Boynton's that I had provided to one person and one person only. And I had asked Ronald E. Burr to treat it as confidential information when I handed it directly to him. At the time I had no reason to suspect that he would do otherwise. There was nothing out of the ordinary in the ledger, but for troublemakers trying to create maximum suspicion, it was temporarily beneficial to them. Ironically, those same paragons who had spent a lifetime railing against government waste, had themselves contributed to a witch-hunt that had cost the government $millions. The cost to their employer, *The American Spectator*, wasn't insignificant either. Their delusions raise serious questions about their judgment, their worth, and their honor. I don't include loyalty; that question has already been answered. They had accepted their paychecks without protest, in some instances for decades. When the Office of Independent Counsel (OIC) issued its press release on July 27, 1999, it stated in part, "Many of the allegations, suggestions, and insinuations regarding the tendering and receipt of things of value were shown to be unsubstantiated or, in some cases, untrue." In my memory, nothing that harsh had ever been said about reporting in *The American Spectator*.

CHAPTER THIRTY-FOUR ~
ISOLATION

The year 1998 ended quietly and little had been heard about the investigation by the Office of Special Review. Word had gotten around that Bob Kaiser, a writer for the Washington Post, was preparing to write a major article, one of those multi-part serials that the Post is famous for. It was to be about Richard M. Scaife. I expected to hear from Bob Kaiser any day. That day came on January 20, 1999. We had been hearing, off and on, that the investigation had been completed and that a report was expected soon. Kaiser confirmed those rumors in his call to me. Or at least he thought he did. I was willing to take his call although I did not intend to be interviewed for his article. In what I took to be an attempt at flattery, he told me that we had met during the Westmoreland trial. I did not remember having ever met him and I told him that. I had worked closely with another Washington Post reporter who had covered the Westmoreland story, Eleanor Randolph, now a member of the editorial board of The New York Times. My respect for Eleanor exceeds that of any other journalist that I have known. When I mentioned that to Kaiser he told me that he had talked to Eleanor about me. I was pleased to hear that. He explained to me that he had been doing exhaustive research for a story that he was writing about Dick Scaife and said he would like to ask me about "The Arkansas Project." I explained to him that I had decided to remain silent during the investigation, but that I would have plenty to say after it was concluded. For the record, I am saying it now.

Bob Kaiser told me that he had talked to Shaheen and had been told by him that the investigation was over. He said that he expected the report to be out by the end of January. Because that was so soon, that he would wait and try again to interview me after the report came out. He also mentioned that he knew one of the judges that Shaheen was reporting to. He planned to talk with him. Kaiser said The Washington Post was expecting a full report and I told him that I shared their interest. I wanted to have the story told to put an end to the lies, distortions and character assassination that had accompanied this story from day one.

I learned that Bob Kaiser was not as well informed as he thought he was. The judges, for whatever their reasons, had read the Shaheen report and then asked for more follow-up work by the investigators. It became obvious to me what at least a part of the follow-up was when Dick Leon called me sometime after my conversation with Bob Kaiser. Dick told me that several of Shaheen's staff wanted to have a conference call with me. I readily accepted that arrangement. It was more convenient than going to their office. Dick Leon was, of course, on the conference call from his office.

The conference lasted for what seemed to me to be more than an hour, and it was primarily about the alleged role of Ted Olson in "The Arkansas Project." I was aware from reading many published accounts that someone was determined to connect Ted to events and activities that simply had not occurred. But, Olson's friendship with Kenneth Starr and his brief representation of David Hale was too tempting for the "Dream Weavers" to ignore. As we have seen, "insinuations and suggestions" can take these investigations a very long way. Gene Lyons even tied Ted Olson in as co-author of Bob Tyrrell's bestselling book, "The Impeachment of William Jefferson Clinton", the prophetic novel by Tyrrell and Anonymous. No, Lyons, it was not Olson. Try a former White House aide who knew the law and had worked there during an earlier impeachment. Ok, try William Safire or Vic Gold.

The end of that conference call was the end of my contact with the Office of Special Review. One of the Assistant U.S. Attorneys who was on the conference call told me that they were sorry for the inconvenience of the call. I told him that it was not an inconvenience to me, that it had to be done, and I understood that. Altogether, those people had conducted themselves in a very professional manner, as far as I could tell.

There would be a lot of waiting before we would get the final results. During this time the strain of not being able to resume normal communication with friends was suffocating. I received notice from my telephone company that my phone records had been subpoenaed for a period of time subsequent to my grand jury testimony. These things are oppressive and lead to speculation about how far a corrupt government will intrude into the lives of supposedly free men. I did have the opportunity to talk to a former United States Attorney, then a member of congress, about being cut off from my friends. He told me that it was by design, a tool of prosecutors. Guilt by association?

[According to Google's service, Bob Kaiser retired from the Washington Post in 2014. Noting that he is not much younger than I am, I'm pleased that he is retired and I hope he is in good health. I also hope he reads this book.]

In just a few words, the press release from the OIC described what was at play. "...many of the allegations [and there were many], suggestions [a favorite word for some journalists trying to link dark motives to simple actions], and insinuations [they did it, don't ask me how, but they did it] regarding the tendering and receipt of things of value were shown to be unsubstantiated [where's the proof?] or, in some cases, untrue." Well, now we finally have a crime. It is illegal to give false statements to the FBI. It is also illegal to give false sworn testimony (perjury) to a grand jury, or to a federal team of investigators. Who did? When is their trial to start? When can we testify against them?

There are so many questions to be asked and answered. Will the future of this country offer the promise to the yet unborn that it had to my generation? That troubles me because my generation responded to hope and promise more than it did to stark reality. We believed that things would get better, and because we believed they
would, they did. Our families were our hope, and our friends were our treasures. Sacrifice was a noble undertaking, and expected of each citizen in the darkest hours faced by this young nation. Roosevelts and Churchill's inspired millions by their words and deeds. Because of their accomplishments, the world was rid of many of the impediments to a better life. The better life was the national ambition of the post-World War II generation, and for the most part, it was realized. There were inequities remaining in our society, but in the generosity of the

American spirit, they were addressed, and in time, largely alleviated. The great black underclass emerged and slowly flourished by the force of their will, and the rightness of their cause. And their accomplishments would be diminished by the emulation of less deserving groups, who shrouded themselves in the garment of "civil rights." An industry arose the grievance community, whose actions delayed the acceptance by the majority, of the real injustices committed against the American Black.

Now, may I posit that my friends who endured this series of events with me are above reproach? That they, too, were maligned and subjected to ridicule? And may I apologize to the American taxpayer for the $millions of dollars that this exercise costs them? I feel that I must because they will not receive it from those whose oaths of office require that they protect the interests of the public. And isn't it natural, in this "new age" to apologize for the actions of others? Confession, it is said, if good for the soul. Especially, if you confess the sins of others, rather than your own.

CHAPTER THIRTY-FIVE ~
HUNTING

It is Sunday, April 9, 2000, and those of us who awakened early in Northern Virginia found snow on the ground. Through much of the northeast, there was substantial snow, far more than we observed here. High winds and falling temperatures yesterday had wreaked havoc on the Master's Tournament in Augusta, Georgia, and a phone call last night from a friend in New Orleans had informed me that the cooling weather pattern was affecting them.

I mention this only to let the reader know of the progression of my story. It was a good day to curl up with newspapers, and later, to open a book that I had set aside to read, but did not want to read until I had finished my story.

"The Hunting of The President," Joe Conason and Gene Lyons' book, published by St. Martin's Press and released in early 2000 has received many favorable reviews by left-wing partisans, from Sidney Blumenthal on the Amazon.com web pages to The Arkansas Times, a small weekly. Their uniform praise most often congratulates the authors for their "truth" at last. Some reviewers who take issue with the book even get nasty phone calls from Conason, who usually accuses them of having not read the book. Another tactic of Conason and Lyons is their repetitious boast of the documentation that they so fastidiously include in their "Sources" section, beginning on page 375. But wait. Is it documentation or verification that we are looking for? It is a simple matter to document a lie once it has appeared in print, but to verify the truthfulness of a claim is an altogether different standard. Conason and Lyons point out in their acknowledgments that they relied heavily on the previous work of others "...most notably Murray S. Waas, whose intrepid investigations guided so much of our own reporting." And in their preface they decry "...*the abuse of criminal prosecution to resolve political disputes...*" followed by this delightful paragraph, which deserves analysis:

"It is also the story of important journalists and news

organizations succumbing to scandal fever, *credulously and sometimes dishonestly* promoting charges against the Clintons in heavily biased, *error-filled dispatches, columns, bestselling books, and TV news specials*, and thus bestowing "mainstream" prestige upon what was often little more than a *poisonous mixture of half-truths and partisan malice..."*

I have added emphasis to show that what they decry, they also use. Since I and some of my friends are cited repeatedly in their book, I wish to add, *untruths and partisan malice* to their mixture. And now I will prove it.

The authors, still in the preface, make reference to what they refer to as an influential 1994 profile in the *New York Times Magazine* by Michael Kelly. Their selection of passages from Kelly's profile departed momentarily to their own use of this bit of information, "It would later emerge that Kelly had spent much of his time in Arkansas in the company of political operatives employed by a reactionary Pittsburgh tycoon named Richard Mellon Scaife..." Now I must ask, where did it emerge later, and why was I not aware of it. I found no source notes to back up that claim, and must assume that they do not exist. Since neither Steve Boynton nor I have ever met Michael Kelly, and I presume that the authors were referring to us as "political operatives" there appears to be a problem here. They continued their dissection of Kelly's profile, writing, "...the article went so far as to claim that "Arkansas is not really a democracy." Rather it was a benighted rural fiefdom where a tiny, incestuous elite "holds sway over a small and politically disorganized middle class and a large but well-beaten population of the poor." But they seem to confirm Kelly's point just five pages after the preface ended when they write about the Stephens brothers, Jack and Witt. "Unlike his older brother Witt, a traditional conservative southern Democrat who had run Arkansas like a country store during the six terms of segregationist governor Orval Faubus, Jack was quite literally a country-club Republican..."

"The Hunting of The President" is filled with people that I have never met, and covers areas that I have no knowledge of, but in a great deal of it, I am infinitely more knowledgeable than the authors. The story and the stories began on page 105. The authors' report a trip made by Steve Boynton to Pittsburgh on November 12, 1993. Like a John Gresham novel, they track Steve Boynton breathlessly, "...Stephen S. Boynton took a taxi from his home in Vienna, Virginia, to Washington National Airport and flew from there to Pittsburgh. Ten days earlier, David Hale's accusations about President Clinton's role in an illegal loan scheme had broken in the *Washington Post* and *The New York Times*. Only the previous evening, NBC *Nightly News* had explicitly linked Hale's allegation to the Vince Foster suicide, setting off a cascade of speculation in Washington newsrooms."

"Traveling on confidential *Spectator business,* Boynton's destination was the Mellon Bank building downtown, and specifically the thirty-ninth floor offices of the Sarah Scaife and Carthage Foundations. That is where Richard Larry oversaw the charitable and educational interests of Richard Mellon Scaife, heir to the Mellon banking, oil, and steel fortune. (In their book they could have told of a similar journey to the same location by Steve Kangas. That would have really rivaled John Grisham.) *Boynton knew Dick Larry well, as a friend and fellow sportsman...*"

Although Conason and Lyons cite Boynton in their source notes, and quote him in those notes, "...We've fished together many times.", the facts are somewhat different. Conason obtained that quote from Steve Boynton in 1998 as he was preparing a story, mentioned earlier, for The New York Observer. By 1998 Steve Boynton and Dick Larry had come to know each other quite well, but on November 12, 1993, they were meeting for only the second time. The first had been a few weeks earlier, as guests of mine on a fishing trip. Lyons and Conason report that "...*a few days later*, Boynton took another flight this time to Little Rock. In Arkansas, he had dinner with Parker Dozhier..." The story continues with a description of Dozhier's bait shop, on Lake Catherine, as a "Resort." The "few days later" that they had referred to in describing Steve Boynton's trip to Little Rock, had actually been November 19, 1993, and he had not been alone. And, the trip had not been for the purpose of having dinner with Dozhier. I was taking Steve

Boynton to introduce him to David Hale and to meet Randy Coleman, Hale's lawyer. Contrary to the assertion on page 111 that I had renewed my relationship with David Hale through Boynton and Dozhier, it was exactly the opposite. And in the Alice in Wonderland fashion of this book, "The Hunting of The President", black would continue to be portrayed as white, and of course, up would be down.

It continues, "On November 22, according to telephone records, Boynton received a call from Hale himself." Of course, he did. We had given him our phone numbers when we were in Little Rock the previous Saturday. "That was the first of a flurry of calls from Hale to the offices and homes of both Boynton and David W. Henderson, Vice President and director of *The American Spectator* Educational Foundation."

That last sentence is both redundant and incorrect. Redundant, since both Steve Boynton and I maintained offices in our homes and incorrect since I was a director of *The American Spectator*. I did not become Vice President until July 1997. Then I was no longer a director. But why nit-pick? There are far more weighty matters to deal with in this polemic.

On page 109 a meeting at Ted Olson's law offices is mentioned... "Sometime during that same period, Boynton and Henderson attended a meeting at the Washington Law offices of Gibson, Dunn & Crutcher. Their host was Theodore B. Olson..." "...That day Ted Olson agreed to join David Hale's defense team." That is as false as George Washington's teeth. As I have stated earlier, David Hale had two meetings with Ted Olson in 1994 before reaching an agreement to have Ted represent him before congress. Ted had nothing to do with his defense in Federal or State matters.

One page later steam came out of my ears when I read the two paragraphs at the bottom of the page:

"But Boynton did have important connections, particularly through his hunting and fishing buddies Dave Henderson and Dick Larry. Boynton and Henderson had known Larry for well over a decade, dating back at least to the celebrated libel case brought by General William Westmoreland against CBS News in the early 1980's. Larry's boss Scaife had secretly funded the bulk of Westmoreland's $3 million legal expenses, including the cost of hiring Henderson to handle public relations for the retired general. Boynton had played a supporting legal role in the case, which ended in a victory for CBS. In the years since, Henderson and Boynton had often fished and hunted on Maryland's Eastern Shore with Dick Larry. Henderson had eventually joined Westmoreland on *The American Spectator* Educational Foundation's board of directors."

I must deal with this paragraph before I continue, for in it, the authors' badly overreach. And, they even identify me as a source. [p.110] "Boynton and Henderson had known Larry..." Author's interviews with Boynton and Henderson." I have talked with Joe Conason exactly once, on February 3, 1998. I told him that I knew David Hale, and how I had come to know him. Nothing else. I have never talked with Gene Lyons.

Practically every sentence in those two paragraphs is wrong, either through ignorance or intent. And, in spite of my distaste for these writers, I do not believe either of them to be ignorant. That is my last compliment to them. Each of them, in their own way, had pushed for the investigation of "The Arkansas Project." They started writing this book, "The Hunting of The President," hoping to take credit for the outcome. When the investigation ended in exoneration, they relegated it to a footnote in their book.

Specifically, though Steve Boynton and I are hunting and fishing buddies, the same was not true of Dick Larry. I, but not Steve Boynton, had fished, but not hunted with Dick Larry prior to the fall of 1993. I, but not Steve Boynton, had known Dick Larry for more than a decade (it is now three decades) and in the years since the Westmoreland case I had fished many times with Dick Larry, as I had before the Westmoreland case, but Steve Boynton was never with us before the fall of 1993. There is a reason why I have never hunted with Dick Larry. He does not hunt. And I did not eventually join Westmoreland on the Board of Directors of *The American Spectator* Educational Foundation, since it was I who invited him, on behalf of the board, to join me there. I save the most egregious untruth in that paragraph for last. I was paid by no one to handle public relations for General Westmoreland. For more than three years I contributed my services to him, and that is a fact that has been widely documented, and may I say, is verifiable. Lexus/Nexis is a wonderful, if expensive, tool.

I can cite many news articles and books that contemporaneously reported that fact, but since I am not going to serve as a researcher or fact checker for Lyons and Conason, I will get them started by directing their attention to a front page article in The New York Times, written by Peter W. Kaplan. To narrow their search, it was published on Tuesday, October 23, 1984, and the title of the article was, "Public Relations a facet of Westmoreland Trial." Some of the books include; *WESTMORELAND A Biography of General William C. Westmoreland*, by Samuel Zaffiri, William Morrow New York, *A Matter of Honor*, by Don Kowet, New York: Macmillian, *Vietnam on Trial,* By Bob Brewin and Sidney Shaw. New York: Atheneum, *Beyond Malice,* by Richard M. Clurman. Transaction Books: New Brunswick (USA) and Oxford (UK), Renata Adler's *Reckless Disregard,* Knopf, 1986, and Peter Boyer's *Who Killed CBS?* Random House, New York. Each of these resources could have helped Conason and Lyons to better understand and report accurately the events concerning Westmoreland v. CBS.

The second paragraph that I referred to at the bottom of page 110 is an illustration of their technique of implying guilt by association, but in this case, there was no association. "Equally significant were Boynton and Henderson's connections in Arkansas. Jim Johnson knew and trusted both men, having met them through Parker Dozhier years earlier. Say what? Neither Steve Boynton nor I have ever seen, met or spoken to Jim Johnson. I do know why these authors tried to make the association, however. Jim Johnson is characterized as a segregationist throughout the book, and they have evidence to support that characterization. They are inferring... through this ill-concealed ploy... to cast both Boynton and me as racists. The strongest weapon in the left-wing arsenal was aimed at us... and it missed. But they keep trying. On the very next page, in an obvious attempt at reinforcing the connection, they continue, "Through Boynton, Henderson too had met Jim Johnson and Parker Dozhier. Oddly, Henderson had known David Hale in a different context for many years. Back when Hale had presided over the national Jaycees in the early 1970's, Henderson had served as the civic group's executive director. Through Boynton and Dozhier, he said, they had renewed their old friendship..." Here, too, they get it all wrong, and even put quotes in my mouth. "Through Boynton and Dozhier, he said, they had renewed their old relationship." He said it to whom? I am not in the habit of lying to myself or others, and had I said that I would have been doing both. When David Hale was President of The United States Jaycees I was living in Northern Virginia and I was never executive director of the U.S. Jaycees, though I had served in that position for the Virginia Jaycees in the late 1960's. I had met David Hale while I was on the staff of The United States Jaycees before he became the National President. As to my supposed meeting with Jim Johnson, it was through Dozhier on page 110 and through Boynton on page 111. In an earlier age, Conason's and Lyon's teachers would have looked them up and spanked them. In the one time that Joe Conason talked to me, about one subject, he had an opportunity to at least get that right, and he blew it. Or did he blow it off?

On page 125 in an account of the Paula Jones case, citing Caryn Mann as their source, they offer this:

"Apparently, word went out in right-wing circles that Jones needed help, because at some point that spring Stephen Boynton and David Henderson, the duo directing the Scaife-funded Arkansas Project, tried to find her better legal assistance. Their eagerness to assist her was a sign that Traylor's threat to sue *The American Spectator* had been hollow. The little Rock lawyer, in over his head, hadn't realized that his client's right-wing sponsors would never approve such a lawsuit.

It was during a fishing trip on the Chesapeake Bay that Boynton and Henderson--joined by their associate Parker Dozhier and their benefactor, Richard Larry, the Scaife Foundation executive--placed a series of calls to Republican lawyers and conservative organizations seeking additional counsel for Jones. Dozhier's ex-girlfriend, Caryn

Mann, recalled that on the fishing trip, "They wore out the batteries on six cell phones trying to find someone, but didn't do much fishing."

May 8, 1994, was a Sunday, and it was also Mother's Day. Conason and Lyons report on page 125 that 8 May 1994 was the filing deadline in the Paula Jones lawsuit and that Gilbert Davis and Joseph Cammarata had met it. Would they do that on Mother's Day? Of course not. It had been filed in the United States District Court for the Eastern District of Arkansas Western Division on Friday, May 6, 1994.

My memory of the cell phone burn-out fishing trip referred to by the authors, and enhanced by the mystical powers of Caryn Mann, differed. So do the photographs taken of that trip that in and of themselves are revealing, both for what they show and what they don't show. What they don't show is Dick Larry. Parker Dozhier joins the list of those who have not fished with Dick Larry. On board Captain Mike Harris' boat, "Compensation", on that particular trip were Parker Dozhier, Bob Tyrrell, Patrick Tyrrell, Steve Boynton and his stepson, Chris Strong and me. The pictures also show the fish that we caught while we "didn't do much fishing." That trip was on the actual date that the Paula Jones suit was filed. Yes, some cell phone battery power was expended in calls to Little Rock to ascertain that the suit had been filed. It was a newsworthy occurrence and we were in the news business.

Page 169 has Steve Boynton and me bringing Terry Reed to the offices at *The American Spectator* to "tell his amazing revelations." We met Reed there, but we didn't bring him there. Someone else must take credit for that. Steve and I were at the magazine's office when an employee of *The American Spectator* came and asked if we would like to meet Terry Reed. Since I had labored through his painfully constructed book, "Compromised", I did want to meet him. We were led to Ron Burr's office to meet him. I don't remember Ron having been there.

Then, in the following paragraph, Rex Armistead is introduced. Rex is a private investigator whom Steve Boynton and I used and this is how Conason and Lyons say we found him. "Boynton and Henderson had engaged the services of Rex Armistead, a sixty-five-year-old private

detective recommended by their trusted adviser, Justice Jim Johnson."
They just don't quit. The reality is that a businessman from Mississippi,
who had dealings with Steve Boynton on wildlife concerns suggested
that we talk to Rex Armistead, and in good old boy humor, said that if
Rex told him that the sun wouldn't rise in the morning, he would go out
and buy batteries. Steve and I traveled to Lula, Mississippi to meet Rex.
We spent most of a day with him and concluded that he would be an
asset to our team. He was.

In just three more pages comes another whopper, this time
supposedly based on the notes and memory of David Brock.
"Armistead's costly investigative efforts for the Arkansas Project
focused largely upon Mena and the death of Vince Foster, according to
David Brock, who met with the detective at an airport hotel in Miami
during the winter of 1995. For two days the young writer sat listening
and taking notes as Armistead, Henderson, Boynton and Tyrrell
discussed their theories about the Foster and Mena cases. The short
version was that Armistead had spent a small fortune, traveling as far as
Belize and Costa Rica, without producing evidence that implicated
Clinton in any wrongdoing at the rural airport or anywhere else. As they
talked, Brock recalled, Armistead occasionally dropped a racist remark.
Henderson and Boynton didn't seem to notice. They thought Armistead
'was great', but he struck me as a shady character. Actually, I thought
they were all putting on a show for Bob, to make the money they were
spending look worthwhile..."

Here is the issue of the money we were spending again." Much
has been made of it in the press as well as with some former Spectator
employees." That issue was not an issue with the donor. Our
relationship was solid, based on many years of mutual trust and
friendship. After I left the US Jaycees I had occasion to recommend
funding for others on several occasions and my recommendations were
usually met favorably. I never sought anything for myself, and when I
sent Steve Boynton to Pittsburgh to meet with Dick Larry I had no
intention of being a part of the project other than to be a sounding
board for Steve Boynton. Upon Steve's return, he informed me that Dick

Larry wanted me to be involved. At that point, we all thought it was going to be about issues affecting our wildlife interests. It was after I learned through a story in the Washington Post that David Hale was the Special Counsels' (Robert Fiske) chief witness in the Whitewater Investigation that the focus changed overnight. I understood that money was not an issue, nor did it ever come up between the donor and me. I knew exactly where we stood.

Yes, David Brock was invited to attend the meeting so inaccurately reported here. I personally asked him to go and we traveled together, to Orlando, Florida, not Miami. I still had faith in David at the time but realize now that it was a misplaced faith. He was the only American Spectator writer who ever met or talked at any length to Rex Armistead, and it was my mistake that he had. Bob Tyrrell had once stopped by the table where Rex was having dinner with Steve Boynton, me and another friend. It was at the Hyatt Regency Hotel, on New Jersey Avenue in Washington D. C. We introduced Bob to Rex and he briefly visited and parted for another meeting. It was the first...and, next to last time that Bob Tyrrell would ever see Rex Armistead. He had once hitched a ride from Armistead to the Little Rock airport after interviewing sources in Arkansas. Bob was not present at the meeting in Orlando, and neither was Steve Boynton. So the whole premise of the story is shot. Since Bob Tyrrell was not there, how could we have been "putting on a show" for him? And since Steve Boynton was not there, he couldn't have sat impassively through Armistead's racist remarks. This selective augmentation of fact with fiction may play well with the left-wing, but it will not wash with me. There was, however, someone there who should have been in Brock's notes, because it was he whom we had gone to see. His name was John Hull, the Indiana native, who owned a very famous ranch in Costa Rica. It was used by Oliver North's Nicaraguan Contra operation, and the reason for Rex Armistead's trip to Central America.

Then on page 173, "...Soon after the Miami conference, Brock decided to avoid the Kerry piece [the hit-piece the absent Tyrrell had supposedly commissioned in Miami but was, in reality, Orlando.] and any assignments related to the Arkansas Project, or Rex Armistead." "...If Brock, Plesczynski, and most of their colleagues weren't buying Armistead's goods, other journalists were. Ambrose Evans-Pritchard of the London Sunday Telegraph and Micah Morrison of the Wall Street Journal editorial page both spent considerable time at Parker Dozhier's bait shop picking up leads and documents." "...The few Spectator staffers like Brock who spent any time in Arkansas eventually realized that the project's material was turning up in other publications."

Ahem. So Brock validates my earlier claim that he was exercising editorial judgments over Plesczynski. He was avoiding any assignments related to the Arkansas Project. Remind me again, who was wasting the magazine's money? Then Brock "realized that the project's material was turning up in other publications." My God, how awful. Other editors with different views about what was newsworthy? The stories were there and The American Spectator had all the opportunity in the world to use them, but fits of pique prevented their use. No story remains under wrap forever. Finally, if reporters were going to Dozhier's to get information about Rex Armistead's "goods" they went to the wrong place. Dozhier and Armistead had no connection.

The Kerry piece referred to by Brock was not a piece, although I acknowledge that the Kerry Hearings [Iran-Contra hearings chaired by Senator John Kerry in 1986 during which John Hull had participated] had been discussed, but the discussions were based on John Hull's personal experiences, not Armistead's research. Ironically Salon Magazine had reported on Kerry's hearings and they were certainly relevant to drug smuggling. If Tyrrell had discussed Kerry with Brock, it would not have been in Orlando, I state redundantly because R. Emmett Tyrrell Jr. was not with us at our Florida meeting. By Brock's own admission, if properly quoted by Conason and Lyons, he did just what pleased him for his $170,000 salary, and little more.

In early 1986, the 42-year-old Massachusetts Democrat stood almost alone in the U.S. Senate demanding answers about the emerging evidence that CIA-backed Contras were filling their coffers by collaborating with drug traffickers then flooding U.S. borders with cocaine from South America.

The authors trot out Caryn Mann again on page 174 to concoct this scenario: "Parker Dozhier, however, was very jealous and angry about Armistead, because when Rex was hired, P.D. went into rages, [saying] Armistead was getting money he should be getting. Logic is missing here, and we must find it. Parker Dozhier ran a bait shop twelve months of the year, seven days each week, from very early to very late. Rex Armistead had his own airplane, and he is a professional investigator. Each of them had a role to play. Much has been made of Dozhier's role in this episode and though it was of value, his was not the central role. He provided hospitality to us when we visited and kept us informed of developments in Arkansas, particularly in the media when we were out of state. But, his worms and his customers required his presence.

Digressing to page 166, "But according to Caryn Mann, Parker Dozhier told her that he and Henderson had tried to bolster this fresh support for Hale. She claims that Dozhier told her they had debriefed Brown in a motel room while Hale sat in an adjacent room, providing questions as Dozhier went back and forth. Unable to offer a specific date for the meeting, Mann cannot be certain whether Henderson and Dozhier were trying to prepare Brown for his testimony..." Here the authors were describing the testimony of former Arkansas State Trooper and member of Governor Clinton's security detail, Lawrence Douglas "LD" Brown.

James Ring Adams wrote many articles about various aspects of Whitewater for *The American Spectator,* and he worked very closely with Steve Boynton and me. In Adams' first and lengthy article, published in February 1994, he quoted David Hale describing a chance encounter with then Governor Bill Clinton on the steps of the

Arkansas State Capitol Building. Hale had said that while he stood outside waiting for a ride, the Governor had approached him and had asked if he was going to be able to help them out? According to Hale's account, the governor was making reference to a loan that he later made to Susan McDougal. Though the Adams article was in the

February issue of *The American Spectator*, it was based on interviews Adams had with Hale in late 1993 and January 1994.

L.D. Brown was in the offices of *The American Spectator* being interviewed by Danny Wattenburg for a story that would become the cover story in a later edition. Brown read Adams' article and commented to someone on the staff of *The American Spectator* that he had witnessed that chance encounter between Hale and Clinton. Though I had not met Brown at the time, his comments were passed along to me. In a later meeting in Little Rock, I had told David Hale that there was someone, whom I would not identify, who claimed to have witnessed the brief encounter between him and Clinton. With no hesitation and the hint of a smile, Hale asked, "What are his initials?" I didn't reply, but his question told me enough.

There was a meeting in a hotel between "L.D." Brown, me, and Parker Dozhier. It was at the Holiday Inn in North Little Rock. It was the first and only meeting between the three of us, and to the best of my knowledge, it was the only time Brown and Dozhier ever met. I had, by then, met Brown and his wife, Becky on several occasions. The meeting in North Little Rock was many months after I had first met the Browns. Bob Tyrrell was working on a story using L.D. Brown as a source. Brown had told us of supporting documents in his possession that he was willing to share, but he was unwilling to let them out of his control. We reached a compromise. Parker Dozhier had been a professional photographer. I arranged, with Brown's consent, to have Dozhier bring camera and lights to the Holiday Inn to photograph the documents. That was it, pure and simple. The roll of film was delivered to *The American Spectator*, developed, and the contents appeared in Bob Tyrrell's book, "Boy Clinton."

Mention was also made, on page 181 in "The Hunting of The President" that L. D. Brown had received some $5,000 dollars paid through Tom Golden for unspecified services. That was an act of true compassion on the part of Bob Tyrrell, and it happened while I worked at *The American Spectator* in 1997. L. D. was unemployed at the time and seeking work. Bob called a few friends in an effort to assist L. D. He raised $5000 and Brown was employed to do research in Little Rock.

In the Conason-Lyons account of the events leading to Ron Burr's firing, they are very revealing with this sentence on page 314, "He eventually took the deal and has never spoken publicly about the Arkansas Project or *The American Spectator* since." Their use of the adverb, publicly, is no doubt their idea of an inside joke. How did so many of his misleading or inaccurate documents and memo's get into their hands? "The Hunting of The President" variously refers to Burr as Tyrrell's partner and Publisher, as on page 103. Then on page 314, "...Tyrrell had made it perfectly plain that he wanted Burr to vacate the post he had held for thirty years." Although Ron Burr had joined the *Alternative* two years after its founding and had held various administrative positions over the years, he would first be listed on the magazine's masthead as publisher in the April 1978 issue, and then it was a shared role with John Von Kannon. From June 1979-March 1980, Burr was listed on the masthead as General Manager, with John Von Kannon as Publisher. One news account, published elsewhere, identified Burr as "founding publisher." Though Burr had been an important employee at the magazine for two years after Tyrrell founded it, it was only after his firing that he became "co-founder."

Today, April 11, 2000, Joe Conason is again on the attack. In the familiar Salon Magazine, he punches back at other reviews of his book. His main target is Neil Lewis of The New York Times, but he makes a small detour, to The Washington Post. Each of those publications has reviewed "The Hunting of The President" as fairly and accurately as their information at the time of publication would allow them to, though Joe Conason believes otherwise. In his crybaby manner, he throws his rattle at the Post for having Jim Bowman, a writer for *The American Spectator*, review "The Hunting of The President." "...The same was true of the Washington Post, whose book editor actually assigned the book review to a writer from *The American Spectator*--the conservative monthly that consorted with billionaire Richard Mellon Scaife in the Byzantine "get Clinton" scheme known as the "Arkansas Project--events we described in all their comical detail." Well, OK, it was comical. Not the events themselves, but the way you described them.

This book was reviewed on Amazon.com website. The overwhelming majority of those reviews are rave reviews. Amazon.com helpfully reports that "Customers who bought titles by Joe Conason also bought titles by these authors: James Carville, Jeffrey Toobin, Molly Ivins, J. H. Hatfield, and Jim Hightower.

Amazon.com allows customers to review its books on their pages and the people who have bought titles by the authors just mentioned, mostly, applaud the efforts of Conason and Lyons, and take what they have written at face value. Here is a sampling of review titles: excellent the real truth, It's not the sex, it's the fascism, True Blue Liberalism at Its Best, Scandal of Scandal's, The Truth Comes out, What journalism is all about, Conspiracy against us, This important book will make you mad, and it should, A season of Treason, tell me lies, tell me right wingers' lies, scary, A Pulitzer, please, A CANCER ON THE JUDICIARY, Hillary found her authors, A Godsend!, I Lived to See It!, required Reading, Finally, the Truth, A TRUE VIEW OF WHITEWATER, ETC., Any fair-minded person will see the truth of this book., Named sources, documentation--what a concept!, Great Nonfiction, Great journalism, The truth shall set us free!, AT LAST SOMEONE HAS THE COURAGE TO PRESENT THE TRUTH, The Best Book of the Year 2000, Unimpeachable, A fantastic insight, Finally, the Truth.

Maybe ten of the reviews didn't offer sufficient praise, or perhaps they actually took objection to the findings in the book. The thin-skinned Conason responded:

"Our Book is Carefully Documented"

"We greatly appreciate the interest in our book shown by Amazon customers. But in a few of the reviews posted here, our research and even our truthfulness has been questioned. Although it would be miraculous if there were no errors in "The Hunting of The President," we did make every effort to check facts. Unlike some current nonfiction authors, we also provide copious source citations, both in the text and in 27-page end notes."

It is worth repeating, there is a substantial difference between documentation and verification. Documents themselves, such as some of the news articles relied upon by Conason and Lyons, can, and often do, contain distortions, half-truths, untruths, shaded truth, and even honest mistakes. Much of the documentation that the authors cite come from Associated Press articles by Karen Gullo, David Brock's unreliable notes, the flawed reporting by Greg Gordon and Tom Hamburger in the Minneapolis Star-Tribune, and the vendetta laced reporting of Murray Waas in Salon Magazine. Some future writer will cite their book as documentation, and we can see where that leads.

One last thing before we leave this subject. On page 163 in this tendentious book, two people that I know personally, Micah Morrison and Chris Ruddy, get Mann handled. "The more she saw of Dozhier and his Arkansas Project colleagues, however, the less credible she found their stories. (No stranger to speculation, Mann was something [Something?] of an amateur astrologer.) To her there appeared to be a strong element of paranoia and make believe among Dozhier's crowd. Although the guns frightened her, she also found it faintly comical to watch Chris Ruddy and Micah Morrison swaggering around the fishing camp, carrying the semiautomatic pistols Dozhier furnished to them on the pretext that their lives were in danger." Now you know what Conason and Lyons meant when they wrote of "comical detail." Here is one of their comedies. It is a side-splitter. Chris Ruddy has never been to Dozhier's. Micah Morrison has, but it is totally out of character for him to play cowboy, and he certainly was smart enough to realize that there had been no casualties at Dozhier's Bait Shop.

Perhaps Caryn remembers seeing me target shoot a nifty .22 pistol that someone had at Dozhier's on one of my many visits. That is in character for me. I have handled firearms most of my life and I instructed young officers in the United States Air Force in the use of the .38 pistol, which replaced the old service .45. I also shot competitively on an Air Force Rifle Team. And, I have never had an occasion to use a gun defensively or have one loaded in my home. It seems unlikely that a self-described member of a mafia family would have a fear of guns.

I have now spent most of three days with this nonsense and it is time to quit and let others make of the remainder whatever they will. In the relatively few pages that I have addressed there have been an enormous number of distortions, untruths, invented scenes, manipulated associations, and, overall, the kind of "Creative Reporting" that has killed countless newspapers and magazines. I invite the reader to give the same scrutiny to any story published in *The American Spectator*, from its initial Troopergate revelations to its revelations that CIA shipped arms out of Mena Airport in an operation that was corrupted by drug trafficking. *The American Spectator* has never argued that Clinton was involved-- only that he knew about the operation. In "The Hunting of The President", there are slights galore and insinuations too numerous to bother with. I hope that what I have written will illustrate the cause and intent of this overblown book. Assuming that everything else in the book is accurate, and I for one would not, I have demonstrated the lengths to which the authors will go to try to make their heroes, Bill and Hillary Clinton, look good, but as most cats are aware, not everything can be covered up. For conspiracy hunters, these two sound suspiciously...conspiratorial.

The fact that Parker Dozhier met Caryn Mann as a result of the death of his father is clear. It was the hand of fate. Her motives when she came to him months later and initiated an affair are not clear.

The purveyors of the vast-right-wing conspiracy theory suggest that our efforts were super-secret and that they only found out about them because of news accounts, based on Caryn Mann's tales, is laughable. Admittedly, we were as discreet as possible, but we operated on the realistic assumption that our every move was scrutinized. There had been two break-ins at the office of *The American Spectator*, a fact little noticed by the watch-dog press. For years our home telephones did funny things, and I never felt alone.

"She was a real piece of work" according to Jim Peck. "In 1995, Caryn Mann once went ballistic and shrieked that David needed to hide, go to ground, leave Arkansas, and go to Chicago where her friends would hide him and he would never be found." Peck never reported that to the OIC, and in retrospect wonders if perhaps he should have. He was prepared to if any overt efforts were made toward that end. At any rate, Peck was on full alert, and he took steps to minimize the time that David spent at Dozhier's. David was very uncomfortable when she was lurking around trying to intercept conversations

Mann's son, Josh Rand, had many well-documented problems, but I see no use in revealing his juvenile past. I am sure that he was under some pressure from Caryn and he had scores to settle with Parker. Surely Parker remembers Steve Boynton's oft repeated, "Don't get mad at me. I haven't done anything for you." Maybe time will help Josh to see that his role in this debacle was one of shame.

And finally, I quote Jim Peck, again. "She [Caryn Mann] did not come to her decision belatedly as she declared on Geraldo Rivera's television show, 1.5 years after she left Dozhier's. No, she was flying a false flag from day one, trying to screw up the bona fides of the witness, and then when she was told, she "dropped the dime." She wanted to believe that there were vast right-wing sums of money, and she had not been given her percentage. She used her rage about money to believe her own lie."

"From weird questions put to me before and during my grand jury appearance, there must have been some wild and twisted allegation they were trying to evaluate. Putting it all in one question: Did David Hale fabricate evidence in prison, leave Texarkana Federal Prison at night, steal a plane, fly to Hot Springs, pick up Parker Dozhier, fly to Little Rock, drive to southwest Little Rock where a tornado had gone through hours before, place documents in the trunk of an old car marked for salvage, and return that night, undetected to federal prison, to the best of your knowledge...? Serious. Apparently the psychic got twisted by a tornado that struck Little Rock. Dave's lawyer nearly lost his house, his dog, his life, and all of his family in that storm...and he had been on the case for only two weeks. That storm damaged a salvage yard. A car in it was damaged, the trunk was opened and a box of Whitewater-related documents were found inside, having been placed there years ago at Jim McDougal' direction. Pete Yost of the Associated

Press covered that story in depth. The salvage yard owner died under mysterious circumstances not all that long afterward. Being flush with cash, he purchased a new muscle car that went out of control, crashed, and he died of medical complications. A tree did it, as was wryly diagnosed by the botanist."

Some of us were aware that Caryn Mann was telling that story to reporters. Not just to reporters it seems. None of the reporters wrote the story for obvious reasons. I cannot put myself in the minds of the Assistant United States Attorney, or grand juror, who asked those questions of the "country botanist", Jim Peck. If I were a betting man, I would wager that it was to impeach the witness. Enough is enough.

CHAPTER THIRTY-SIX ~
GOOD FRIDAY:BLACK SATURDAY

In my mind, a memoir gives the writer considerable latitude to share reflections on his or her life and experiences. In my case, it has been bittersweet. A memoir offers the opportunity to leave impressions with the reader most favorable to the author. There is an element of that in this book. I do not wish to be defined by people whom I have never met, yet they do have their opinions, based on the information available to them. The reality is, I know me, better than anyone else possibly could. In my case, brutally honest self-appraisal comes rather late in life. We all see imperfect actions and missed opportunities. We are pleased with noble endeavors, however small. We suppress our failings, however large. There have been accomplishments in my life, for which I have been excessively proud and failures that I either didn't recognize or minimalized, at the time. Shame has caused me private pain, the result of bad choices, internalized, but unspoken. I tell the reader this because I recognize that each person's experiences help them to reach conclusions about right and wrong, good and bad, acceptable and unacceptable. I can deceive you, or you can deceive me, but unless we have serious cognitive problems, we cannot deceive ourselves.

Our public lives offer insights into our actions and motives. Wise observers can draw certain insights and conclusions based on those observations. Unwise observers can do the same. Our bias guides our conclusions, and I, like most, possess bias. Therefore, you may accept or reject my conclusions, based on that understanding.

We now know, thanks to Newsweek magazine, that The President of The United States has had access to federal grand jury testimony since September 21, 1993. How fortunate for him. How timely for him. The Department of Justice had provided a memo authorizing him to obtain grand jury testimony for a variety of purposes, and one of those purposes was of paramount interest to Co-Presidents Clinton. A federal grand jury was getting ready to indict David Hale. Who would have a greater interest in knowing what had been presented to his grand jury than the Clintons? On September 22, 1993, the day after the Justice Department's memo authorizing him access to grand jury information, the United States Senate approved President Clinton's appointments of an old law school student, Paula Casey, to the position of United States Attorney in Little Rock, and P. K. Holmes United States Attorney for the western district of Arkansas. The next day, September 23, 1993, the grand jury, in open court indicted David Hale. Were these events random? Did the Clinton Administration use grand jury testimony to leak information to the press? If so, did they blame their enemies for the leaks? I would answer those questions; no, yes and yes. The largest question of all is this: Did the President of The United States have access to grand jury information wherein he was the target of the investigation? Will anyone have the courage to answer that question?

PHOTOGRAPHS AND DOCUMENT COPIES

Standing L to R: General William C. Westmoreland, Charles Wall, G. Ray Arnett, David Henderson, and Steve Boynton. Kneeling: Thomas R. Donnelly, Wilson Reynolds, and Howard Pollock.
   * *See below for more dtail...*

Right to left. Richard M. Larry, Joseph Lackner, the Author Dave Henderson, Paul Kraus and the Skipper.

Professor Jim Peck and his Arkansas minnow

*An evening at Fort Point Point Hunt Club, Chestertown, Maryland. This was in the early days of the Reagan Administration and of the hunt club. Standing Left to Right: General William C. Westmoreland, Charles Wall, New Orleans businessman, G. Ray Arnett, Assistant Secretary of Interior for Fish, Wildlife and Parks and later Executive Vice President of the NRA, David Henderson, co-founder of Fort Point Hunt Club, and Steve Boynton, co-founder of Fort Point Hunt Club. Kneeling: Thomas R. Donnelly, Club member and Assistant Secretary of Health and Human Services, HHS, Wilson Reynolds, Hunt Club guide and manager, and Howard Pollock, former member of Congress from Alaska, and Former President of the NRA.

Peggy Henderson

Author David W. Henderson

Steve Boynton

Rex Armistead holding the
newborn child, Jonathan

Author's grandson, Jonathan T. Kelly

Author Dave Henderson and wife Peggy
with President George H.W. Bush

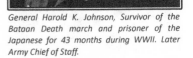

General Harold K. Johnson, Survivor of the
Bataan Death march and prisoner of the
Japanese for 43 months during WWII. Later
Army Chief of Staff.

Republican Nixon loses 18 min of tape and left office; Democrat Hillary erased 30,000 emails and expects to enter office.
Artwork by John Taylor – © 2016

221

Office of the Independent Counsel
Office of Special Review

950 Pennsylvania Avenue, N.W.
Washington, D.C. 20530
(202) 633-1100
Fax (202) 633-1125

July 30, 1998

Re: David Henderson

Please find enclosed a Grand Jury subpoena for your client David Henderson, for which you have agreed to accept service. He is scheduled to appear in Fort Smith, Arkansas, at 9:00 a.m. on August 4, 1998.

Please have your client contact Kim Nicholson, Witness Coordinator, at 202-633-1100 so that she may coordinate travel and hotel arrangements for him. Please be advised that non-Federal employees (military or civilian) are entitled to a $40 witness fee, as well as reimbursement for accommodations in an amount not to exceed $50 for hotel and $30 for meals and incidental expenses. These amounts are payable to your client upon completion of his Grand Jury testimony and the return to this office of all original receipts and the executed Fact Witness Voucher.

Sincerely,

Kimatrell R. Nicholson
Witness Coordinator

Notice of Grand Jury Subpeona to David Henderson by the Office of Special Review, July 1998

AO 110 (Rev. 12/89) Subpoena to Testify Before Grand Jury

United States District Court

WESTERN ——————————— DISTRICT OF —————— ARKANSAS

TO:

David Henderson

SUBPOENA TO TESTIFY
BEFORE GRAND JURY

SUBPOENA FOR:
☒ PERSON   ☒ DOCUMENT(S) OR OBJECT(S)

YOU ARE HEREBY COMMANDED to appear and testify before the Grand Jury of the United States District Court at the place, date, and time specified below.

PLACE	COURTROOM
JUDGE ISAAC C. PARKER FEDERAL BUILDING 6TH & ROGERS STREET FORT SMITH, ARKANSAS	Room 1028
	DATE AND TIME
	August 4, 1998 9:00 a.m.

YOU ARE ALSO COMMANDED to bring with you the following document(s) or object(s):*

(See Subpoena Rider)

☐ *Please see additional information on reverse*

This subpoena shall remain in effect until you are granted leave to depart by the court or by an officer acting on behalf of the court.

CLERK	DATE
CHRISTOPHER R. JOHNSON	
(BY) DEPUTY CLERK	July 30, 1998

This subpoena is issued on application of the United States of America

NAME, ADDRESS AND PHONE NUMBER OF ASSISTANT U.S. ATTORNEY
MICHAEL E. SHAHEEN, COUNSEL
OFFICE OF SPECIAL REVIEW
950 PENNSYLVANIA AVENUE, N.W.,
WASHINGTON D.C.   20530
(202) 633-1100

Subpeona to Testify Before the Grand Jury served to David Henderson by the Office of Special Review, with an appearance date of August 04, 1998

To: David Henderson

SUBPOENA RIDER

All records of any type relating in any way to disbursements made to, or on behalf of, David Hale or members of his family including but not limited to canceled checks, check registers, check stubs, money orders, money order receipts, wire transfers and wire transfer receipts, credit card statements, expense vouchers and receipts.

All records relating in any way to any account at a financial institution (personal or institutional) through or from which any payments or disbursements were made to, or on behalf of, David Hale or members of his family.

All records of any type relating in any way to disbursements made to, or on behalf of, Parker Dozhier, Rex Armistead or Stephen Boynton or members of their families including but not limited to canceled checks, check registers, check copies, check stubs, money orders, money order receipts, wire transfers and wire transfer receipts, credit card statements, expense vouchers and receipts.

All records relating in any way to any account at a financial institution (personal or institutional) through or from which any payments were made to, or on behalf of, Parker Dozhier, Rex Armistead or Stephen Boynton or members of their families.

All records related to receipt of funds from any source used to make payments or disbursements, directly or indirectly, to, or on behalf of, Parker Dozhier, Rex Armistead or Stephen Boynton or members of their families.

All records relating in any way to any account at a financial institution (personal or institutional) into which were deposited, and any funds used to make payments or disbursements to, or on behalf of, Parker Dozhier, Rex Armistead or Stephen Boynton or members of their families.

All records of funds received directly or indirectly from Stephen Boynton, the American Spectator Educational Fund, the American Spectator Magazine, the Carthage Foundation, the Sara Scaife Foundation, the Editorial Enhancement Project (also known as the "Arkansas Project") or Andrew Mellon Scaife or any entity associated with him, including but not limited to records of deposits, expense statements, vouchers and receipts.

All records relating in any way to any account at a financial institution (personal or institutional) into which were deposited, and any funds received directly or indirectly from Stephen Boynton, the American Spectator Educational Fund, the American Spectator Magazine, the Carthage Foundation, the Sara Scaife Foundation, the Editorial Enhancement Project (also known as the "Arkansas Project") or Andrew Mellon Scaife or any entity associated with him.

Subpeona Rider to the Subpeona to Testify Before the Grand Jury set for August 04, 1998

ACKNOWLEDGEMENTS

Shortly after the July 28, 1999, announcement by the Office of Independent Counsel that the Office of Special Review had concluded its investigation of "The Arkansas Project", I began preparations for this book. In late August, my wife Peggy and I journeyed to Arkansas where I introduced her to the state, and I also touched base with an old friend, Jim Peck, a Botany professor at the University of Arkansas - Little Rock. I was aware of his vast insights into the subject matter to be written as well as his formidable trove of documents. I had my own documents, and of course, my own personal recall of events in which I had been personally involved, but I shared my desire to write this book with Jim. His generosity of spirit included the gift of his time, as well as some terrific research on my behalf.

This is my first effort at writing a book, and if it fails it will be due to me, but if it succeeds, much credit goes to others:

Each night, often following twelve hours at the keyboard, Peggy would read my copy, usually after I had gone to bed. I would find her corrections and comments awaiting me in the morning. They were helpful, and in most case, heeded.

My dear little grandson Jonathan soon learned that "Grandad" was not always available to play, but nonetheless, he tried several times each day. I had to restore his deletions on occasion due to his "help", and rename several files that he had changed, but most often he settled for a hug and kiss, then returned to other activities, leaving me to continue my efforts.

Our daughter, Marki Kelly, and her husband Ron each in their own way offered their support and encouragement. Few others knew what I was writing, or even that I was writing.

Above all else, I want them to know that I have been blessed with the friendships and acquaintances named in this book, however, maligned some of them may have been. Particularly, those of Steve Boynton, Bob Tyrrell, Dick Larry, Jim Peck, David Hale, General Westmoreland, General Harold K. Johnson, Andre Le Tendre, Jim

McCauley, Tom Donnelly, Bob Dunbar, Gordon Thomas, Dan McMichael, Dick Scaife, Jack Marsh, Phil Kirkpatrick, Rex Armistead, James Ring Adams, Ambrose Evans Pritchard, Frenchie Boutitette, Parker Dozhier, Micah Morrison, Ted Olson, Sam Winer, Rick Clayton, and others unnamed.

My family; Peggy, my wife, and our daughter, Marcail and her husband Ron Kelly, parents of the joy of my life, Jonathan Kelly. Each of them has added more than I could have ever expected from life.

In August of 2007, we sold our home in Virginia and moved to Olive Branch, Mississippi. Jonathan, his mother and father, Peggy and I shared a home together. He had been with the four of us his entire life.

Friends absent:

Steve Boynton died the day after we closed on our home. He had been battling lung cancer. It was August 24, 2007

Parker Dozhier died August 29, 2012

Jonathan continued to need regular care for his heart condition and on June 13, 2013, he died following a routine Heart Catheterization. He was sixteen years old.

Richard M. Larry died on July 6, 2013 [Ten Years ago Lois Larry, wife of Richard M. Larry, asked me if I would give Dick's Eulogy should he precede me in death. I had agreed. He died soon after Jonathan and when I got the call from Lois she asked If I could do it. It was so soon after we had lost Jonathan that I knew my emotions would not allow me to do so, however, I promised that I would be there for the funeral, and I was. I was amazed to find that I was the only person there who had been the recipient of Scaife Family funds, and I knew most of them. It was sad to see the absence of people whose own aspirations had been achieved in part because Richard M. Larry had believed in them and supported them.]

Richard M. Scaife died July 4, 2014

Rex Armistead died on Christmas Eve, 2015